RESTORATION VERSE
1660-1715

MACMILLAN AND CO., LIMITED
LONDON · BOMBAY · CALCUTTA · MADRAS
MELBOURNE

THE MACMILLAN COMPANY
NEW YORK · BOSTON · CHICAGO
DALLAS · ATLANTA · SAN FRANCISCO

THE MACMILLAN COMPANY
OF CANADA, LIMITED
TORONTO

RESTORATION VERSE
1660-1715

CHOSEN AND EDITED BY
WILLIAM KERR

MACMILLAN AND CO., LIMITED
ST. MARTIN'S STREET, LONDON
1930

COPYRIGHT

TO CLARICE

The best is not too good for you

CONTENTS

	PAGE
INTRODUCTION - - - - - - - -	ix
RESTORATION VERSE - - - - -	1
NOTES - - - - - - - -	361
LIST OF AUTHORS - - - - - -	426
ANONYMOUS POEMS - - - - -	429
INDEX OF FIRST LINES - - - - -	431

INTRODUCTION

RESTORATION poetry was until recently neglected or misunderstood, and its representation in anthologies has been perfunctory and unsympathetic. This must be the excuse for an attempt to bring together typical examples of the verse of the period, and to consider them in relation to their own rather than to other aims and ideals. The better-known poets are represented at some length, to illustrate the individual characters of their contributions to the general accomplishment : the minor and anonymous verse of the period is almost for the first time [1] made available to the general reader. It is hoped that at least one-third of the verse now collected will be new to all but professed students. An anthology can never be more than an introduction to its subject, but perhaps this book will make it possible for the first time to appreciate Restoration poetry as not a negligible part of our poetic heritage. The period has often been hurried over as merely transitional between Caroline and Eighteenth Century, or suppressed as a rather disgraceful interruption to a conveniently regular development of English poetry. One reason for this is the course of critical research and re-discovery : to the eighteenth cen-

---

[1] Mr. Ault in his *Seventeenth Century Lyrics* has covered the ground before me, and I have elsewhere acknowledged the debt I owe him, but the scale and method of his book are different enough to justify my essay.

tury the Restoration was merely old-fashioned, as the Victorian age is to-day ; the Romantics re-discovered the Elizabethans, the Victorians the Carolines : recently Eighteenth Century poetry has been revived, and perhaps at last the current interest in Restoration drama will be extended to the neglected interval between Milton and Pope.   But there are other non-literary explanations of that neglect.   One is political prejudice, conscious or unconscious. The Whig legend of English history, though now to be seen in nude innocence in elementary text-books only, was potent so long that it still colours or distorts judgment ; the efficiency of Macaulay's consummate advocacy leaves the defendants damaged if not condemned.   Closely connected with this, more explicit and more damaging, is the legend of Restoration immorality.   This unfortunately cannot be dismissed as merely Whiggish, for the greatest of Tories did much to confirm it in *The Lives of the English Poets*. Moral judgments are seldom supported by citations or proofs ;   the moralist relies upon adjectives, and a list [1] of the adjectives applied to Restoration poets has its own moral splendour. Restoration Englishmen were much as other Englishmen, judged either by the standard of mundane common sense or by that Divine and immutable standard which makes all men ashamed.   In such matters it is well to recall the counsel of the great Pantagruelist, " Ne vous fiez jamais aux gens qui regardent par un pertuys."   I know Tory prejudice is no more a

[1] Poisonous, indecent, filthy, vicious, gross, savage, lewd, licentious, impudent, malignant, goatish, sordid, shameless, false, affected, tawdry, insincere, dissolute, foppish, outrageous, depraved, heartless, callous, nauseating, petty, artificial, waxwork, squalid, grimy, decaying, fulsome, reeking, debauched.   Mr. Masefield uses all these in twenty pages, and no doubt forgot some more he meant to use.

judicial qualification than Whig prejudice and
that reply to Mr. Podsnap is as irrelevant as
his own eloquence, so that I could wish my
notes more conciliatory in tone.   But whoever
has to do with this period must beware of fire
under cold ashes; to be impartial would be an
anachronism.

The year 1660 is obviously a turning point in
literature as in history.   The civil wars are over,
the great epoch of Louis XIV begins in France,
the King comes to his own in England.   The
men who rang the bells in those May days had
much to rejoice for.   The corrupt and gloomy
tyranny of the Commonwealth had gone like a
bad dream ; the theatres were open, the Maypoles set up, the silenced organs sang in the
churches. Christian men could rejoice once more
at Christian feasts. They had not yet realised how
much had been scattered along with the King's
pictures, how much smashed along with the
carvings and the windows of the cathedrals ; it
was enough for them that England could be
merry again after twenty years.   In poetry there
is no such sudden change ; most of the poets
were King's men, who had lasted the winter
through as singing-birds best might ; they went
on in the old tradition, and it is gradually only
that newcomers try new ways ; Cotton is a
contemporary of Dryden, Traherne of Sedley.
There had been two poets on the other side ;
Marvell was now driven out of his garden-plot into
satire ; Milton, the greatest of Puritans, and the
greatest of seventeenth century poets, had yet
his epic to build.   Milton was never a Caroline
poet ; he despised vain and amatorious rhyming
and his haughty heresy is worlds away from
Vaughan's walks of prayer.   It is not paradoxical to call *Paradise Lost* baroque and to see in

it something of the newer quality (which in his case it would be absurd to call " Restoration ") : it has more in common with St. Peter's (which Milton saw in 1638) and with St. Paul's (planned in the year of *Paradise Regained*) than with George Herbert and Laudian Gothic, or with the cooler, severer classicism of Ben Jonson and Inigo Jones. Those sudden transitions which the literary historian sees do but falsify literary history; how gradually change came in the sixteen-sixties may be noted in the first fifty poems in this book.

The death of Dryden, and the retirement of Congreve, might well be taken to define the end of the epoch as 1700. But here again there is a gradual transition to the achieved manner of the eighteenth century which fills the years of Anne's reign. This is illustrated by the selections at the end of the book, which aim not so much at representing the poets between Dryden and Pope as at illustrating the persistence of elder traditions. In 1715 Pope was only twenty-seven ; it was the translation of the *Iliad* beginning to appear in that year, that established his dynasty as securely as the Hanoverian succession. The political change is definite enough ; the accession of George I, the death of Louis XIV, marks the end of the older kingship. Toryism was dead " and men stamped down the earth on its coffin." The parallel literary change establishes the narrower, more domestic Eighteenth Century, eschewing ecstasies and subtleties. The Renaissance is over, the true and vast Renaissance which began with the Provencal poets and the architects of Romanesque.[1] Generalisations and general

[1] It is significant that the Royal Commission on Ancient Monuments takes 1715 as its *terminus ad quem*.

terms are dangerous to use, but it seems true to say that Baroque now gave way to Rococo ; Dryden is baroque, Pope rococo. The Renaissance had the seeds of Baroque just as the Rococo had the seeds of Romanticism : Pope leads on to Shelley, as Shakespeare led on to Dryden. We do wrong to the unity of history by these sections, and the idea of a series of jumps is best corrected by allowing their proper place to minor figures, whose work fills the gaps and keeps the line unbroken.

Halfway between 1660 and 1715 comes the turning point of 1688, when again a political change is the index of a literary and artistic change. The Glorious Revolution has yet to be re-considered by the historians and it still needs some independence of mind to see that politically we lost more than we gained then. Certainly in literature there is a change of weather if not of season ; many generalisations about the Restoration period go wrong through failure to recognise the succession of one generation to another about that time. The younger generation looked back on the days of Charles II as a romantic time of freedom and chivalry ; it was the men of William's reign and not of Charles the Second's, who ignored Caroline poetry and thought the Renaissance Gothic. They ignored Milton, just as the young men of to-day ignore Tennyson : theirs was the coarseness in moral tone, the slovenliness in diction, which is so often confused with the rather self-conscious elegance and profligacy of Dorset and Buckingham. But that decade of 1680 marks a decline all over Europe ; Bernini dies in Italy, Calderon in Spain, and a century of great artistic achievement dies with them ; the Dutch painters are going or gone ; the brief summer of French classicism is over already. And for a time too there is a decline in the birth-rate of ability ; the only great artist born in Europe in the sixteen-fifties is Purcell ; it is the insufficiently filled gap between Rochester and Prior in this book. This is again the sort of change that is clearer to observers from a distance than to those close at hand. It is vain to seek any explanation of these European climatic variations ; there are too many causes which might have operated.

Certainly a political cause need not be advanced for spiritual changes ; there is a tide moved by forces outside human control to which literature and politics, philosophy and art, swing together. The mediæval conception of a Divine order, of which Kingship is at once symbol and sacrament, the Renaissance conception of men following each his own will, with the Prince the first and strongest among men—these give place about 1660 to the modern conception of the State. Men feel themselves but citizens of the State, the King a servant of the State. Divergent effects of this change in conception are to be seen in England and in France, with divergent influence on literature. Louis XIV identifying himself with the State (it absorbed him, not he it) established something like an Augustan order, which is reflected in the balance and order and permanence of the classical French achievement in literature. The Stuarts, fighting by craft or by violence for an older Kingship, could only prolong the civil strife of the previous twenty years. English men of letters in that generation never had before them, like their French contemporaries, the vision of a State in which reason and tradition had been reconciled.

The achievement of Louis XIV was illusory ; the reaction against him was ethical rather than political ; Jansenism and libertinism were its two wings, and they stood for those French elements which broke down his Principate. The year 1687 has been taken to mark the end of French classicism, as it does the oncoming decay of the French monarchy. For another generation French literature, lately so assured and magnificent, is frozen into sterility. By 1715, when Louis XIV died in defeat, the classical tradition was gone, and Voltaire could begin to build the French philosophical synthesis of the eighteenth century. In England the turning point is about the same time, at the Revolution of 1688, which transforms the English state into a Republic with a crowned President. Yet here again stability is not attained ; the long winning struggle of Whig against Tory becomes the long losing struggle of Tory against Whig, settled at last in 1715 by the Protestant succession and its allied Whig ascendancy. Over this whole period, while in France there is the peace of submission or decay, in England there is the fight between two factions for the right to control this external organisation, the State. Poetry is not subordinate to politics ; political causes, like the stars, do but incline and not control the poets. In this period politics was as much a pre-occupation of men as religion had been in the first part of the century. All the poets, small and great, with more or less of enthusiasm, were on one side or the other and so were distracted by these contemporary turmoils from their own work of the imagination. Their loyalty was divided between a party identified with the State, and the State as transcending party.

Parallel with this political development and with its effect on poetry also, is the philosophical revolution of the later seventeenth century. Here again is something not directly a concern of the poet, which yet moves and directs him : philosophy underlies poetry as geological structure does landscape.[1] The philosophical revolution defined by Descartes and culminating with Locke, destroyed the unity of men's conceptions of the universe. By its separation of mind from matter it made possible the acquisition of scientific knowledge and took away the hope or illusion of rational certainty. No longer could the syntheses of scholasticism or humanism fill the imagination : *Religio Medici* is as obsolete philosophically for the men of that day as *Pseudodoxia Epidemica* is scientifically. From 1660 onwards, a consistently material order of things, governed by laws capable of discovery and definition, is conceived as existing side by side with an irrational and undefined spiritual order, which may be ignored or exalted according to the accident of individual conviction. And here again is a state of struggle, of divided allegiance, of the necessity for taking sides and denying one of two apparently inconsistent truths. This is proper to the philosopher, a soldier sworn to this war : to the poet, who must have belief rather than knowledge, it is an inhibition from imaginative creation.

Religion, too, is an energy of the imagination, the highest poetry, a transfiguration of human life itself into an imaginative form. Men are drawn by philosophical uncertainty to interpret

[1] This attempt to define the philosophic development of the period, as subsidiary to its poetry, owes any value it has to what I have been able to understand and adapt of Mr. Whitehead's great book, *Science and the Modern World*.

religion in the lower terms of morality and so to
divorce it from their imaginative life.   South
and Tillotson are typical religious teachers of
such an epoch, and their outlook is comparable
to that of Bossuet and Bourdaloue in France,
upheld though these were by the richer and
stronger tradition of Catholicism.   This change
from the attitude of the earlier seventeenth
century is illustrated by the fact that almost all
the religious poetry in this book is in the form of
the hymn (which thus re-enters literature after
three hundred years).   A Caroline anthology
passes from unconscious to conscious devotion
without sense of incongruity ; a reader of this
book may perhaps except to the transitions
from love-song to hymn I must present to him.
Yet, as I have tried to show here and there in
the notes, the division between religious and
other poetry is not as complete as might appear,
or as definite as in the next century.   There is
something very noble and complete in the best
religious poetry of this age, because of its
moderation and humility ; the hymn, expressing
a common measure of public devotion, chooses
to leave rarer individual experiences in devout
silence.

The consideration of Restoration religion
leads on inevitably to the difficult question of
Restoration morals.   Each generation in this
matter has its own standard of criticism as well
as of practice.   The moral standard of to-day,
disquieting to those whose own morality is
merely inherited convention, makes it easier
for us to condone Restoration ways, as far
as condonation is necessary.   We understand,
better than the Victorians, how prudence and
even timidity too often pose as moral principle.
The morality of Puritanism has been described

by a historian as " the triumph of the economic
virtues " ; its outlook was that of a commercial
middle-class. As against this, there flamed up
for twenty years the last revival of Renaissance
self-expression and self-expense in extravagant
and dangerous pleasure. I have said something
in the notes of the tragedy of Rochester ; it is
unnecessary to confuse his solitary example of
perverse athleticism or asceticism with the
graceful carelessness of Etherege or the elegant
amorality of Sidley or the supreme artistic
detachment of Congreve. Criticism has little to
do with a poet's morals ; to criticise Shelley's
pre-occupation in his work with his own fantastic
moral dogmas is dangerously allowable, but to
vituperate him as an adulterer is mere impertinence. The moralist whose theme is Restoration degradation will impute corruption not only
to half-a-dozen extravagant aristocrats, but to
most of the Englishmen [1] of two generations.
Like the simpleton who hisses the villain from
the gallery, he will judge that society by
Mr. Horner and Sir John Brute, as some day the
twentieth century may be judged in the eroto-
maniac heroes of admired contemporary novels.
Jeremy Collier, born too soon for Sunday news-
papers, is taken seriously, and the anecdotes of
memoir writers pass for authentic. The more
innocent of literary historians seem to suppose
that adultery was first practised in England
after 1660, under the influence of the notoriously
immoral French, and encouraged by the unique
royal example of Charles II. It follows that the
poems such wicked people read or wrote would

[1] Englishwomen too ; a learned lady in a learned book just
published has referred to " a phase of decadence which has left an
ineradicable stain on the fair fame of English gentlewomen." The
glibness of this—without authorities or references—recalls irresistibly
a Drydenian jest about a parrot and an almond.

have been wicked too, and this is conveyed
without actual quotation by the use of such
terms as " unquotable " and " unprintable."
The present selection is likely to be disappoint-
ing in this respect, although here too, the proper
may discover their cream-tarts.

The greater men of the period, such as Temple
and Savile, Dryden and Wren, in their balance
and sanity illustrate the ideal of Molière's
" honnête homme." (The characters and
manners of politicians may be left to those
curious in such matters.) The typical grace and
dignity of the period, in literature and in life,
has something of seventeenth century nobility
together with something of eighteenth century
urbanity, free from the suspicion of the fantastic
in its grandfathers and of the self-conscious in its
grandsons. The same golden mean of carriage
and conduct is seen in the women of the time,
who need no more be confounded with the fast
and noisy set whose doings interested the memoir-
writers, than the women of to-day with the
heroines of newspaper-paragraphs. In the love-
lyrics they may be seen walking, not in an air of
glory, but in the cheerful sunshine of their
England, at once gracious and free, merry and
serene. Women are good and beautiful in every
age ; to see the characteristic mode of their
goodness and beauty we must look through the
eyes of their lovers. Nor are we left without
evidence from themselves ; women in this period
wrote verse often and well, as never before except
in Italy of the Cinquecento, as never again for
two centuries more. This fact may be left to be
explained or explained away by those who
cherish among the other myths of Progress, that
of the gradual Emancipation of Woman. In
the women of Chaucer, the women of Spenser, as

in the women of to-day, may be seen the same
joyous and sober freedom : there have been
intervals of Puritan repression and of snobbish
formalism, as there will be again.

Half the poems in this book are love-poems ;
perhaps half the poems in any representative
anthology of any period would be love-poems,
and certainly it is not for a generation which
demands a love-interest even in detective stories
to except to the proportion. The Restoration
love-poem has its own character ; it has more of
the lady and less of the lover than any previously
or most since. It is possible to see the heroine
of almost every song here, while the goddess of
the Renaissance sonnet or the mediæval tale is
generally conventionalised out of existence.
The novel had not yet reached maturity, and
much of the interplay and comedy of love,
which later was to fill the looser form of the
novel, is here concentrated in lyric form. It is
true that there is something lost as compared
with the great love-song of the past, the canzone
form which Dante bequeathed to Europe, or the
softer tradition of Petrarch. Of Dante's " mag-
nalia quae sint maxime pertrectanda "—Arms
and Love and Right Living—Love suffered least
from the inhibitions that hampered the age ; it
had to come down from the heights of imagination like the other two (although its full scientific explanation was reserved for our own
day). Yet Restoration love poetry is rather a
golden mean than a mere compromise ; no
period of poetry will furnish more of profitable
meditation for hours of desolation or of hymns
of thanksgiving for the use of the practising
lover : at the last lovers alone can best judge
love-poetry.

I have not inquired whether the verse of the

Restoration should properly be termed Classical ;
the word, like Romantic, begs several questions
and is generally employed for the expression of
prejudice. This poetry is contemporary with
and shares the accomplishment of Wren's
architecture and Purcell's music. A generation
which could so make the best of both worlds in
St. Paul's Cathedral and Hampton Court is
obviously not negligible, and its expression in
poetry is a part of our literary heritage not to be
forgotten. A word is not perhaps out of place
as to French influence on English poetry ; this,
for the period under review, is a commonplace of
the text-books, but it is assumed without pro-
duction of proofs, and what little research I have
been able to do makes one think that proofs
would be hard to come by. Literary historians
find over-simplification a device which saves
much labour ; it is easier to talk of an Age of
Prose beginning in 1660 and to suggest French
influence [1] than to define the relation of Restoration to Caroline poetry. There is in English,
certainly from the days of Jonson, a tradition as
English as any other, which for convenience only
may be called Classical. This tradition holds
to our Latin heritage, which in literature, as in
religion, is denied by those who would forget our
membership of the European unity. This runs
all through the seventeenth century, in Carew
and Herrick as well as in Milton and Marvell,
and it is sufficient to account for the lucidity and
discipline of the Restoration verse method as
far as explanation is necessary.

The particular virtue of this poetry is in two
matters—diction and measure. The anonymous
editor of Waller (perhaps Atterbury, as Bullen

[1] Charles II and his Court in exile spent very little time in France ;
Mazarin had to propitiate Cromwell by denying them hospitality.

suggests) spoke plain truth when he said, " I
question whether in Charles the Second's reign
English did not come to its full perfection."
How true this is in prose only those can understand who have had to praise Dryden with the
sound of his prose in their ears. Even rarer and
harder to attain is the clarity and directness of
this Augustan diction in verse. Its best
examples have the quality of early line engrav-
ing ; the words have no aura of distorting and
wavering suggestion ; and the whole has the
Florentine achievement of colour subordinated
to form. " What kind of Intellects must he
have who sees only the Colours of things and not
the Forms of things," says Blake, who in many
passages of his art-criticism praises an ideal
which was consciously that of the Restoration
poet. It is indeed true that for reasons suggested earlier, this remains a matter of method
only and never finds in verse (as Wren and
Purcell found for their arts, informed by the
same ideal) any work to do worthy of the
possibilities. What those possibilities were may
be guessed from the contemporary mastery of
La Fontaine and Racine, who in French attain
the same clarity and chastity in choice and order
of words. The quality of the period in verse-
form is less exquisite and exceptional ; yet here
too it strikes the golden mean between over-
laxity and over-stiffness. English has nothing
to show more admirably accomplished than the
couplet of Dryden, the Common Measure of so
many songs and hymns, and the laughing triple-
time of Prior. Keats went back to Dryden for
the form of his *Lamia* ; our own generation for
the moment has gone astray after the illusion of
freedom towards something like the Pindaric
anarchy of the Restoration, but signs are not

lacking of a return also to its more excellent way.

Almost anxiously does one let a selection like this go out into the world ; many misgivings cloud the mind of an anthologist. Partiality perhaps has dimmed judgment and these poems, grown friends after long companionship, may not be as good as they have come to seem. Perhaps the Accuser will be justified in dismissing them again to the limbo of the merely interesting ; perhaps some clumsiness or oversight in advocacy will repel a possible friend. Go they must, and good luck go with them. If they give as much delight as I hope they may, I shall have done a little to repay my own debt to all poets.

My texts are as good as I could make them ; in all but a very few cases (when I have had to be content with Chalmers) I have gone to original editions. They do not claim to be critically final ; this is a book for the general reader, and I have studied his comfort in matters of spelling and the choice of readings. I hope no serious errors will be found, although the misfortunes of other anthologists in this respect warn me to hope humbly. As for the notes, they should be regarded as suggestive and tentative only ; ten years of research would not be too much to spend on this little-explored period. For their shortcomings, and for those of this Introduction I will, with all modest exceptions, quote an apology of Dryden's. " I am sensible that I have written this too hastily and too loosely ; I fear I have been tedious, and, which is worse, it comes out from the first draught and uncorrected. This, I grant, is no excuse ; for it may be reasonably urged, why did he not write with more leisure, or, if he had it not (which was certainly my case), why did he attempt to write on so nice a subject ? The objection is unanswerable ; but, in part of recompense, let me assure the reader that in hasty productions, he is sure to meet with an author's present sense, which cooler thoughts would possibly have disguised. There is undoubtedly more of spirit, though not of judgment, in these uncorrect essays ; and consequently, though my hazard be the greater, yet the reader's pleasure is not the less.''

WILLIAM KERR.

LEEDS,
October, 1929.

ACKNOWLEDGEMENTS

I wish to thank all those who have so kindly
helped me. To Mr. Norman Ault my debt is
considerable. His *Seventeenth Century Lyrics*
has been always under my hand and in a sense
has made this book possible ; his Short-Title
List of Miscellanies has saved me hours of
searching catalogues ; in addition to all this he
has generously given me permission (duly
acknowledged where I have taken advantage of
it) to use any of his copyright texts and has
answered questions with the greatest kindness.
Mr. Geoffrey Woledge, Assistant Librarian at
Leeds University, has helped me very greatly
with bibliographical and general information,
while the Introduction and Notes owe much to
his criticism. To these services he has added the
labour of reading the proofs. My friends, Mr.
Wilfred Childe, Lecturer in English at Leeds
University, and Mr. John Haines, have given me
much encouragement. Mr. R. E. W. Flower,
of the British Museum, and Mr. H. F. B. Brett-
Smith, I thank for information freely given ;
Mr. Gerald Crow assisted me in the transcription
of texts.

I have also to thank Dr. R. Offor, Librarian
at Leeds University, and Mr. R. J. Gordon,
Leeds City Librarian, for many courtesies ; the
Librarian and Staff of the London Library for
their usual kindness ; Mr. Clive Murray and

Mr. Denis Botterill for the loan of books ; Miss H. M. Rhodes for typing my transcripts.

I have drawn freely upon Mr. Saintsbury's *History of English Prosody*, Mr. Elton's *Augustan Age*, and Mr. Spingarn's *Critical Essays of the Seventeenth Century*, while Birkbeck Hill's edition of Johnson's *Lives* has been indispensable. I have had also much assistance from previous anthologies—Mr. J. C. Squire's *Book of Women Poets*, Mr. Iolo Williams's *Shorter Poems of the Eighteenth Century*, Bullen's *Musa Proterva* and Arber's *Dryden Anthology*.

I have to acknowledge permission to use copyright texts in the following cases : The Oxford University Press for Wanley, Traherne, Flatman, Ayres and Katherine Philips ; the Cambridge University Press for Prior's *Jinny the Just* ; the University of Chicago Press for two poems from their edition of Lady Winchilsea ; Messrs. Constable & Co., and Professor de Sola Pinto for Sedley ; the Nonesuch Press for Rochester and Wycherley ; and the Fortune Press for Shadwell.

EDMUND WALLER (1606-87)

I

TRANSLATED OUT OF FRENCH

Fade, flowers, fade, nature will have it so ;
'Tis but what we must in our autumn do ;
And as your leaves lie quiet on the ground,
The loss alone by those that loved them found,
So in the grave shall we as quiet lie,
Missed by some few that loved our company ;
But some so like to thorns and nettles live,
That none for them can, when they perish,
    grieve.

II

ON ST. JAMES'S PARK

Of the first paradise there's nothing found,
Plants set by Heaven are vanished, and the
    ground ;
Yet the description lasts ; who knows the fate
Of lines that shall this paradise relate ?
  Instead of rivers rolling by the side
Of Eden's garden, here flows in the tide ;
The sea, which always served his empire, now
Pays tribute to our Prince's pleasure too.
Of famous cities we the founders know ;
But rivers, old as seas to which they go,
Are nature's bounty ; 'tis of more renown
To make a river, than to build a town.
  For future shade, young trees upon the banks
Of a new stream appear in even ranks ;

A   I   Œ

The voice of Orpheus, or Amphion's hand,
In better order could not make them stand ;
May they increase as fast, and spread their
        boughs,
As the high fame of their great owner grows !
May he live long enough to see them all
Dark shadows cast, and as his palace tall !
Methinks I see the love that shall be made,
The lovers walking in that amorous shade ;
The gallants dancing by the river's side ;
They bathe in summer, and in winter slide.
Methinks I hear the music in the boats,
And the loud echo which returns the notes ;
While overhead a flock of new-sprung fowl
Hangs in the air, and does the sun control ;
Darkening the sky, they hover o'er, and shroud
The wanton sailors with a feathered cloud.
Beneath, a shoal of silver fishes glides,
And plays about the gilded barges' sides ;
The ladies, angling in the crystal lake,
Feast on the waters with the prey they take ;
At once victorious with their lines, and eyes,
They make the fishes, and the men, their prize.
A thousand Cupids on the billows ride,
And sea-nymphs enter with the swelling tide,
From Thetis sent as spies, to make report,
And tell the wonders of her sovereign's court . . .

1661.

III

THE TRIPLE COMBAT

When through the world fair Mazarine had run
Bright as her fellow-traveller, the sun,
Hither at length the Roman eagle flies,
As the last triumph of her conquering eyes.
As heir to Julius, she may pretend
A second time to make this island bend.

But Portsmouth, springing from the ancient race
Of Britons, which the Saxon here did chase,
As they great Caesar did oppose, makes head,
And does against this new invader lead.
That goodly nymph, the taller of the two,
Careless and fearless to the field does go.
Becoming blushes on the other wait,
And her young look excuses want of height.
Beauty gives courage ; for she knows the day
Must not be won the Amazonian way.
Legions of Cupids to the battle come,
For little Britain these, and those for Rome.
Dressed to advantage, this illustrious pair
Arrived, for combat in the list appear.
What may the Fates design ? For never yet
From distant regions two such beauties met.
Venus had been an equal friend to both,
And Victory to declare herself seems loath ;
Over the camp with doubtful wings she flies,
Till Chloris shining in the field she spies.
The lovely Chloris well-attended came,
A thousand graces waited on the dame :
Her matchless form made all the English glad,
And foreign beauties less assurance had.
Yet, like the three on Ida's top, they all
Pretend alike, contesting for the ball :
Which to determine, Love himself declined,
Lest the neglected should become less kind.
Such killing looks ! so thick the arrows fly !
That 'tis unsafe to be a stander-by.
Poets, approaching to describe the fight,
Are by their wounds instructed how to write ;
They with less hazard might look on, and draw
The ruder combats in Alsatia ;
And, with that foil of violence and rage,
Set off the splendour of our golden age :
Where Love gives law, Beauty the sceptre sways,
And, uncompelled, the happy world obeys.

SIR WILLIAM DAVENANT (1606-68)

IV

THE DYING LOVER

Dear Love, let me this evening die !
  Oh, smile not to prevent it ;
Dead with my rivals let me lie,
  Or we shall both repent it.
Frown quickly then, and break my heart,
  That so my way of dying
May, though my life was full of smart,
  Be worth the world's envying.

Some, striving knowledge to refine,
  Consume themselves with thinking ;
And some, who friendship seal in wine,
  Are kindly killed with drinking.
And some are wrecked on the Indian coast
  Thither by gain invited ;
Some are in smoke of battles lost,
  Whom drums, not lutes, delighted

Alas, how poorly these depart,
  Their graves still unattended !
Who dies not of a broken heart
  Is not of death commended.
His memory is only sweet,
  All praise and pity moving,
Who kindly at his mistress' feet
  Does die with over-loving.

And now thou frown'st, and now I die,
  My corpse by lovers followed ;
Which straight shall by dead lovers lie—
  That ground is only hallowed.
If priests are grieved I have a grave,
  My death not well approving,

The poets my estate shall have,
  To teach them the art of loving.

And now let lovers ring their bells
  For me, poor youth, departed,
Who kindly in his love excels
  By dying broken-hearted.
My grave with flowers let virgins strow,
  Which, if thy tears fall near them,
May so transcend in scent and show,
  As thou wilt shortly wear them.

Such flowers how much will florists prize,
  Which, on a lover growing,
Are watered with his mistress' eyes,
  With pity ever flowing.
A grave so decked will—though thou art
  Yet fearful to come nigh me—
Provoke thee straight to break thy heart,
  And lie down boldly by me.

Then everywhere all bells shall ring,
  All light to darkness turning ;
While every choir shall sadly sing,
  And Nature's self wear mourning.
Yet we hereafter may be found,
  By destiny's right placing,
Making, like flowers, love under ground,
  Whose roots are still embracing.

Works, 1673 (*first printed*, 1655).

v

My lodging it is on the cold ground,
  And very hard is my fare,
But that which troubles me most is
  The unkindness of my dear.

Yet still I cry, ' Oh turn, Love,
    And I prithee, Love, turn to me ;
For thou art the man that I long for,
    And, alack ! what remedy ?

' I'll crown thee with a garland of straw then ;
    And I'll marry thee with a rush ring ;
My frozen hopes shall thaw then,
    And merrily we will sing.
Oh turn to me, my dear Love,
    And prithee, Love, turn to me ;
For thou art the man that alone canst
    Procure my liberty.

' But if thou wilt harden thy heart still,
    And be deaf to my pitiful moan,
Then I must endure the smart still,
    And tumble in straw alone.
Yet still I cry, Oh turn, Love,
    And I prithee, Love, turn to me ;
For thou art the man that alone art
    The cause of my misery.'

The Rivals, 1668.

ROBERT WILD (1609-79)

VI

IN MEMORY OF MRS. E. T., WHO DIED APRIL 7, 1659

It was the spring, and flowers were in contest
Whose smells should first reach Heaven, and
    please it best :
Then did Eliza's sweetness so surpass
All rival virgins, that she sent for was.

'Twas April when she died : no month so fit
For Heaven to be a mourner in, as it.
'Twas Easter too : that time did Death devise
Best for this lamb to be a sacrifice.
It was the spring : the way 'twixt Heaven and
    earth
Was sweetened for her passage, by the birth
Of early flowers which burst their mother's
    womb
Resolved to live and die upon her tomb.
It was the spring : between the earth and sky
To please her soul, as it was passing by,
Birds filled the air with anthems, every nest
Was on the wing, to chant her to her rest :
Not a pen-feathered lark, who ne'er tried wing
Nor throat, but ventured then to fly and sing,
Following the saint to Heaven, whose entrance
    there
Damped them, and changed their notes. Then
    pensive air
Dissolved to tears, which spoiled the feathered
    train,
And sunk them to their nests with grief again.
Meantime, methought I saw at Heaven's fair
    gate
The glorious virgins meet and kiss their mate.
They stood awhile her beauty to admire,
Then led her to her place in their own choir :
Which seemed to be defective until she
Added her sweetness to their harmony.
As medals scattered when some prince goes by
So lay the stars that night about the sky.
The Milky Way too (since she passed it o'er)
Methinks looks whiter than it was before.

Iter Boreale, 1668.

SAMUEL BUTLER (1612-80)

VII

Man is supreme lord and master
Of his own ruin and disaster ;
Controls his fate, but nothing less
In ordering his own happiness ;
For all his care and providence
Is too, too feeble a defence,
To render it secure and certain
Against the injuries of Fortune ;
And oft, in spite of all his wit,
Is lost with one unlucky hit,
And ruined with a circumstance,
And mere punctilio, of chance.

Miscellaneous Thoughts ("*The
Genuine Remains*," 1759).

VIII

Love is too great a happiness
For wretched mortals to possess
For, could it hold inviolate
Against these cruelties of Fate,
Which all felicities below
By rigid laws are subject to,
It would become a bliss too high
For perishing mortality,
Translate to Earth the joys above ;
For nothing goes to Heaven but love.

Ibid.

IX

How various and innumerable
Are those who live upon the rabble !
'Tis they maintain the church and state,
Employ the priest and magistrate ;

Bear all the charge of government,
And pay the public fines and rent ;
Defray all taxes and excises,
And impositions of all prices ;
Bear all th' expense of peace and war,
And pay the pulpit and the bar ;
Maintain all churches and religions,
And give their pastors exhibitions ;
And those who have the greatest flocks
Are primitive and orthodox ;
Support all schismatics and sects,
And pay them for tormenting texts ;
Take all their doctrines off their hands,
And pay them in good rents and lands ;
Discharge all costly offices,
The doctor's and the lawyer's fees,
The hangman's wages, and the scores
Of caterpillar bawds and whores ;
Discharge all damages and costs
Of knights and squires of the post ;
All statesmen, cutpurses, and padders,
And pay for all their ropes and ladders ;
All pettifoggers, and all sorts
Of markets, churches, and of courts ;
All sums of money paid or spent,
With all the charges incident,
Laid out, or thrown away, or given
To purchase this world, Hell, or Heaven.

Ibid.

JOHN AUSTIN (1613-69)

x

Hark my soul, how every thing
Strives to serve our bounteous King ;
Each a double tribute pays,
Sings its part and then obeys.

Nature's chief and sweetest choir
Him with cheerful note admire,
Chanting every day their Lauds,
While the grove their song applauds.

Though their voices lower be
Streams have too their melody ;
Night and day they warbling run,
Never pause, but still sing on.

All the flowers that gild the spring
Hither their still music bring.
If Heaven bless them, thankful they
Smell more sweet and look more gay.

Devotions in the Ancient Way of
Offices, 1688.

XI

With all the powers my poor soul hath
Of humble love and loyal faith,
Thus low, my God, I bend to thee
Whom too much love bowed lower for me.

Down, busy sense ; discourses die ;
And all adore faith's mystery.
Faith is my skill, faith can believe
As fast as love new laws can give.

Faith is my eye, faith strength affords,
To keep pace with those powerful words ;
And words more sure, more sweet than they,
Love could not think, truth could not say.

O dear memorial of that death,
Which still survives and gives us breath !
Live ever, Bread of Life, and be
My food, my joy, my all to me.

Come, glorious Lord, my hopes increase,
And fill my portion in thy peace ;
Come hidden life, and that long day
For which I languish, come away,

When this dry soul those eyes shall see,
And drink the unsealed source of thee ;
When glory's sun faith's shade shall chase
And for thy veil, give me thy face.

Ibid.

XII

And now, my Lord, my God, my all,
    What shall I most in thee admire ?
That power which made the world and shall
    The world again dissolve with fire ?

O no, thy strange humility ;
    Thy wounds, thy pain, thy cross, thy death :
These shall alone my wonder be,
    My health, my joy, my staff, my breath.

Ibid.

SIR WALTER KIRKHAM BLOUNT (-1717)

XIII

VICTIMAE PASCHALI

Bring, all ye dear-bought nations, bring
Your richest praises to your king,

That spotless Lamb, who more than due
Paid for his sheep, and those sheep you ;

That guiltless Son, who wrought you peace,
And made his Father's anger cease.

Life and death together fought,
Each to a strange extreme were brought.

Life died, but soon revived again,
And even death by it was slain.

Say, happy Magdalen, oh say,
What didst thou see there by the way ?

' I saw the tomb of my dear Lord ;
I saw himself and him adored ;

I saw the napkin and the sheet,
That bound his head and wrapt his feet ;

I heard the angels witness bear,
" Jesus is risen ; he's not here :

Go, tell his followers, they shall see
Thine and their hope in Galilee." '

We, Lord, with faithful heart and cheerful
    voice,
On this thy glorious rising-day rejoice ;

O thou, whose conquering power o'ercame the
    grave,
By thy victorious grace us sinners save.

Complete Office of the Holy Week, 1670.

ANONYMOUS

XIV

VENI, SANCTE SPIRITUS

Come into us, Holy Ghost ;
From thy bright celestial coast,
  Send us a resplendent beam.
Come, thou Father of the poor,
Come, thou willing gift-bestower,
  Come thou heart-reviving gleam.

Thou, of comforters the best,
Thou, the soul's delightful guest,
    A refreshing sweet relief.
Thou, in toil a resting seat,
Temper in excessive heat,
    Solace to a soul in grief.

O thou blessedest of lights,
Those that love to observe thy rites,
    With thyself their bosoms fill.
While thou art absent nothing can
Be regardable in man,
    Nothing can he act but ill.

What is sordid mundify,
Water what is over-dry,
    What is wounded render sound.
Pliant make what's hard to yield,
Cherish what with cold is chilled,
    Govern what is vagabond.

In the faithful that confide
In thy mercies, cause reside
    All the train of seven-fold grace.
Give what virtue's merit is,
Give the accomplishment of bliss,
    Joys of an eternal race.

Primer, 1685.

ABRAHAM COWLEY (1618-67)

XV

BACON

From the ODE TO THE ROYAL SOCIETY

Authority, which did a body boast,
Though 'twas but air condensed, and stalked
    about

Like some old giant's more gigantic ghost,
  To terrify the learned rout,
With the plain magic of true reason's light,
  He chased out of our sight,
Nor suffered living men to be misled
  By the vain shadows of the dead :
To graves, from whence it rose, the conquered
    phantom fled ;
  He broke that monstrous god which stood
In midst of th' orchard, and the whole did
    claim,
  Which with a useless scythe of wood,
  And something else not worth a name,
  (Both vast for shew, yet neither fit
  Or to defend, or to beget ;
  Ridiculous and senseless terrors !) made
Children and superstitious men afraid.
  The orchard's open now, and free ;
Bacon has broke that scarecrow deity ;
  Come, enter, all that will,
Behold the ripened fruit, come gather now your
    fill.
  Yet still, methinks, we fain would be
  Catching at the forbidden tree,
  We would be like the Deity,
When truth and falsehood, good and evil, we
Without the senses' aid within our selves would
    see ;
  For 'tis God only who can find
  All nature in his mind.

From words, which are but pictures of the
    thought,
  (Though we our thoughts from them perversely
    drew)
To things, the mind's right object, he it brought ;
Like foolish birds to painted grapes we flew,
He sought and gathered for our use the true ;

And when on heaps the chosen bunches lay,
He pressed them wisely the mechanic way,
Till all their juice did in one vessel join,
Ferment into a nourishment divine,
    The thirsty soul's refreshing wine.
Who to the life an exact piece would make,
Must not from others' work a copy take ;
    No, not from Rubens or Vandyke ;
Much less content himself to make it like
Th' ideas and the images which lie
In his own fancy, or his memory.
    No, he before his sight must place
    The natural and living face ;
    The real object must command
Each judgment of his eye, and motion of his
    hand.

From these and all long errors of the way,
In which our wand'ring predecessors went,
And like th' old Hebrews many years did stray
    In deserts but of small extent,
Bacon, like Moses, led us forth at last,
    The barren wilderness he passed,
    Did on the very border stand
    Of the blest promised land,
And from the mountain's top of his exalted wit,
    Saw it himself, and shewed us it.
But life did never to one man allow
Time to discover worlds, and conquer too ;
Nor can so short a line sufficient be
To fathom the vast depths of Nature's sea.
Works, 1668.

XVI

TO J. EVELYN, ESQUIRE

  Happy art thou whom God does bless
With the full choice of thine own happiness ;

And happier yet, because thou'rt blessed
With prudence how to choose the best.
In books and gardens thou hast placed aright,—
Things which thou well dost understand,
And both dost make with thy laborious hand—
Thy noble, innocent delight,
And in thy virtuous wife, where thou again dost
meet
Both pleasures more refined and sweet :
The fairest garden in her looks,
And in her mind the wisest books...

Essays (in *Works*, 1668).

THE SAME

XVII

...If we could open and intend our eye,
We all like Moses should espy
Even in a bush the radiant Deity.
But we despise these his inferior ways
Though no less full of miracle and praise ;
Upon the flowers of heaven we gaze,
The stars of earth no wonder in us raise,
Though these perhaps do more than they
The life of mankind sway...

Ibid.

ROWLAND WATKYNS

XVIII

UPON CHRIST'S NATIVITY
OR CHRISTMAS

From three dark places Christ came forth this
day,
First from his Father's bosom, where he lay
Concealed till now ; then from the typic Law,
Where we his manhood but by figures saw ;

And lastly from his mother's womb he came
To us a perfect God, and perfect Man.
Now in a manger lies th' eternal Word ;
The Word he is, yet can no speech afford.
He is the Bread of Life, yet hungry lies,
The living Fountain, yet for drink he cries ;
He cannot help, or clothe himself at need,
Who did the lilies clothe, and ravens feed :
He is the Light of Lights, yet now doth shroud
His glory with our nature as a cloud :
He came to us a little one, that we
Like little children might in malice be ;
Little he is, and wrapped in clouts, lest he
Might strike us dead, if clothed with majesty.
Christ had four beds, and those not soft, nor
    brave,
The Virgin's womb, the manger, cross and grave.
The angels sing this day ; and so will I
That have more reason to be glad, than they.

Flamma sine Fumo, 1662.

XIX

THE SPRING

See how the wanton Spring
    In green is clad,
Hark how the birds do sing,
    I'll not be sad.
Doth not the blushing rose
    Breath sweet perfume ?
I will my spice disclose,
    But not presume.
The dew falls in the grass
    And hastes away,
Which makes me mind my glass
    Which will not stay.

Now plants and herbs do grow
   In every place,
Lord, let me not be slow
   In growth of grace.
Behold the fruitful trees
   And fertile ground ;
Observe the painful bees
   Whose hives abound.
I will not barren be
   Nor waste my days,
Like sluggards, that are free
   From virtuous ways.

Ibid.

HENRY VAUGHAN (1622-95)

xx

TO ETESIA LOOKING FROM HER CASE-MENT AT THE FULL MOON

See you that beauteous queen, which no age
   tames ?
Her train is azure, set with golden flames :
My brighter fair, fix on the East your eyes,
And view that bed of clouds, whence she doth
   rise.
Above all others in that one short hour
Which most concerned me, she had greatest
   power.
This made my fortunes humorous as wind,
But fixed affections to my constant mind.
She fed me with the tears of stars, and thence
I sucked in sorrows with their influence.
To some in smiles, and store of light she broke,
To me in sad eclipses still she spoke.
She bent me with the motion of her sphere,
And made me feel what first I did but fear.

But when I came to age, and had o'ergrown
Her rules, and saw my freedom was my own,
I did reply unto the laws of fate,
And made my reason my great advocate :
I laboured to inherit my just right.
But then—Oh hear, Etesia !—lest I might
Redeem myself, my unkind starry mother
Took my poor heart, and gave it to another.

Thalia Rediviva, 1678.

XXI

LOOKING BACK

Fair shining mountains of my pilgrimage
    And flowery vales, whose flow'rs were stars,
The days and nights of my first happy age,
    An age without distaste and wars :
When I by thoughts ascend your sunny heads,
    And mind those sacred midnight lights
By which I walked, when curtained rooms and
      beds
    Confined or sealed up others' sights,
        Oh then, how bright
        And quick a light
Doth brush my heart and scatter night,
        Chasing that shade
        Which my sins made ;
While I so spring, as if I could not fade.
How brave a prospect is a bright back-side
    Where flowers and palms refresh the eye !
And days well spent like the glad East abide,
    Whose morning glories cannot die.

Ibid.

XXII

THE SHOWER

Waters above ! eternal springs !
· The dew that silvers the Dove's wings !
Oh welcome, welcome, to the sad ;
Give dry dust drink drink that makes glad.
Many fair ev'nings, many flow'rs
Sweetened with rich and gentle showers
Have I enjoyed, and down have run
Many a fine and shining sun ;
But never, till this happy hour,
Was blest with such an evening-shower.

Ibid.

XXIII

THE REQUEST.

O Thou who didst deny to me
This world's adored felicity,
And ev'ry big imperious lust,
Which fools admire in sinful dust,
With those fine subtle twists, that tie
Their bundles of foul gallantry :
Keep still my weak eyes from the shine
Of those gay things which are not Thine
And shut my ears against the noise
Of wicked, though applauded, joys.
For Thou in any land hast store
Of shades and coverts for Thy poor ;
Where from the busy dust and heat,
As well as storms, they may retreat.
A rock or bush are downy beds,
When Thou art there, crowning their heads
With secret blessings, or a tire
Made of the Comforter's live fire.

And when Thy goodness in the dress
Of anger will not seem to bless,
Yet dost Thou give them that rich rain
Which, as it drops, clears all again.
　　Oh what kind visits daily pass
'Twixt Thy great self and such poor grass :
With what sweet looks doth Thy love shine
On those low violets of Thine,
While the tall tulip is accurst,
And crowns imperial die with thirst !
Oh give me still those secret meals,
Those rare repasts which Thy love deals ;
Give me that joy, which none can grieve,
And which in all griefs doth relieve.
This is the portion Thy child begs,
Not that of rust, and rags, and dregs.

Ibid.

JOHN BUNYAN (1628-88)

XXIV

OF THE CHILD WITH THE BIRD AT THE BUSH

My little bird, how canst thou sit
　　And sing amidst so many thorns ?
Let me but hold upon thee get,
　　My love with honour thee adorns.

Thou art at present little worth,
　　Five farthings none will give for thee ;
But prithee, little bird, come forth,
　　Thou of more value art to me.

'Tis true it is sun-shine to-day,
　　To-morrow birds will have a storm ;
My pretty one, come thou away,
　　My bosom then shall keep thee warm.

Thou subject art to cold o' nights
   When darkness is thy covering,
At days thy danger's great by kites ;
   How canst thou then sit there and sing ?

Thy food is scarce and scanty too,
   'Tis worms and trash which thou dost eat ;
Thy present state I pity do,
   Come, I'll provide thee better meat.

I'll feed thee with white bread and milk,
   And sugar-plums, if them thou crave ;
I'll cover thee with finest silk,
   That from the cold I may thee save.

My father's palace shall be thine,
   Yea, in it thou shalt sit and sing ;
My little bird, if thou'lt be mine,
   The whole year round shall be thy spring.

I'll teach thee all the notes at court ;
   Unthought-of music thou shalt play ;
And all that thither do resort
   Shall praise thee for it every day.

I'll keep thee safe from cat and cur,
   No manner o' harm shall come to thee :
Yea, I will be thy succourer,
   My bosom shall thy cabin be.

But lo ! behold, the bird is gone ;
   These charmings would not make her yield :
The child's left at the bush alone,
   The bird flies yonder o'er the field.

A Book for Boys and Girls, 1686.

XXV

OF THE CUCKOO

Thou booby, say'st thou nothing but Cuckoo ?
The robin and the wren can thee out-do :
They to us play thorough their little throats
Not one, but sundry pretty taking notes.
    But thou hast fellows, some, like thee, can do
    Little but suck our eggs and sing Cuckoo.
Thy notes do not first welcome in our Spring,
Nor dost thou its first tokens to us bring :
Birds less than thee by far, like prophets, do
Tell us 'tis coming, though not by Cuckoo :

Nor dost thou summer have away with thee,
Though thou a yawling, bawling cuckoo be.
When thou dost cease among us to appear
Then doth our harvest bravely crown our year.
    But thou hast fellows, some, like thee, can do
    Little but suck our eggs and sing Cuckoo.
Since cuckoos forward not our early Spring
Nor help with notes to bring our harvest in ;
And since, while here, she only makes a noise
So pleasing unto none as girls and boys ;
The formalist we may compare her to,
For he doth suck our eggs and sing Cuckoo !
Ibid.

XXVI

OF THE BOY AND THE BUTTERFLY

Behold how eager this our little boy
Is of this butterfly, as if all joy,
All profits, honours, yea and lasting pleasures
Were wrapt up in her, or the richest treasures
Found in her would be bundled up together,
When all her all is lighter than a feather.

He holloas, runs, and cries out, " Here, boys;
    here,"
Nor doth the brambles or the nettles fear ;
He stumbles at the mole-hills, up he gets,
And runs again, as one bereft of wits ;
And all this labour and this large outcry
Is only for a silly butterfly.

EMBLEM

This little boy an emblem is of those
Whose hearts are wholly at the world's dispose.
The butterfly doth represent to me
The world's best things at best but fading be :
All are but painted nothings and false joys
Like this poor butterfly to these our boys.
  His running thorough nettles, thorns and briars
To gratify his boyish, fond desires,
His tumbling over mole-hills to attain
His end, namely his butterfly to gain,
Doth plainly show what hazards men will run
To get what will be lost as soon as won.
Men seem in choice, than children far more wise,
Because they run not after butterflies :
When yet alas ! for what are empty toys
They follow children, like to beardless boys.
Ibid.   •

MARGARET CAVENDISH, DUCHESS OF NEWCASTLE (1624-74)

XXVII

WIT

... Those verses still to me do seem the best
Where lines run smooth, and wit's with ease
    expressed ;

Where fancies flow, as gentle waters glide,
And flow'ry banks of rhet'ric on each side,
Which with delight the readers do invite
To read again, wishing they could so write ;
For verses should, like to a beauteous face ,
Both in the eye and in the heart take place,
That readers may, like lovers, wish to be
Always in their dear mistress' company.

Poems and Fancies, 1664.

XXVIII

WHEREIN POETRY CHIEFLY CONSISTS

Most of our modern writers nowadays
Consider not the fancy, but the phrase,
As if fine words were wit, or one should say,
A woman's handsome, if her clothes be gay,
Regarding not what beauty's in her face,
Nor what proportion doth the body grace ;
As when her shoes be high, to say she's tall,
And when she is strait lac'd, to say she's small ;
When painted, or her hair is curl'd with art,
Though of itself but plain, and her skin swart,
We cannot say, that from her thanks are due
To Nature, nor those arts in her we view,
Unless she them invented, and so taught
The world to set forth that which is stark
     naught ;
But fancy is the eye, gives life to all,
Words, the complexion, as a whited wall ;
Fancy the form is, flesh, blood, skin and bone,
Words are but shadows, substance they have
     none :
But number is the motion, gives the grace,
And is the count'nance of a well-formed face.

Ibid.

NATURE'S DESSERT

Sweet Marmalade of Kisses newly gathered
Preserved Children, which were never fathered ;
Sugar of Beauty, which away melts soon,
Marchpane of Youth and childish Macaroon ;
Sugar-Plum words, which fall sweet from the
    lips,
And Water-promises mouldering like chips ;
Biscuits of Love, which crumble all away,
Jelly of Fear, which shaked and quivering lay
Then was a fresh Green-sickness cheese brought
    in,
And tempting Fruit, like that which Eve made
    sin,
With Cream of Honour, which was thick and
    good.
Firm Nuts of sincere Friendship by it stood,
Grapes of Delight, dull Spirits to revive,
Whose Juice, 'tis said, doth Nature keep alive.
All this Dessert did Nature greatly please,
She eat and drank, then went to rest in Ease.

Ibid.

XXX

NATURE'S DRESS

The Sun crowns Nature's head with beams so
    fair,
The Stars do hang as jewels in her hair ;
Her garment's made of pure bright watchet sky,
Which round her waist the Zodiac doth tie ;
The Polar Circles, bracelets for each wrist,
The Planets round about her neck do twist ;

The Gold and Silver mines shoes for her feet,
And for her garters are the flowers sweet ;
Her stockings are of grass that's fresh and green,
The rainbow is like coloured ribands seen,
The powder for her hair is milk-white snow,
And when she comes, her locks the winds do
　　blow ;
Light, a thin veil, doth hang upon her face,
Through which her creatures see in every place.
Ibid.

XXXI

OF SHADOW AND ECHO

Pale Shadow once in love fell with bright Light
Which makes her still walk always in his sight,
And when he's absent, then, poor soul, she dies,
But when he shows himself, her life revives.
She sister is to Echo, loud and clear,
Whose voice is heard, no body doth appear ;
She hates to see or show herself to men
Unless Narcissus could revive again :
But these two souls (for they no bodies have)
Do wander in the air to seek a grave.
Silence would bury one, the other Night,
But was denied by Repercussion's spite ;
And both are subject to the eye and ear,
For one we see, and th' other we do hear.
Ibid.

XXXII

(*MELANCHOLY SPEAKS*)

I dwell in groves that gilt are with the sun,
Sit on the banks by which clear waters run ;

In summers hot, down in the shade I lie,
My music is the buzzing of a fly ;
Which flies do in the sunbeams dance all day
And harmlessly do pass their time away.
I walk in meadows, where grows fresh green
    grass,
In fields, where corn is high, I often pass ;
Walk up the hills, where round I prospects see,
Some brushy woods, and some all champains be ;
Returning back, I in fresh pastures go,
To hear how sheep do bleat, and cows do low ;
They gently feed, and do no evil know,
Have no designs each other wrong to do.
In winter cold, when nipping frosts come on,
Then I do live in a small house alone ;
Which being little and close, doth make it warm.
No wind or weather cold can do it harm.
Altho' 'tis plain, yet cleanly 'tis within
Like to a soul that's pure and clear from sin ;
And there I dwell in quiet and still peace,
Not filled with cares how riches to increase ;
I wish nor seek for vain and fruitless pleasures.
No riches are, but what the mind intreasures.
Thus am I solitary, live alone,
Yet better loved, the more that I am known.
For I am like a shade : who sits in me
He shall not wet, nor yet sunburned be.

Ibid.

XXXIII

A poet I am neither born nor bred,
But to a witty poet married,
Whose brain is fresh and pleasant as the spring,
Where fancies grow, and where the Muses sing.
There oft I lean my head, and listening hark
To observe his words, and all his fancies mark ;

And from that garden flowers of fancies take
Whereof a posy up in verse I make :
Thus I that have no garden of my own,
There gather flowers that are newly blown.
Ibid.

MATTHEW STEVENSON (1627?-85)

XXXIV

APRIL

Hail, April, true Medea of the year,
That makest all things young and fresh appear.
What praise, what thanks, what commendation
   due
For all thy pearly drops of morning dew ?
When we despair, thy seasonable showers
Comfort the corn, and cheer the drooping
   flowers ;
As if thy charity could not but impart
A shower of tears to see us out of heart.
Sweet, I have penned thy praise and here I bring
   it
In confidence the birds themselves will sing it.

The Twelve Months, 1661.

XXXV

TO BOSCOBELLA

Madam, I love and truly, should I not
I must have both you and myself forgot :
I talk not of the little winged Boy
Nor his fair flattering mother that burnt Troy ;
Nor clothe I my discourse in pastoral dress,
Call myself swain, nor you my shepherdess.
I rank you not with Heaven's bright tutelars,
Nor rival you unto the moon or stars,

Condemn not then my plainness, for I mean
No feigned story, but Love's faithful scene,
And send you therefore to augment its fuel
This present of plain dealing for a jewel.

Poems, 1665.

XXXVI

. . . No, I'll to tavern, where being come,
The first attendant shows a room.
The next presents a glancing lass
Like Venus in a Venice glass.
With that I knock and as some sprite,
I conjure up pure red and white.
My circle's a round table, and
In midst thereof does Hymen stand,
With a light taper, when I call
To celebrate my nuptial.
Here do I a French madam place,
And there a sweet-lipped Spanish lass.
Here all in white a lady dances,
And there in red another glances,
And lest mine eyes want fresh delight,
Here sits Claretta, red and white.
Nor do I compliment, I trow,
But tell 'em plain, 'tis so and so.
They struggle not, nor are they coy,
But I may what I will enjoy.
No, there's no coil made for a kiss,
Though melting, melting, melting bliss,
No shifting from the friendly cup
But I may freely all take up.
And in each face, if so I please,
I'll court my own effigies.
Who would not then on this stage act Narcissus,
Where lively lips so sweetly say, come kiss us ?

Ibid.

XXXVII

THE WILLOW GARLAND

How many coronets of daffodillies
Of purer roses and of Paphian lilies
Wove thy false hope for her thou thoughtst thy
    own
When Fate was wreathing willows for thy
    crown . . .

Ibid.

XXXVIII

UPON THE VIRTUOUS BROWN (I KNOW WHO) AT THE POPINJAY

Lilies and roses, let who will go suit ye
I'm for the lovely brown, the lasting beauty.
Her cheeks are roses need no thorny fence,
And there's no lily like her innocence.
Their blossoms are but slaves to every blast,
But she's the same, when Spring and Autumn's
    past.
Her May's eternal : she, when envious Time
Shall be no more, is then but in her prime.
She shall bid all these fading forms adieu
And Heaven and Earth shall for her sake be new.

Poems, 1673.

SIR ROBERT HOWARD (1626-98)

XXXIX

TO THE UNCONSTANT CYNTHIA

Tell me once, dear, how it does prove
    That I so much forsworn could be ?

I never swore always to love,
   I only vow'd still to love thee :
And art thou now what thou wert then,
Unsworn unto by other men ?

In thy fair breath, and once fair soul,
   I thought my vows were writ alone ;
But others' oaths so blurred the scroll,
   That I no more could read my own.
And am I still obliged to pay,
When you had thrown the bond away ?

Nor must we only part in joy,
   Our tears as well must be unkind :
Weep you that could such truth destroy,
   And I, that could such falseness find.
Thus we must unconcerned remain
In our divided joys and pain.

Yet we may love, but on this different score,
You what I am, I what you were before.

Poems, 1660.

JAMES HOWARD

XL

Ladies, farewell ! I must retire,
Though I your faces all admire,
And think you heavens in your kinds,
Some for beauties, some for minds :
If I stay and fall in love,
One of these heavens, hell would prove.

Could I love one, and she not know it,
Perhaps I then might undergo it ;
But if the least she guess my mind,
Straight in a circle I'm confined ;

By this I see, who once doth dote,
Must wear a woman's livery coat.

Therefore, this danger to prevent,
And still to keep my heart's content,
Into the country I'll with speed,
With hounds and hawks my fancy feed :
Both safer pleasures to pursue,
Than staying to converse with you.

The English Monsieur, 1674.

GEORGE VILLIERS, DUKE OF
BUCKINGHAM (1628-87)

XLI

*AN EPITAPH ON THOMAS,
THIRD LORD FAIRFAX*

*Under this stone does lie
One born for Victory.*

Fairfax the valiant ; and the only he
Who e'er, for that alone a conqueror would be.
    Both sexes' virtues were in him combined :
He had the fierceness of the manliest mind,
And yet the meekness too of womankind.
    He never knew what envy was, or hate.
His soul was filled with worth and honesty ;
    And with another thing, quite out of date,
        Called modesty.

He ne'er seemed impudent but in the field, a
    place
Where impudence itself dares seldom show its
    face.

B

Had any stranger spied him in the room
With some of those he had overcome,
And had not heard their talk, but only seen
   Their gestures and their mien,
They would have sworn he had the vanquished
    been.
For as they bragged and dreadful would appear
While they their own ill lucks in war repeated,
His modesty still made him blush to hear
   How often he had them defeated.

Through his whole life, the part he bore
   Was wonderful and great,
And yet it so appeared in nothing more
   Than in his private last retreat,
   For it's a stranger thing to find
   One man of such a glorious mind,
   As can dismiss the power he has got,
Than millions of the sots and braves
(Those despicable fools and knaves),
   Who such a pother make,
   Through dulness and mistake,
In seeking after power and get it not.

When all the nation he had won,
And with expense of blood had bought
   Store great enough, he thought,
   Of fame and of renown,
   He then his arms laid down
   With full as little pride
As if he had been of his enemies' side ;
Or one of them could do, that were undone.

   He neither wealth nor places sought ;
   For others, not himself, he fought.
     He was content to know
     (For he had found it so)
That when he pleased to conquer he was able,
And left the spoil and plunder to the rabble.

He might have been a king,
  But that he understood
How much it is a meaner thing
To be unjustly great, than honourably good.

This from the world did admiration draw,
And from his friends both love and awe,
Remembering what in fight he did before.
  Nay his foes loved him too,
  As they were bound to do,
Because he was resolved to fight no more.
So, blessed of all, he died.   But far more blessed
  were we,
If we were sure to live till we could see
A man as great in war, in peace as just, as he.

Miscellany Poems, 1692
  [Broadside, 1677].

XLII

TO HIS MISTRESS

Phillis, though your all-powerful charms
Have forced me from my Celia's arms,
That sure defence against all powers
But those resistless eyes of yours,
Think not your conquest to maintain
By rigour or unjust disdain ;
In vain, fair nymph, in vain you strive,
Since love does seldom hope survive :
Or if I languish for a time,
While all your glories in their prime
May justify such cruelty
By the same force that conquered me ;
When age shall come, at whose command
Those troops of beauties must disband,
A tyrant's strength once took away,
What slave so dull as to obey ?

These threatening dangers then remove :
Make me at least believe you love ;
Dissemble, and by that sly art
Preserve and govern well my heart ;
Or if you'll learn a nobler way
To keep your empire from decay,
And here for ever fix your throne,
Be kind, but kind to me alone.

1665.

XLIII

TO HIS MISTRESS

What a dull fool was I,
  To think so gross a lie
As that I ever was in love before !
  I have, perhaps, known one or two
  With whom I was content to be
At that which they call ' keeping company.'
  But, after all that they could do,
    I still could be with more.
Their absence never made me shed a tear ;
    And I can truly swear,
  That, till my eyes first gazed on you,
I ne'er beheld that thing I could adore.

A world of things must curiously be sought,
A world of things must be together brought,
To make up charms which have the power to
    move,
  Through a discerning eye, true love.
  That is a masterpiece, above
  What only looks and shape can do ;
  There must be wit, and judgment too,
  Greatness of thought, and worth, which draw
  From the whole world, respect and awe.

She that would raise a noble love, must find
Ways to beget a passion for her mind,
She must be that, which she to be would seem ;
For all true love is grounded on esteem.
Plainness and truth gain more a generous heart
Than all the crooked subtleties of art.
At least, I'm sure, thus much I plainly see,
None but yourself e'er did it upon me.
'Tis you alone, that can my heart subdue
    To you alone, it always shall be true.

Miscellaneous Works, 1704.

XLIV

FORTUNE

Fortune, made up of toys and impudence,
That common jade, that has not common sense ;
But fond of business, insolently dares
Pretend to rule, and spoils the world's affairs ;
She, flutt'ring up and down, her favours throws
On the next met, not minding what she does ;
Nor why, nor whom she helps or injures, knows.
Sometimes she smiles, then like a fury raves ;
And seldom truly loves, but fools or knaves.
Let her love whom she please, I scorn to woo her ;
Whilst she stays with me, I'll be civil to her,
But if she offers once to move her wings,
I'll fling her back all her vain gew-gaw things,
And, armed with virtue, will more glorious stand,
Than if the bitch still bow'd at my command.
I'll marry Honesty, tho' ne'er so poor,
Rather than follow such a dull blind whore.

Miscellany Poems, iv, 1694.

WALTER POPE (1627?-1714

XLV

THE WISH

If I live to be old, for I find I go down,
Let this be my fate : in a country town
May I have a warm house, with a stone at the
gate
And a cleanly young girl to rub my bald pate.
  May I govern my passion with an absolute
    sway,
  And grow wiser and better as my strength
    wears away,
  Without gout or stone, by a gentle decay.

Near a shady grove, and a murmuring brook,
With the ocean at distance, whereupon I may
  look,
With a spacious plain without hedge or stile,
And an easy pad-nag to ride out a mile.
  May I govern my passion with an absolute
    sway,
  And grow wiser and better as my strength
    wears away,
  Without gout or stone, by a gentle decay.

With Horace and Petrarch, and two or three
  more
Of the best wits that reigned in the ages before,
With roast mutton, rather than venison or veal,
And clean though coarse linen at every meal.
  May I govern my passion with an absolute
    sway,
  And grow wiser and better as my strength
    wears away,
  Without gout or stone, by a gentle decay.

With a pudding on Sundays, with stout humming
    liquor,
And remnants of Latin to welcome the vicar,
With Monte-Fiascone or Burgundy wine,
To drink the King's health as oft as I dine.
    May I govern my passion with an absolute
        sway,
      And grow wiser and better as my strength
        wears away,
    Without gout or stone, by a gentle decay.

With a courage undaunted may I face my last
    day,
And when I am dead may the better sort say,
In the morning when sober, in the evening when
    mellow,
He's gone, and left not behind him his fellow.
    May I govern my passion with an absolute
        sway,
      And grow wiser and better as my strength
        wears away,
    Without gout or stone, by a gentle decay.

CHARLES COTTON (1630-87)

XLVI

*RESOLUTION IN FOUR SONNETS, OF A
    POETICAL QUESTION PUT TO ME
    BY A FRIEND, CONCERNING FOUR
    RURAL SISTERS*

I

Alice is tall and upright as a pine,
White as blanched almonds, or the falling snow,
Sweet as are damask roses when they blow,
And doubtless fruitful as the swelling vine.

Ripe to be cut, and ready to be pressed,
Her full-cheeked beauties very well appear;
And a year's fruit she loses every year,
Wanting a man t' improve her to the best.

Full fain she would be husbanded, and yet,
Alas! she cannot a fit labourer get
To cultivate her to her own content:

Fain would she be (God wot) about her task,
And yet (forsooth) she is too proud to ask,
And (which is worse) too modest to consent.

2

Margaret of humbler stature by the head
Is (as it oft falls out with yellow hair)
Than her fair sister, yet so much more fair,
As her pure white is better mixed with red.

This, hotter than the other ten to one,
Longs to be put unto her mother's trade,
And loud proclaims she lives too long a maid,
Wishing for one t'untie her virgin zone.

She finds virginity a kind of ware
That's very very troublesome to bear,
And being gone, she thinks will ne'er be missed;

And yet withal, the girl has so much grace,
To call for help I know she wants the face,
Though asked, I know not how she would resist.

3

Mary is black, and taller than the last,
Yet equal in perfection and desire,
To the one's melting snow, and t' other's fire,
As with whose black their fairness is defaced.

She pants as much for love as th' other two,
But she so virtuous is, or else so wise,

That she will win (or will not love) a prize,
And but upon good terms will never do :

Therefore who her will conquer ought to be
At least as full of love and wit as she,
Or he shall ne'er gain favour at her hands ;

Nay, though he have a pretty store of brains,
Shall only have his labour for his pains,
Unless he offer more than she demands.

4

Martha is not so tall, nor yet so fair
As any of the other lovely three,
Her chiefest grace is poor simplicity ;
Yet were the rest away, she were a star.

She's fair enough, only she wants the art
To set her beauties off as they can do,
And that's the cause she ne'er heard any woo,
Nor ever yet made conquest of a heart :

And yet her blood's as boiling as the best,
Which, pretty soul, does so disturb her rest,
And makes her languish so, she's fit to die.

Poor thing, I doubt she still must lie alone,
For being like to be attacked by none,
She's no more wit to ask than to deny.

Poems, 1689.

XLVII

OLD TITYRUS TO EUGENIA

I

Eugenia young, and fair and sweet,
  The glory of the plains,

In thee alone the graces meet
   To conquer all the swains :
Tall as the poplar of the grove,
Straight as the winged shaft of Love,
As the Spring's early blossoms white,
Soft as the kisses of the light,
Serene and modest as the morn,
   Ere vapours do from fens arise,
   To dim the glory of the skies,
Untainted, or with pride or scorn,
T'oblige the world, bright Nymph, thou sure
   wast born.

2

Oh ! be still fair, thou charming maid,
   For beauty is no crime ;
May thy youth's flower never fade,
   But still be in its prime :
Be calm, and clear, and modest still,
Oblige as many as you will,
Still, still be humble, still be sweet ;
By those ways conquer all you meet ;
But let them see 'tis undesigned,
   Natural virtues, not put on
   To make a prize of any one,
The native goodness of your mind ;
And have a care of being over-kind :

3

That's (my Eugenia) a mistake
   That noblest ardours cools,
And serves on th' other side to make
   Damn'd over-weening fools.
Be courteous unto all, and free,
As far as virgin modesty ;
Be not too shy, but have a care
Of being too familiar ;

The swain you entertain alone,
   To whom you lend your hand or lip,
   Will think he has you on the hip,
And straight conclude you are his own,
Women so easy, men so vain are grown.

4

Reservedness is a mighty friend
   To form and virtue too,
A shining merit should pretend
   To such a star as you ;
'Tis not a roundelay well played,
A song well sung, a thing well said,
A fall well given, a bar well thrown,
Should carry such a lovely one.
Should these knacks win you, you will be
   (Of all the Nymphs that with their beams
   Gild swift Columba's crystal streams)
Lost to the world, your self and me,
And more despised than freckled Lalage.

5

Maintain a modest kind of state,
   'Tis graceful in a maid ;
It does at least respect create,
   And makes the fools afraid.
Eugenia, you must pitch upon
A Sylvia, not a Corydon ;
'Twould grate my soul to see those charms
In an unworthy shepherd's arms.
A little coldness (girl) will do,
   Let baffled lovers call it pride,
   Pride's an excess o' th' better side,
Contempt to arrogance is due,
Keep but state now, and keep 't hereafter too.

Ibid.

XLVIII

NIGHT QUATRAINS

. . . Nyctimine now freed from day,
From sullen bush flies out to prey,
And does with ferret note proclaim
Th' arrival of th' usurping Dame.

The rail now crakes in fields and meads,
Toads now forsake the nettle-beds,
The tim'rous hare goes to relief,
And wary men bolt out the thief.

The fire's new raked, and hearth swept clean
By Madge, the dirty kitchen-quean,
The safe is locked, the mouse-trap set,
The leaven laid, and bucking wet.

Now in false floors and roofs above,
The lustful cats make ill-tuned love,
The ban-dog on the dunghill lies,
And watchful nurse sings lullabies.

Philomel chants it whilst she bleeds,
The bittern booms it in the reeds,
And Reynard entering the back yard,
The Capitolian cry is heard.

The goblin now the fool alarms,
Hags meet to mumble o'er their charms ;
The night-mare rides the dreaming ass,
And fairies trip it on the grass.

The drunkard now supinely snores,
His load of ale sweats through his pores,
Yet when he wakes the swine shall find
A crapula remains behind.

The sober now and chaste are blest
With sweet, and with refreshing rest,
And to sound sleeps they've best pretence,
Have greatest share of innocence.

We should so live then that we may
Fearless put off our clouts and clay,
And travel through death's shades to light ;
For every day must have its night.

Ibid.

XLIX

THE NEW YEAR

Hark, the cock crows, and yon bright star,
Tells us the day himself's not far ;
And see where, breaking from the night,
He gilds the western hills with light.
With him old Janus does appear,
Peeping into the future year
With such a look as seems to say
The prospect is not good that way.
Thus do we rise ill sights to see,
And 'gainst our selves to prophesy,
When the prophetic fear of things
A more tormenting mischief brings,
More full of soul-tormenting gall
Than direst mischiefs can befall.
    But stay ! but stay ! methinks my sight,
Better informed by clearer light,
Discerns sereneness in that brow,
That all contracted seemed but now :
His reverse face may shew distaste,
And frown upon the ills are past ;
But that which this way looks is clear,
And smiles upon the new-born year.
He looks too from a place so high,

The year lies open to his eye,
And all the moments open are
To the exact discoverer ;
Yet more and more he smiles upon
The happy revolution.
Why should we then suspect or fear
The influences of a year
So smiles upon us the first morn,
And speaks us good so soon as born ?
Pox on't ! the last was ill enough,
This cannot but make better proof ;
Or at the worst, as we brushed through
The last, why so we may this too ;
And then the next in reason should,
Be superexcellently good :
For the worst ills we daily see
Have no more perpetuity
Than the best fortunes that do fall ;
Which also brings us wherewithal
Longer their being to support,
Than those do of the other sort ;
And who has one good year in three,
And yet repines at Destiny,
Appears ingrateful in the case,
And merits not the good he has.
Then let us welcome the new guest,
With lusty brimmers of the best ;
Mirth always should good Fortune meet,
And renders e'en disaster sweet :
And though the Princess turn her back,
Let us but line ourselves with sack
We better shall by far hold out,
Till the next year she face about.

Ibid.

L

WINTER

. . . Then let the chill Scirocco blow,
And gird us round with hills of snow ;
Or else go whistle to the shore,
And make the hollow mountains roar.

Whilst we together jovial sit
Careless, and crowned with mirth and wit ;
Where though bleak winds confine us home,
Our fancies round the world shall roam.

We'll think of all the friends we know,
And drink to all worth drinking to :
When having drunk all thine and mine,
We rather shall want healths than wine.

But where friends fail us, we'll supply
Our friendships with our charity ;
Men that remote in sorrows live,
Shall by our lusty brimmers thrive.

We'll drink the wanting into wealth,
And those that languish into health,
The afflicted into joy, the oppressed
Into security and rest.

The worthy in disgrace shall find
Favour return again more kind,
And in restraint who stifled lie,
Shall taste the air of liberty.

The brave shall triumph in success,
The lovers shall have mistresses,
Poor unregarded virtue praise,
And the neglected poet bays.

Thus shall our healths do others good
Whilst we ourselves do all we would ;

For freed from envy and from care,
What would we be, but what we are ?

'Tis the plump grape's immortal juice
That does this happiness produce,
And will preserve us free together,
Maugre mischance, or wind and weather.

Then let old Winter take his course,
And roar abroad till he be hoarse,
And his lungs crack with ruthless ire ;
It shall but serve to blow our fire.

Let him our little castle ply,
With all his loud artillery,
Whilst sack and claret man the fort
His fury shall become our sport.

Or, let him Scotland take, and there
Confine the plotting Presbyter ;
His zeal may freeze, whilst we kept warm
With love and wine, can know no harm.

Ibid.

LI

THE RETIREMENT

Stanzes Irreguliers

To MR. IZAAK WALTON

Farewell thou busy World, and may
    We never meet again :
Here I can eat, and sleep, and pray,
And do more good in one short day,
    Than he who his whole age out-wears
Upon thy most conspicuous theatres,
Where nought but vice and vanity do reign.

Good God ! how sweet are all things here,
How beautiful the fields appear !

How cleanly do we feed and lie !
Lord ! what good hours do we keep !
    How quietly we sleep !
What peace ! what unanimity !
How innocent from the lewd fashion
Is all our bus'ness, all our conversation !

Oh how happy here's our leisure !
Oh how innocent our pleasure !
O ye valleys, O ye mountains,
O ye groves and crystal fountains,
    How I love at liberty,
By turn to come and visit ye !

O Solitude, the Soul's best friend,
That man acquainted with himself dost make,
And all his Maker's wonders to intend ;
    With thee I here converse at will,
    And would be glad to do so still ;
For it is thou alone that keep'st the soul awake.

    How calm and quiet a delight
        It is alone
    To read, and meditate, and write,
By none offended, nor offending none :
To walk, ride, sit, or sleep at one's own ease,
And pleasing a man's self, none other to dis-
    please !

O my beloved Nymph ! fair Dove,
Princess of rivers, how I love
    Upon thy flow'ry banks to lie,
    And view thy silver stream,
When gilded by a summer's beam,
And in it all thy wanton fry
    Playing at liberty,
And with my angle upon them,
    The all of treachery
I ever learned to practise and to try ! . . .

O my beloved rocks ! that rise
To awe the earth, and brave the skies,
From some aspiring mountain's crown
How dearly do I love,
Giddy with pleasure, to look down ;
And from the vales to view the noble heights
above ! . . .

Lord ! would men let me alone,
What an over-happy one
Should I think myself to be,
Might I in this desert place
Which most men by their voice disgrace,
Live but undisturbed and free !
Here, in this despised recess,
Would I maugre winter's cold,
And the summer's worst excess,
Try to live out to sixty full years old,
And all the while
Without an envious eye
Or any thriving under Fortune's smile,
Contented live, and then contented die.

Ibid.

LII

From ' THE JOYS OF MARRIAGE '

. . . Yet with me 'tis out of season
To complain thus without reason,
Since the best and sweetest fair
Is allotted to my share ;
But alas ! I love her so
That my love creates my woe ;
For if she be out of humour,
Straight displeased I do presume her,
And would give the world to know
What it is offends her so :

Or if she be discontented,
Lord, how am I then tormented !
And am ready to persuade her
That I have unhappy made her :
But if sick I then am dying,
Meat and med'cine both defying :
So uneasy is his life
Who is married to a wife. . . .

KATHERINE PHILIPS (1631-64)

LIII

AN ANSWER TO ANOTHER PERSUADING
A LADY TO MARRIAGE

Forbear, bold youth, all's Heaven here,
    And what you do aver,
To others courtship may appear,
    'Tis sacrilege to her.

She is a public deity,
    And were 't not very odd
She should dispose herself to be
    A petty household god ?

First make the sun in private shine,
    And bid the world adieu,
That so he may his beams confine
    In compliment to you.

But if of that you do despair,
    Think how you did amiss,
To strive to fix her beams which are
    More bright and large than this.

Poems, 1667.

LIV

AGAINST LOVE

Hence Cupid, with your cheating toys,
Your real griefs, and painted joys,
Your pleasure which itself destroys.
    Lovers like men in fevers burn and rave,
    And only what will injure them do crave.

Men's weakness makes love so severe,
They give him power by their fear,
And make the shackles which they wear.
    Who to another does his heart submit,
    Makes his own idol, and then worships it.

Him, whose heart is all his own,
Peace and liberty does crown,
He apprehends no killing frown,
    He feels no raptures which are joys diseas'd,
    And is not much transported, but still pleas'd.

Ibid.

FRANCES BOOTHBY

LV

ERICINIA'S SONG

O you powerful Gods ! If I must be
An injured offering to Love's deity ;
Grant my revenge ! this plague on men :
That women ne'er may love again !
Then I'll, with joy, submit unto my fate,
Which, by your justice, gives their empire date.

Depose that proud insulting Boy,
Who most is pleased, when he can most destroy !

Oh, let the World no longer governed be
By such a blind and childish deity !
For if you Gods be in your power severe,
We shall adore you, not from love, but fear.

   But if you'll his divinity maintain,
O'er men, false men, confine his torturing reign.
And when their hearts Love's greatest torments
      prove,
Let that not pity, but our laughter move.
Thus scorned, and lost to all their wishes' aim,
Let rage, despair, and death then end their flame.

Marcelia, 1670.

JOHN DRYDEN (1631-1700)

LVI

SONG

Ah fading joy, how quickly art thou past !
     Yet we thy ruin haste :
As if the cares of human life were few,
     We seek out new,
And follow Fate that does too fast pursue.

See how on ev'ry bough the birds express
   In their sweet notes their happiness.
   They all enjoy and nothing spare ;
But on their mother Nature lay their care :
Why then should Man, the lord of all below,
   Such troubles choose to know,
As none of all his subjects undergo ?

Hark, hark, the waters fall, fall, fall,
   And with a murmuring sound
   Dash, dash, upon the ground,
    To gentle slumbers call.

The Indian Emperor, 1667.

LVII

SECRET LOVE

I feed a flame within which so torments me
That it both pains my heart, and yet contents
   me :
'Tis such a pleasing smart and I so love it,
That I had rather die, than once remove it.

Yet he for whom I grieve shall never know it,
My tongue does not betray, nor my eyes shew it :
Not a sigh, not a tear my pain discloses,
But they fall silently like dew on roses.

Thus to prevent my love from being cruel,
My heart's the sacrifice as 'tis the fuel :
And while I suffer thus to give him quiet,
My faith rewards my love, though he deny it.

On his eyes will I gaze, and there delight me ;
While I conceal my love, no frown can fright me :
To be more happy I dare not aspire ;
Nor can I fall more low, mounting no higher.

The Maiden Queen, 1668.

LVIII

You pleasing dreams of love and sweet delight,
Appear before this slumb'ring virgin's sight :
Soft visions, set her free
From mournful piety.
Let her sad thoughts from Heaven retire ;
And let the melancholy love
Of those remoter joys above
Give place to your more sprightly fire.

Let purling streams be in her fancy seen,
And flowery meads, and vales of cheerful green,
And in the midst of deathless groves
Soft smiling wishes lie
And smiling hopes fast by,
And just beyond 'em ever-laughing Loves.

Tyrannic Love,
    Or, The Royal Martyr, 1670.

LIX

SONG A L'ANGLOISE

After the pangs of a desperate lover,
    When day and night I have sighed all in vain,
Ah what a pleasure it is to discover
    In her eyes pity, who causes my pain !

When with unkindness our love at a stand is,
    And both have punished ourselves with the
        pain,
Ah what a pleasure the touch of her hand is,
    Ah what a pleasure to press it again !

When the denial comes fainter and fainter,
    And her eyes give what her tongue does deny,
Ah what a trembling I feel when I venture,
    Ah what a trembling does usher my joy !

When, with a sigh, she accords me the blessing,
    And her eyes twinkle 'twixt pleasure and pain ;
Ah what a joy 'tis, beyond all expressing,
    Ah what a joy to hear, shall we again ?

An Evening's Love, 1671.

LX

DAMON

Celimena, of my heart
None shall e'er bereave you :
If with your good leave I may
Quarrel with you once a day
I will never leave you.

CELIMENA

Passion's but an empty name
Where respect is wanting :
Damon, you mistake your aim ;
Hang your heart and burn your flame,
If you must be ranting.

DAMON

Love as dull and muddy is,
As decaying liquor :
Anger sets it on the lees,
And refines it by degrees,
Till it works it quicker.

CELIMENA

Love by quarrels to beget
Wisely you endeavour ;
With a grave physician's wit,
Who to cure an ague fit
Put me in a fever.

DAMON

Anger rouses love to fight,
And his only bait is,
'Tis the spur to dull delight,
And is but an eager bite,
When desire at height is.

CELIMENA

If such drops of heat can fall
In our wooing weather,
If such drops of heat can fall
We shall have the devil and all
When we come together.

An Evening's Love, 1671.

LXI

SONG OF THE ZAMBRA DANCE

Beneath a myrtle shade
Which love for none but happy lovers made,
I slept, and straight my love before me brought
Phillis the object of my waking thought;
Undressed she came my flames to meet,
While love strowed flowers beneath her feet;
Flowers, which so pressed by her, became more
      sweet.

From the bright vision's head
A careless veil of lawn was loosely spread:
From her white temples fell her shaded hair,
Like cloudy sunshine, not too brown nor fair:
Her hands, her lips did love inspire;
Her ev'ry grace my heart did fire:
But most her eyes which languished with
      desire . . . .

The Conquest of Granada (Part I), 1672.

LXII

Can life be a blessing,
Or worth the possessing,
Can life be a blessing if love were away?

Ah no ! though our love all night keep us
    waking,
And though he torment us with cares all the day,
  Yet he sweetens, he sweetens our pains in the
    taking,
There's an hour at the last, there's an hour to
  repay.

    In ev'ry possessing
    The ravishing blessing,
In ev'ry possessing the fruit of our pain,
  Poor lovers forget long ages of anguish,
Whate'er they have suffered and done to obtain ;
  'Tis a pleasure, a pleasure to sigh and to
    languish,
When we hope, when we hope to be happy again.

Troilus and Cressida, 1679.

LXIII

Farewell ungrateful traitor,
  Farewell my perjured swain,
Let never injured creature
  Believe a man again.
The pleasure of possessing
Surpasses all expressing,
But 'tis too short a blessing,
  And love too long a pain.

'Tis easy to deceive us
  In pity of your pain,
But when we love you leave us
  To rail at you in vain.
Before we have descried it
There is no bliss beside it,
But she that once has tried it
  Will never love again.

The passion you pretended
 Was only to obtain,
But when the charm is ended
 The charmer you disdain.
Your love by ours we measure
Till we have lost our treasure ;
But dying is a pleasure,
 When living is a pain.

The Spanish Friar, 1681.

LXIV

Fair Iris I love and hourly I die,
But not for a lip nor a languishing eye :
She's fickle and false, and there I agree ;
For I am as false and as fickle as she :
We neither believe what either can say ;
And, neither believing, we neither betray.

'Tis civil to swear and say things of course ;
We mean not the taking for better or worse.
When present we love, when absent agree ;
I think not of Iris, nor Iris of me :
The legend of love no couple can find
So easy to part, or so equally joined.

Amphitryon, 1690.

LXV

No, no, poor suff'ring heart, no change endeavour,
Choose to sustain the smart, rather than leave
 her ;
My ravished eyes behold such charms about her,
I can die with her, but not live without her :
One tender sigh of hers to see me languish,
Will more than pay the price of my past anguish :
Beware, O cruel fair, how you smile on me,
'Twas a kind look of yours that has undone me.

Love has in store for me one happy minute,
And she will end my pain who did begin it ;
Then no day void of bliss or pleasure leaving,
Ages shall slide away without perceiving ;
Cupid shall guard the door the more to please us,
And keep out Time and Death, when they would
    seize us ;
Time and Death shall depart, and say in flying,
Love has found out a way to live by dying.

Cleomenes, 1692.

LXVI

THE SECULAR MASQUE

Enter JANUS

JANUS

Chronos, Chronos, mend thy pace :
An hundred times the rolling sun
Around the radiant belt has run
    In his revolving race.
Behold, behold, the goal in sight ;
Spread thy fans, and wing thy flight.

> *Enter* CHRONOS, *with a scythe in his
> hand and a great globe on his back,
> which he sets down at his entrance.*

CHRONOS

Weary, weary of my weight,
Let me, let me drop my freight,
    And leave the World behind.
      I could not bear
      Another year
    The load of human kind.

Enter MOMUS *laughing*

MOMUS

Ha   ha! ha! Ha! ha! ha! Well hast thou
    done
  To lay down thy pack,
  And lighten thy back.
The world was a fool, e'er since it begun,
And since neither Janus, nor Chronos, nor I
  Can hinder the crimes
  Or mend the bad times,
'Tis better to laugh than to cry.

CHORUS

'Tis better to laugh than to cry.

JANUS

Since Momus comes to laugh below,
  Old Time begin the show,
That he may see, in every scene,
What changes in this age have been.

CHRONOS

Then Goddess of the silver bow begin.

Horns, or hunting music within.

Enter DIANA

DIANA

With horns and with hounds I waken the day,
And hie to my woodland walks away ;
I tuck up my robe, and am buskined soon,
And tie to my forehead a wexing moon.
I course the fleet stag, unkennel the fox,
And chase the wild goats o'er summits of rocks,
With shouting and hooting we pierce thro' the
    sky ;
And Echo turns hunter, and doubles the cry.

Chorus

With shouting and hooting we pierce through the
    sky,
And Echo turns hunter, and doubles the cry.

Janus

Then our age was in its prime :

Chronos

Free from rage.

Diana

    And free from crime.

Momus

A very merry, dancing, drinking,
Laughing, quaffing and unthinking time.

Chorus

Then our age was in its prime,
Free from rage, amd free from crime,
A very merry, dancing, drinking,
Laughing, quaffing and unthinking time.

(Dance of Diana's Attendants)

Enter Mars

Mars

Inspire the vocal brass, inspire ;
The world is past its infant age :
    Arms and honour,
    Arms and honour,
Set the martial mind on fire,
And kindle manly rage.
    Mars has looked the sky to red,
And Peace, the lazy good, is fled.

Plenty, Peace and Pleasure fly;
The sprightly green
In woodland walks no more is seen;
The sprightly green has drunk the Tyrian dye.

CHORUS

Plenty, Peace, etc.

MARS

Sound the trumpet, beat the drum;
Through all the world around,
Sound a reveille, sound, sound,
The warrior God is come.

CHORUS

Sound the trumpet, etc.

MOMUS

Thy sword within the scabbard keep,
And let mankind agree;
Better the world were fast asleep,
Than kept awake by thee.
The fools are only thinner,
With all our cost and care;
But neither side a winner,
For things are as they were.

CHORUS

The fools are only, etc.

Enter VENUS

VENUS

Calms appear, when storms are past;
Love will have his hour at last:
Nature is my kindly care;
Mars destroys, and I repair;
Take me, take me, while you may,
Venus comes not ev'ry day.

CHORUS

Take her, take her, etc.

CHRONOS

The world was then so light,
I scarcely felt the weight ;
Joy ruled the day, and Love the night.
But since the Queen of Pleasure left the ground
I faint, I lag,
And feebly drag
The pond'rous Orb around.

MOMUS

All, all of a piece throughout !

Pointing to DIANA

Thy chase had a beast in view.

To MARS

Thy wars brought nothing about ;

To VENUS

Thy lovers were all untrue.

JANUS

'Tis well an old age is out.

CHRONOS

And time to begin a new.

CHORUS

All, all of a piece throughout : etc.

*Dance of Huntsmen, Nymphs, Warriors and
Lovers*

FINIS

LXVII

ALMANZOR

Fair though you are
As summer mornings, and your eyes more bright
Than stars that twinkle in a winter's night ;
Though you have eloquence to warm and move
Cold age and praying hermits into love ;
Though Almahide with scorn rewards my care,—
Yet, than to change, 'tis nobler to despair.
My love's my soul ; and that from fate is free ;
'Tis that unchanged and deathless part of me.

Conquest of Granada (Part ii), 1672.

LXVIII

AURUNGZEBE

When I consider life, 'tis all a cheat ;
Yet, fooled with hope, men favour the deceit ;
Trust on, and think to-morrow will repay :
To-morrow's falser than the former day ;
Lies worse, and, while it says we shall be blest
With some new joys, cuts off what we possessed.
Strange cozenage ! None would live past years
    again,
Yet all hope pleasure in what yet remain ;
And, from the dregs of life, think to receive,
What the first sprightly running could not give.
I'm tired with waiting for this chemic gold,
Which fools us young, and beggars us when old.

Aurungzebe, 1676.

C

ANTONY

But I have lost my reason, have disgraced
The name of soldier with inglorious ease.
In the full vintage of my flowing honours,
Sat still, and saw it pressed by other hands.
Fortune came smiling to my youth, and wooed
    it,
And purple greatness met my ripened years.
When first I came to empire, I was borne
On tides of people crowding to my triumphs,
The wish of nations ; and the willing world
Received me as its pledge of future peace ;
I was so great, so happy, so beloved,
Fate could not ruin me : till I took pains   ,
And worked against my fortune, chid her from
    me,
And turned her loose ; yet still she came again.
My careless days, and my luxurious nights,
At length have wearied her, and now she's gone,
Gone, gone, divorced for ever. Help me,
    soldier,
To curse this madman, this industrious fool,
Who laboured to be wretched :   Pr'ythee, curse
    me.

All for Love, 1678.

ANTONY'S FAREWELL

Think we have had a clear and glorious day
And Heaven did kindly to delay the storm,
Just till our close of evening.   Ten years' love
And not a moment lost, but all improved
To the utmost joys,—what ages have we lived ?

And now to die each other's ; and, so dying,
While hand in hand we walk in groves below,
Whole troops of lovers' ghosts shall flock about
  us,
And all the train be ours.

Ibid.

LXXI

CLEOPATRA

'Tis sweet to die, when they would force life
    on me,
To rush into the dark abode of death,
And seize him first ; if he be like my love
He is not frightful, sure.
We're now alone, in secrecy and silence ;
And is not this like lovers ? I may kiss
These pale, cold lips ; Octavia does not see me :
And, oh ! 'tis better far to have him thus,
Than see him in her arms,—Oh, welcome,
    welcome !

Ibid.

LXXII

FORTUNE

Happy the man, and happy he alone,
    He, who can call to-day his own :
    He who, secure within, can say,
To-morrow do thy worst, for I have lived
    to-day.
    Be fair, or foul, or rain, or shine,
The joys I have possessed, in spite of fate, are
    mine.
Not Heaven itself upon the past has power ;
But what has been, has been, and I have had my
    hour.

Fortune, that with malicious joy
  Does man her slave oppress,
Proud of her office to destroy,
  Is seldom pleased to bless :
Still various, and unconstant still,
But with an inclination to be ill,
    Promotes, degrades, delights in strife,
    And makes a lottery of life.
I can enjoy her while she's kind ;
But when she dances in the wind,
  And shakes the wings, and will not stay,
  I puff the prostitute away :
The little or the much she gave, is quietly
    resigned :
  Content with poverty, my soul I arm ;
  And virtue, tho' in rags will keep me warm.

    What is't to me,
Who never sail in her unfaithful sea,
  If storms arise, and clouds grow black ;
  If the mast split, and threaten wreck ?
Then let the greedy merchant fear
  For his ill gotten gain ;
And pray to gods that will not hear,
While the debating winds and billows bear
    His wealth into the main :
  For me, secure from Fortune's blows
  (Secure of what I cannot lose,)
In my small pinnace I can sail,
Contemning all the blustering roar ;
  And running with a merry gale,
With friendly stars my safety seek
Within some little winding creek ;
  And see the storm ashore.

Sylvae, 1685.

LXXIII

TO MY DEAR FRIEND, MR. CONGREVE
On his Comedy called The Double-Dealer.

Well then, the promised hour is come at last ;
The present age of wit obscures the past :
Strong were our sires, and as they fought they writ,
Conquering with force of arms and dint of wit :
Theirs was the giant race before the flood ;
And thus, when Charles returned, our empire stood.
Like Janus, he the stubborn soil manured,
With rules of husbandry the rankness cured :
Tamed us to manners, when the stage was rude,
And boisterous English wit with art indued.
Our age was cultivated thus at length,
But what we gained in skill we lost in strength.
Our builders were with want of genius cursed ;
The second Temple was not like the first ;
Till you, the best Vitruvius, come at length,
Our beauties equal, but excel our strength.
Firm Doric pillars found your solid base,
The fair Corinthian crowns the higher space ;
Thus all below is strength, and all above is grace.
In easy dialogue is Fletcher's praise ;
He moved the mind, but had no power to raise.
Great Jonson did by strength of judgment please,
Yet, doubling Fletcher's force, he wants his ease.
In diff'ring talents both adorned their age,
One for the study, t'other for the stage.
But both to Congreve justly shall submit,
One matched in judgment, both o'er-matched in wit.
In him all beauties of this age we see,
Etherege his courtship, Southern's purity.
The satire, wit, and strength of manly Wycherly.

All this in blooming youth you have achieved ;
Nor are your foiled contemporaries grieved ;
So much the sweetness of your manners move,
We cannot envy you, because we love.
Fabius might joy in Scipio, when he saw
A beardless consul made against the law,
And join his suffrage to the votes of Rome,
Though he with Hannibal was overcome.
Thus old Romano bowed to Raphael's fame,
And scholar to the youth he taught, became.
    O that your brows my laurel had sustained,
Well had I been deposed, if you had reigned ;
The father had descended for the son,
For only you are lineal to the throne.
Thus, when the State one Edward did depose,
A greater Edward in his room arose :
But now, not I, but poetry is cursed ;
For Tom the Second reigns like Tom the
        First.
But let 'em not mistake my patron's part
Nor call his charity their own desert.
Yet this I prophesy : Thou shalt be seen,
(Though with some short parenthesis between)
High on the throne of Wit ; and, seated
        there,
Nor mine (that's little) but thy laurel wear.
Thy first attempt an early promise made ;
That early promise this has more than paid.
So bold, yet so judiciously you dare,
That your least praise, is to be regular.
Time, place and action may with pains be
        wrought,
But genius must be born, and never can be
        taught.
This is your portion, this your native store :
Heaven, that but once was prodigal before,
To Shakespeare gave as much ; she could not
        give him more.

Maintain your post: that's all the fame you
    need ;
For 'tis impossible you should proceed.
Already I am worn with cares and age,
And just abandoning th'ungrateful stage :
Unprofitably kept at Heaven's expense,
I live a rent-charge on his Providence :
But you, whom ev'ry Muse and Grace adorn,
Whom I foresee to better fortune born,
Be kind to my remains ; and oh, defend,
Against your judgment, your departed friend !
Let not th' insulting foe my fame pursue,
But shade those laurels which descend to you :
And take for tribute what these lines express ;
You merit more ; nor could my love do less.

1694.

LXXIV

TO THE MEMORY OF MR. OLDHAM

Farewell, too little and too lately known,
Whom I began to think and call my own :
For sure our souls were near allied, and thine
Cast in the same poetic mould with mine.
One common note on either lyre did strike,
And knaves and fools we both abhorred alike.
To the same goal did both our studies drive :
The last set out the soonest did arrive.
Thus Nisus fell upon the slippery place,
Whilst his young friend performed and won the
    race.
O early ripe ! to thy abundant store
What could advancing age have added more ?
It might (what Nature never gives the young)
Have taught the numbers of thy native tongue.

But satire needs not those, and wit will shine
Through the harsh cadence of a rugged line.
A noble error, and but seldom made,
When poets are by too much force betrayed.
Thy generous fruits, though gathered ere their
    prime,
Still shewed a quickness ; and maturing time
But mellows what we write to the dull sweets of
    rhyme.
Once more, hail, and farewell ! farewell, thou
    young,
But ah ! too short, Marcellus of our tongue !
Thy brows with ivy and with laurels bound ;
But fate and gloomy night encompass thee
    around.

1684.

LXXV

ELEONORA

   . . . As precious gums are not for lasting fire,
They but perfume the Temple, and expire,
So was she soon exhaled, and vanished hence,
A short sweet odour, of a vast expense.
She vanished, we can scarcely say she died ;
For but a Now, did Heaven and Earth divide :
She passed serenely with a single breath,
This moment perfect health, the next was death.
One sigh, did her eternal bliss assure ;
So little penance needs, when souls are almost
    pure.
As gentle dreams our waking thoughts pursue,
Or, one dream passed, we slide into a new,
(So close they follow, such wild order keep
We think our selves awake, and are asleep)
So softly death succeeded life, in her ;
She did but dream of Heaven, and she was there.

No pains she suffered, nor expired with noise ;
Her soul was whispered out, with God's still
Voice ;
As an old friend is beckoned to a feast,
And treated like a long familiar guest . . .

Eleonora, 1692.

LXXVI

UPON THE DEATH OF THE
VISCOUNT OF DUNDEE

O last and best of Scots ! who didst maintain
Thy country's freedom from a foreign reign :
New people fill the land, now thou art gone,
New Gods the Temples, and new Kings the
Throne.

Scotland and thee did each in other live,
Nor wouldst thou her, nor could she thee survive.
Farewell ! who living didst support the state,
And could'st not fall but with thy country's fate.

Miscellany Poems, v, 1704.

LXXVII

(*REASON AND RELIGION*)

Dim, as the borrowed beams of moon and stars
To lonely, weary, wandering travellers
Is Reason to the soul : and as on high
Those rolling fires discover but the sky,
Not light us here, so Reason's glimmering ray
Was lent, not to assure our doubtful way,
But guide us upward to a better day.
And as those nightly tapers disappear
When day's bright Lord ascends our hemisphere ;
So pale grows Reason at Religion's sight ;
So dies, and so dissolves in supernatural light.

Religio Laici, 1682.

C 2

LXXVIII

(*THE HIND*)

A milk-white Hind, immortal and unchanged,
Fed on the lawns and in the forest ranged ;
Without unspotted, innocent within,
She feared no danger, for she knew no sin.
Yet had she oft been chased with horns and
    hounds
And Scythian shafts ; and many winged wounds
Aimed at her heart ; was often forced to fly,
And doomed to death, though fated not to die.
   Not so her young, for their unequal line
Was hero's make, half human, half divine.
Their earthly mould obnoxious was to fate,
Th' immortal part assumed immortal state.
Of these a slaughtered army lay in blood,
Extended o'er the Caledonian wood,
Their native walk ; whose vocal blood arose
And cried for pardon on their perjured foes ;
Their fate was fruitful, and the sanguine seed,
Endued with souls, increased the sacred breed.
So captive Israel multiplied in chains,
A numerous exile ; and enjoyed her pains.
With grief and gladness mixed, their mother
    viewed
Her martyred offspring, and their race renewed ;
Their corpse to perish, but their kind to last;
So much the deathless plant the dying fruit
    surpassed.
   Panting and pensive now she ranged alone,
And wandered in the kingdoms once her own.
The common hunt, though from their rage
    restrained
By sovereign power, her company disdained ;
Grinned as they passed, and with a glaring eye
Gave gloomy signs of secret enmity.

'Tis true, she bounded by, and tripped so light,
They had not time to take a steady sight,
For truth has such a face and such a mien
As to be loved needs only to be seen.

The Hind and the Panther, 1687.

LXXIX

(*CONVERSION*)

But, gracious God, how well dost thou provide
For erring judgments an unerring guide !
Thy throne is darkness in th' abyss of light,
A blaze of glory that forbids the sight ;
Oh teach me to believe thee thus concealed,
And search no farther than thyself revealed ;
But her alone for my director take
Whom thou hast promised never to forsake !
My thoughtless youth was winged with vain
    desires,
My manhood, long misled by wandering fires,
Followed false lights ; and when their glimpse
    was gone,
My pride struck out new sparkles of her own.
Such was I, such by nature still I am,
Be thine the glory and be mine the shame.
Good life be now my task : my doubts are done.

Ibid.

LXXX

VENI, CREATOR SPIRITUS
Translated in Paraphrase

Creator Spirit, by whose aid
The world's foundations first were laid,
Come, visit ev'ry pious mind ;
Come, pour thy joys on human kind ;

From sin, and sorrow set us free ;
And make thy temples worthy thee.
  O Source of uncreated light,
The Father's promised Paraclite ;
Thrice holy Fount, thrice holy Fire,
Our hearts with heav'nly love inspire ;
Come, and thy sacred unction bring
To sanctify us, while we sing !
  Plenteous of grace, descend from high,
Rich in thy sev'n-fold energy !
Thou strength of his almighty hand,
Whose pow'r does Heav'n and Earth command,
Proceeding Spirit, our defence,
Who dost the gift of tongues dispense,
And crown'st thy gift with eloquence !
  Refine and purge our earthly parts ;
But, oh, inflame and fire our hearts !
Our frailties help, our vice control ;
Submit the senses to the soul ;
And when rebellious they are grown,
Then, lay thy hand, and hold 'em down.
  Chase from our minds th' infernal foe ;
And peace, the fruit of love, bestow ;
And, lest our feet should step astray,
Protect, and guide us in the way.
  Make us eternal truths receive,
And practise, all that we believe ;
Give us thy self, that we may see
The Father and the Son, by thee.
  Immortal honour, endless fame,
Attend th' almighty Father's name :
The Saviour Son be glorified,
Who for lost man's redemption died ;
And equal adoration be
Eternal Paraclite, to thee.

Examen Poeticum, 1693.

HYMNS FROM THE PRIMER (1706)

LXXXI

O SOLA MAGNARUM URBIUM

Let other cities strive, which most
Can of their strength or heroes boast ;
Bethlem alone is chose to be
The seat of heaven-born majesty.

Here, while our God incarnate lay,
The officious stars their homage pay ;
A sun-like meteor quits its sphere
To show the Sun of Justice here.

Hither the faithful sages ran
To own their king, both God and Man ;
And with their incense, myrrh and gold
The mysteries of their vows unfold.

To God the censer's smoke ascends ;
The gold the sovereign king attends ;
In myrrh the bitter type we see
Of suffering and mortality.

Glory to thee, O Christ, whose rays
Illustrated the Gentiles' ways ;
Whilst equal praises still repeat
The Father, and the Paraclete.

LXXXII

AURORA CŒLUM PURPURAT

Aurora spreads her cheerful rays,
The heavens rejoice in hymns of praise ;
The earth resounds in tuneful strains
More loud than hell can shake its chains ;

To see the mighty Jesus lead
The patriarchs ransomed from the dead,
Late sons of shades and heirs of night,
To people realms of endless light.

The dead's first-born resumes his breath,
And forces through the gates of death,
To come victorious, and increase
The triumphs of his own decease.

Cease, mournful tears ; behold, relief ;
Enough you have indulged in grief :
The herald-angels now proclaim
Life's reign restored, and sound his fame.

From death of sin, O Jesus, free
Them that are born again to thee ;
Be thou alone our chosen guest
And everlasting paschal feast.

May endless worlds the glories tell
Of Christ, who vanquished death and hell ;
And one eternal praise repeat
The Father and the Paraclete.

LXXXIII

JESU, DULCIS MEMORIA

Jesus, the only thought of thee
  With sweetness fills my breast ;
But sweeter still it is to see,
  And on thy beauty feast.

No theme so soft, or sound so gay
  Can art of music frame ;
No words, or even thought can say,
  Thy most mellifluous name.

Sole hope, when we our sins repent,
   So bounteous of thy grace ;
If thus thou'rt good when we lament,
   Oh, what when face to face ?

Jesus, that name inspires my mind
   With springs of life and light ;
More than I ask in thee I find,
   And lavish in delight.

No eloquence, nor art can reach
   The joys of those above ;
The blest can only know, not teach
   What they in Jesus prove.

Thee then I'll seek retired apart,
   From world and business free ;
When noise invades I'll shut my heart,
   And keep it all for thee.

An early pilgrim thus I'll come,
   With Magdalen, to find
In sighs and tears my Saviour's tomb,
   And there refresh my mind.

My tears upon his grave shall flow,
   My sighs the garden fill ;
Then at his feet myself I'll throw,
   And there I'll seek his will.

Jesus, in thy blest steps I'll tread,
   And haunt thee through thy ways ;
I'll mourn, and never cease to plead
   Till I'm restored to grace.

Great conqueror of Death ! Thy fire
   Does such sweet flames excite,
That first it raises the desire,
   Then fills it with delight.

Thy quickening presence shines so clear
   Through every sense and way,
That souls, who once have seen thee near,
   See all things else decay.

Come then, dear Lord, possess my heart,
   And chase the shades of night :
Come, pierce it with thy flaming dart,
   And ever-shining light.

Then, I'll for ever Jesus sing,
   And with the blessed rejoice ;
Then all the vaulted towers shall ring,
And echoing hearts and voices sing,
   And still repeat, ' Rejoice.'

WENTWORTH DILLON, EARL OF ROSCOMMON (1633-85)

LXXXIV

ON THE DAY OF JUDGMENT

The day of wrath, that dreadful day,
Shall the whole world in ashes lay,
As David and the Sibyls say.

What horror will invade the mind,
When the strict Judge, who would be kind,
Shall have few venial faults to find !

The last loud trumpet's wondrous sound
Shall through the rending tombs rebound,
And wake the nations under ground.

Nature and Death shall, with surprise,
Behold the pale offender rise,
And view the Judge with conscious eyes.

Then shall, with universal dread,
The sacred mystic book be read,
To try the living and the dead.

The Judge ascends his awful throne,
He makes each secret sin be known,
And all with shame confess their own.

Oh then ! what interest shall I make
To save my last important stake,
When the most just have cause to quake ?

Thou mighty, formidable King,
Thou mercy's unexhausted spring,
Some comfortable pity bring !

Forget not what my ransom cost,
Nor let my dear-bought soul be lost,
In storms of guilty terror tossed.

Thou, who for me didst feel such pain,
Whose precious blood the cross did stain,
Let not those agonies be vain.

Thou, whom avenging powers obey,
Cancel my debt (too great to pay)
Before the sad accounting-day.

Surrounded with amazing fears,
Whose load my soul with anguish bears,
I sigh, I weep : accept my tears.

Thou, who wert moved with Mary's grief,
And, by absolving of the thief,
Hast given me hope, now give relief.

Reject not my unworthy prayer,
Preserve me from that dangerous snare
Which Death and gaping Hell prepare.

Give my exalted soul a place
Among thy chosen right-hand race ;
The sons of God, and heirs of grace.

From that insatiable abyss
Where flames devour, and serpents hiss,
Promote me to thy seat of bliss.

Prostrate my contrite heart I rend,
My God, my Father, and my Friend,
Do not forsake me in my end.

Well may they curse their second breath,
Who rise to a reviving death ;
Thou great Creator of mankind,
Let guilty man compassion find !

Poems, 1717.

LXXXV

THE GROVE

Ah ! happy grove ! Dark and secure retreat
Of sacred silence, rest's eternal seat ;
How well your cool and unfrequented shade
Suits with the chaste retirements of a maid.
Oh ! If kind Heaven had been so much my
    friend
To make my fate upon my choice depend ;
All my ambition I would here confine,
And only this Elysium should be mine.
Fond men by passion wilfully betrayed
Adore those idols which their fancy made :
Purchasing riches, with our time and care
We lose our freedom in a gilded snare ;

And having all, all to ourselves refuse
Oppressed with blessings which we fear to use.
Fame is at best but an inconstant good,
Vain are the boasted titles of our blood.
We sorriest lose what we most highly prize,
And with our youth, our short-lived beauty dies.
In vain our fields and flocks increase our store
If our abundance makes us wish for more.
How happy is the harmless country maid,
Who rich by nature, scorns superfluous aid !
Whose modest clothes no wanton eyes invite,
But, like her soul, preserve the native white.
Whose little store her well-taught mind does
     please,
Not pinched with want, nor cloyed with wanton
     ease ;
Who, free from storms, which on the great ones
     fall
Makes but few wishes and enjoys them all.
No care but love can discompose her breast,
Love, of all cares the sweetest and the best.
Whilst on sweet grass her bleating charge does
     lie,
One happy lover feeds upon her eye.
Not one on whom or gods or men impose,
But one whom Love has for this lover chose.
Under some favourite myrtle's shady boughs
They spend their passion in repeated vows :
And whilst a blush confesses how she burns,
His faithful heart makes as sincere returns.
Thus in the arms of Love and Peace they lie,
And whilst they live, their flames can never die.

Sylvae, 1685.

NATHANIEL WANLEY (1634-80)

LXXXVI

THE RESURRECTION

Can death be faithful or the grave be just
Or shall my tomb restore my scattered dust ?
Shall every hair find out its proper pore
And crumbled bones be joined as before
Shall long unpractised pulses learn to beat
Victorious rottenness a loud retreat,
Or eyes eclipsed with a tedious night
May they once hope to resalute the light ?
What if this flesh of mine be made the prey
Of scaly pirates, cannibals at sea :
Shall living sepulchres give up their dead
Or is not flesh made fish then perished ?
What if the working of a subtle flame
By an unkind embrace dissolve this frame
To ashes ; and the whistling winds convey
Each atom to a quite contrary way :
Shall the small pilgrims that (perhaps) may pass
From grass to flesh and thence from flesh to
        grass
Travel until they meet and then embrace
So strictly as to grow the former face ?
My God, I know thy powerful word did frame
Out of pure nothing all that hath a name,
From the bright Angels bathing in full streams
Of deathless joys, to motes that dance in beams.
And shall I doubt but such a word can call
Flesh out of dust, that out of less made all ?
No, no, I am resolved, that when poor I
Shall slumbering in our mother's bosom lie,
The circling worms shall loose their fast embrace
And kinder turfs that cover me give place ;

The bands of death shall burst at the shrill sound
Of Heaven's summons and I shall be found :
Then will I rise and dress me, Lord, for thee
Who did'st by death undress thee, Lord, for me.

Scintillulae Sacrae [1667].

LXXXVII

HEAVEN AND HELL

Surely that is a stately frame
Which we do Heaven name ;
Where angels feast, where every dish
Outstrips what they can wish.

Of both the Indies all the store
Surely can be but poor
To such a plenty as doth bless
That mine of happiness.

Yet can we slight and scorn that place
When tendered, as if base,
Not worth a look, and which is worse
Eagerly court a curse.

Surely those fires are strange indeed
That upon spirits feed ;
And full of power is that flame
That powers themselves can tame.

Of dreadful darkness' deepest shade
Surely those chains are made,
That can the Prince of darkness bind
And round about him wind.

Yet can we game at sin and make
Our very souls the stake,
As if those flames and all the rest
Were but a fabled jest.

Ibid.

LXXXVIII

THE CASKET

What spendthrifts are we of the day,
    Wasting it vainly while
We deck a cottage made of clay,
    Or somewhat yet more vile.

We prize and hug this idle breath
    As if more than a span,
And pamper up these slaves of death
    Carcases of the man.

We think all little to entrust
    With bodies which yet shall
Shrink to a scuttle full of dust,
    And worthless ashes fall.

But the imprisoned soul distressed
    Languishes quite forgot,
Thus are the caskets gilt and dressed
    When jewels rust and rot.

Ibid.

LXXXIX

SIN

Bewitching sin, hadst thou not been,
Blest Paradise had yet been seen,
Majestic man had graced that bower
And been the garden's choicest flower :
Wasting diseases, that displace
The virgin beauties of the face,
While York thrives in the civil war
And treads on blushing Lancaster,
Had owned no power to invade
Bodies so firm and strongly made ;

The trembling palsies that engage
Most with the weakness of old age
Had then in vain assayed to make
So well a tempered fabric shake ;
Nor was there any art to show
A poison before sin, our foe.
What's deadly now, was wholesome food
While we in innocency stood,
And till himself his death did vote,
Man's self was his own antidote.

Ibid.

THOMAS KEN (1637-1711)

xc

DIVINE POESY

Blest Poetry ! immortal soul refined,
Pure love with bright illumination joined !
The spirit lost in an ecstatic height ;
Imagination soaring out of sight :
Seraphic ardour circling in each vein ;
The majestatic presence in the brain :
Inspired to make mankind with angels vie,
To emulate the anthems sung on high,
To celebrate God's providential care,
His attributes and wonders to declare ;
To vent the adoration which they raise,
To guide the passions with attempered lays :
With amiable strokes each grace to paint,
To eternize the copy of each saint,
Vice in its foul deformities to draw,
And sinners with God's thunderbolts to awe.

XCI

THE EUCHARIST

When at Thy altar, Lord, I prostrate fall,
Thy dolorous crucifixion to recall,
Make my soul fuel to supernal fire,
Into my heart devotion warm inspire,
Shame and contrition vileness to deplore,
Firm resolutions never to sin more :
An humble, pure, and charitable mind,
From all remains of wilful sin refined :
Faith, hope, desire, joy, praise, thanksgiving,
    zeal,
Languor and ardours which Thy lovers feel,
All grateful passions which have ever streamed
From sinners by the blood of God redeemed.
Into all love, my powers, my spirit turn,
Love which unquenchable may ever burn ;
May every thought I of Thy sufferings frame,
Sustain, invigorate, increase the flame.
Nourished by Thee, I no fatigue shall feel,
And tread Thy steps with persevering zeal :
Or if Thou shorten by the Cross my way,
Filled with Thy love I gladly shall obey.
Before Thy death this feast Thou didst ordain,
The antidote against eternal pain :
Thy saints will imitate thy solemn care,
And by the Altar for the Cross prepare.

XCII

MIDNIGHT HYMN

My God, now I from sleep awake,
The sole possession of me take ;
From midnight terrors me secure,
And guard my heart from thoughts impure.

Blest Angels ! while we silent lie,
You Hallelujahs sing on high ;
You joyful hymn the ever Blessed
Before the throne, and never rest.

I with your choir celestial join,
In offering up a hymn divine :
With you in heaven I hope to dwell,
And bid the night and world farewell.

My soul, when I shake off this dust,
Lord ! in Thy arms I will entrust :
O make me Thy peculiar care,
Some mansion for my soul prepare.

Give me a place at Thy saints' feet,
Or some fallen Angel's vacant seat :
I'll strive to sing as loud as they,
Who sit above in brighter day.

Oh may I always ready stand,
With my lamp burning in my hand ;
May I in sight of heaven rejoice
Whene'er I hear the Bridegroom's voice !

All praise to Thee, in light arrayed,
Who light Thy dwelling-place hast made ;
A boundless ocean of bright beams
From Thy all-glorious Godhead streams.

The sun in its meridian height
Is very darkness in Thy sight :
My soul, Oh, lighten and inflame,
With thought and love of Thy great name.

Blest Jesu Thou, on heaven intent,
Whole nights has in devotion spent ;
But I, frail creature, soon am tired,
And all my zeal is soon expired.

My soul !—how canst thou weary grow
Of antedating bliss below ;
In sacred hymns and heavenly love,
Which will eternal be above ?

Shine on me, Lord, new life impart,
Fresh ardours kindle in my heart ;
One ray of Thy all-quickening light
Dispels the sloth and clouds of night.

Lord lest the tempter me surprise,
Watch over Thine own sacrifice ;
All loose, all idle thoughts cast out,
And make my very dreams devout.

Praise God, from whom all blessings flow,
Praise Him, all creatures here below ;
Praise Him above, ye heavenly host,
Praise Father, Son, and Holy Ghost.

A Manual of Prayers, 1709.

THOMAS TRAHERNE (1637-74)

XCIII

SOLITUDE

How desolate !
Ah ! how forlorn, how sadly did I stand
When in the field my woeful state
I felt ! Not all the land,
Not all the skies,
Though Heaven shined before mine eyes,
Could comfort yield in any field to me,
Nor could my mind contentment find or see.

Removed from town,
From people, churches, feasts and holidays,
The sword of state, the mayor's gown,
And all the neighb'ring boys ;

As if no kings
On earth there were, or living things,
The silent skies salute mine eyes, the seas
My soul surround ; no rest I found, or ease.

My roving mind
Searched every corner of the spacious earth,
    From sky to sky, if it could find,
        (But found not) any mirth :
            Not all the coasts,
    Nor all the great and glorious hosts,
In Heaven or Earth, did any mirth afford ;
No welcome good or needed food, my board.

I do believe,
The evening being shady and obscure,
    The very silence did me grieve,
        And sorrow more procure :
            A secret want
    Did make me think my fortune scant.
I was so blind, I could not find my health,
No joy mine eye could there espy, nor wealth.

Nor could I guess
What kind of thing I longed for : But that I
    Did somewhat lack of blessedness,
        Beside the earth and sky,
            I plainly found ;
    It grieved me much, I felt a wound
Perplex me sore ; yet what my store should be
I did not know, nothing would shew to me.

Ye sullen things !
Ye dumb, ye silent creatures, and unkind,
    How can I call you pleasant springs
        Unless ye ease my mind ?
            Will ye not speak
What 'tis I want, nor silence break ?

O pity me, and let me see some joy ;
Some kindness shew to me, although a boy.

They silent stood :
Nor earth, nor woods, nor hills, nor brooks, nor
    skies,
  Would tell me where the hidden good,
      Which I did long for, lies :
        The shady trees,
    The evening dark, the humming bees,
The chirping birds, mute springs and fords,
    conspire,
While they deny to answer my desire.

Bells ringing I
Far off did hear ; some country church they
    spake ;
  The noise re-echoing through the sky
      My melancholy brake ;
        When 't reached mine ear
    Some tidings thence I hoped to hear :
But not a bell me news could tell, or shew
My longing mind, where joys to find, or know.

I grieved the more,
'Cause I thereby somewhat encouraged was
  That I from thence should learn my store ;
      For churches are a place
        That nearer stand
    Than any part of all the land
To Heaven ; from whence some little sense I
    might
To help my mind receive, and find some light.

They louder sound
Than men do talk, something they should dis-
    close ;
  The empty sound did therefore wound
      Because not shew repose.

It did revive
To think that men were there alive ;
But had my soul, called by the toll, gone in,
I might have found, to ease my wound, a thing.

A little ease
Perhaps, but that might more molest my mind ;
One flattering drop would more disease
My soul with thirst, and grind
My heart with grief :
For people can yield no relief
In public sort when in that court they shine,
Except they move my soul with love divine.

Th' external rite,
Although the face be wondrous sweet and fair,
Can satiate my appetite
No more than empty air
Yield solid food.
Must I the best and highest good
Seek to possess ; or blessedness in vain
(Tho' 'tis alive in some place) strive to gain ?

Oh ! what would I
Diseased, wanting, melancholy, give
To find *that* true felicity,
The place where bliss doth live ?
Those regions fair
Which are not lodged in sea nor air,
Nor woods, nor fields, nor arbour yields, nor
springs,
Nor heavens shew to us below, nor kings.

I might have gone
Into the city, market, tavern, street,
Yet only changed my station,
And strove in vain to meet
That ease of mind
Which all alone I longed to find :

A common inn doth no such thing betray,
Nor doth it walk in people's talk, or play.

O Eden fair !
Where shall I seek the soul of holy joy
   Since I to find it here despair ;
      Nor in the shining day,
      Nor in the shade,
   Nor in the field, nor in a trade
I can it see ?   Felicity !   Oh, where
Shall I thee find to ease my mind ?   Oh, where ?

Poems of Felicity.   [1671.]

XCIV

CHRISTENDOM

When first mine infant ear
   Of Christendom did hear,
I much admired what kind of place or thing
   It was of which the folk did talk :
   What coast, what region, what therein
   Did move, or might be seen to walk.
      My great desire
      Like ardent fire
Did long to know what things did lie behind
That mystic name, to which mine eye was blind.

Some depth it did conceal
   Which till it did reveal
Itself to me, no quiet, peace, or rest,
   Could I by any means attain ;
   My earnest thoughts did me molest
   Till some one should the thing explain :
      I thought it was
      A glorious place,

Where souls might dwell in all delight and
    bliss ;
So thought, yet feared that I the truth might
    miss :

      Among ten thousand things
      Gold, silver, cherub's wings,
Pearls, rubies, diamonds, a church with spires,
  Masks, stages, games and plays,
  That then might suit my young desires,
  Feathers, and farthings, holidays,
      Cards, music, dice,
      So much in price ;
A city did before mine eyes present
Itself, wherein there reigned sweet content.

      A town beyond the seas,
      Whose prospect much did please,
And to my soul so sweetly raise delight
  As if a long expected joy,
  Shut up in that transforming sight,
  Would into me itself convey ;
      And blessedness
      I there possess,
As if that city stood on my own ground,
And all the profit mine which there was found.

      Whatever force me led
      My spirit sweetly fed
On these conceits, that 'twas a city strange,
  Wherein I saw no gallant inns,
  No markets, new or old Exchange,
  No childish trifles, useless things ;
      Nor any bound
      That town surround ;
But as if all its streets even endless were ;
Without or gate or wall it did appear.

Things native sweetly grew,
  Which there mine eye did view,
Plain, simple, cheap, on either side the street,
  Which was exceeding fair and wide ;
  Sweet mansions there mine eyes did meet ;
  Green trees the shaded doors did hide :
    My chiefest joys
    Were girls and boys
That in those streets still up and down did play
Which crowned the town with constant holiday.

  A sprightly pleasant time
  (Even summer in its prime)
Did gild the trees, the houses, children, skies,
  And made the city all divine ;
  It ravished my wondering eyes
  To see the sun so brightly shine :
    The heat and light
    Seemed in my sight
With such a dazzling lustre shed on them
As made me think 'twas th' New Jerusalem.

  Beneath the lofty trees
  I saw, of all degrees,
Folk, calmly sitting in their doors ; while some
  Did standing with them kindly talk,
  Some smile, some sing, or what was done
  Observe, while others by did walk ;
    They viewed the boys
    And girls, their joys,
The streets adorning with their angel-faces,
Themselves diverting in those pleasant places.

  The streets like lanes did seem,
  Not paved with stones, but green,
Which with red clay did partly mixed appear ;
  'Twas holy ground of great esteem ;
  The springs choice liveries did wear
  Of verdant grass that grew between

The purling streams,
   Which golden beams
Of light did varnish, coming from the sun,
By which to distant realms was service done.

In fresh and cooler rooms
   Retired they dine ; perfumes
They wanted not, having the pleasant shade
  And peace to bless their house within
  By sprinkled waters cooler made,
For those incarnate cherubin.
      This happy place
      With all the grace
The joy and beauty which did it beseem,
Did ravish me and heighten my esteem

That here to raise desire
   All objects do conspire,
People in years, and young enough to play,
  Their streets of houses, common peace,
  In one continued holy day
  Whose gladsome mirth shall never cease :
      Since these become
      My Christendom,
What learn I more than that Jerusalem
Is mine, as 'tis my Maker's, choicest gem.

Before I was aware
   Truth did to me appear,
And represented to my virgin eyes
  Th' unthought-of joys and treasures
  Wherein my bliss and glory lies ;
  My God's delight, (which gives me measure)
      His turtle dove
      Is peace and love
In towns : for holy children, maids, and men
Make up the King of Glory's diadem.

Ibid.

D

XCV

ON CHRISTMAS DAY

Shall dumpish melancholy spoil my joys
        While angels sing
        And mortals ring
   My Lord and Saviour's praise !
Awake from sloth, for that alone destroys ;
'Tis sin defiles, 'tis sloth puts out thy joys.
  See how they run from place to place,
  And seek for ornaments of grace ;
  Their houses decked with sprightly green,
  In winter makes a summer seen ;
     They bays and holly bring
      As if 'twere spring !

Shake off thy sloth, my drowsy soul, awake ;
        With angels sing
        Unto thy King,
   And pleasant music make ;
Thy lute, thy harp, or else thy heart-strings take,
And with thy music let thy sense awake.
  See how each one the other calls
  To fix his ivy on the walls,
  Transplanted there it seems to grow
  As if it rooted were below :
     Thus He, who is thy King,
      Makes winter, spring.

Shall houses clad in summer liveries
        His praises sing
        And laud thy King,
   And wilt not thou arise ?
Forsake thy bed, and grow (my soul) more wise,
Attire thyself in cheerful liveries :
  Let pleasant branches still be seen
  Adorning thee, both quick and green ;

And, which with glory better suits,
Be laden all the year with fruits ;
   inserted into Him,
      For ever spring.

'Tis He that life and spirit doth infuse :
      Let every thing
      The praises sing
   Of Christ the King of Jews ;
Who makes things green, and with a spring infuse
A season which to see it doth not use :
   Old Winter's frost and hoary hair,
   With garlands crownèd, bays doth wear ;
   The nipping frost of wrath being gone,
   To Him the manger made a throne
     Due praises let us sing,
      Winter and spring.

See how, their bodies clad with finer clothes,
      They now begin
      His praise to sing
   Who purchased their repose :
Whereby their inward joy they do disclose ;
Their dress alludes to better works than those
   His gayer weeds and finer band,
   New suit and hat, into his hand
   The plough-man takes ; his neatest shoes,
   And warmer gloves, he means to use :
     And shall not I, my King,
      Thy praises sing ?

See how their breath doth smoke, and how they
   haste
      His praise to sing
      With Cherubim ;
   They scarce a breakfast taste ;
But through the streets, lest precious time should
   waste
When Service doth begin, to Church they haste.

And shall not I, Lord, come to Thee,
The beauty of Thy Temple see ?
Thy name with joy I will confess,
Clad in my Saviour's righteousness ;
    'Mong all Thy servants sing
        To Thee my King.

'Twas Thou that gavest us cause for fine attires ;
            Even Thou, O King,
                As in the spring,
    Dost warm us with Thy fires
Of love : Thy blood hath bought us new
    desires ;
Thy righteousness doth clothe with new attires.
    Both fresh and fine let me appear
    This day divine, to close the year ;
    Among the rest let me be seen
    A living branch and always green,
        Think it a pleasant thing
            Thy praise to sing.

At break of day, Oh how the bells did ring !
            To Thee, my King,
            The bells did ring ;
    To Thee the angels sing :
Thy goodness did produce this other Spring,
For this it is they make the bells to ring :
    The sounding bells do through the air
    Proclaim Thy welcome far and near ;
    While I alone with Thee inherit
    All these joys, beyond my merit.
        Who would not always sing
            To such a King ?

I all these joys, above my merit, see
            By Thee, my King,
            To whom I sing,
    Entire conveyed to me.

My treasure, Lord, Thou mak'st the people be,
That I with pleasure might Thy servants see.
  Ev'n in their rude external ways
  They do set forth my Saviour's praise,
  And minister a light to me,
  While I by them do hear to Thee
    Praises, my Lord and King,
      Whole churches ring.

Hark how remoter parishes do sound !
    Far off they ring
    For Thee, my King,
  Ev'n round about the town :
The churches scattered over all the ground
Serve for Thy praise, who art with glory crowned.
  This city is an engine great
  That makes my pleasure more complete ;
  The sword, the mace, the magistrate,
  To honour Thee attend in state :
    The whole assembly sings ;
      The minster rings.
Ibid.

XCVI

SHADOWS IN THE WATER

In unexperienced infancy
Many a sweet mistake doth lie,
Mistake tho' false, intending true ;
A seeming somewhat more than view
  That doth instruct the mind
  In things that lie behind,
And many secrets to us show
Which afterwards we come to know.

Thus did I by the water's brink
Another world beneath me think ;

And while the lofty spacious skies
Reversèd there abused mine eyes,
　　I fancied other feet
　　Came mine to touch or meet ;
As by some puddle I did play
Another world within it lay.

Beneath the water people drowned,
Yet with another heaven crowned,
In spacious regions seemed to go
As freely moving to and fro :
　　In bright and open space
　　I saw their very face ;
Eyes, hands and feet they had like mine ;
Another sun did with them shine.

'Twas strange that people there should walk,
And yet I could not hear them talk :
That through a little wat'ry chink,
Which one dry ox or horse might drink,
　　We other worlds should see,
　　Yet not admitted be ;
And other confines there behold
Of light and darkness, heat and cold.

I called them oft, but called in vain ;
No speeches we could entertain :
Yet did I there expect to find
Some other world, to please my mind.
　　I plainly saw by these
　　A new Antipodes,
Whom, though they were so plainly seen,
A film kept off that stood between.

By walking men's reversed feet
I chanced another world to meet
Though it did not to view exceed
A phantasm, 'tis a world indeed,

Where skies beneath us shine,
And earth by art divine
Another face presents below,
Where people's feet against ours go.

Within the regions of the air,
Compassed about with heavens fair,
Great tracts of land there may be found
Enriched with fields and fertile ground ;
　　Where many num'rous hosts,
　　In those far distant coasts,
For other great and glorious ends,
Inhabit, my yet unknown friends.

O ye that stand upon the brink,
Whom I so near me through the chink
With wonder see : What faces there,
Whose feet, whose bodies, do ye wear ?
　　I my companions see
　　In you, another me.
They seemèd others, but are we ;
Our second selves those shadows be.

Look how far off those lower skies
Extend themselves ! scarce with mine eyes
I can them reach.　O ye my friends,
What secret borders on those ends ?
　　Are lofty heavens hurled
　　'Bout your inferior world ?
Are ye the representatives
Of other peoples' distant lives ?

Of all the playmates which I knew
That here I do the image view
In other selves, what can it mean ?
But that below the purling stream

Some unknown joys there be
Laid up in store for me,
To which I shall, when that thin skin
Is broken, be admitted in.
Ibid.

SAMUEL PORDAGE (1633-91)

XCVII

TO LYDIA BEING RETIRED PRIVATELY INTO THE COUNTRY

Now to the secret groves is Lydia gone,
Stolen from us all, meaning to live alone
Among the silent woods, where she may be
From busy servants' entertainments free;
And hear the pleasant songsters of the groves
With whistling lays resound their growing loves;
With uncontrolling freedom view the trammels
Of Flora, which the fragrant meads enamels;
With pleasure walk and see the crystal brooks,
Catching the sportive fish with silver hooks;
Conversing with the flowery Napææ;
Making diversity of flowers agree
Bound up together; 'mong the shady trees
Dance in a circle with the Dryades;
Feeding on cleanly, though but homely food;
Esteemed the only goddess of the wood.
Oh how I fear those rural pleasures may
Entice her there to make a tedious stay:
But I with vows will frosty Hyems move
To haste the ruins of the leavy grove:
Pray cold-mouth Boreas kiss her tender cheek
To make her shelter in the town to seek,
Where conversation and warm fires do bring,
Though frost without doors lies, within a spring.
Poems, 1660.

XCVIII

DAMON ON AMARILLIS DANCING IN A RING

See my fortune, see my fortune,
How she flies me and denies me;
Woe alas! woe alas too soon
Still I follow! Still I follow!
But she flies me and denies me,
And cannot be won.

Cruel sport in this sort
With woes to fill me which will kill me.
Ah, from this pain release me.
For whilst she flies, my eyes
They discover I'm a lover,
And that it is herself must ease me.
Round we go, round we go,
But she flies me and denies me;
Still I follow wrapt in woe.

She moves swiftly and yet sweetly;
Don't forsake me, I'll o'ertake thee
If thou wilt pity bestow:
Cruel sport, in this sort
To increase my fires and desires
And to exhibit my despair;
She shifts her place, apace
I after move
Being urged by Love;
But in vain still my endeavours are.

Ibid.

D 2

ANONYMOUS

XCIX

A RHAPSODY

Now, I confess, I am in love,
Although I thought I never could ;
But 'tis with one dropped from above,
Whose nature's made of better mould :
   So fair, so good, so all divine,
    I'd quit the world to make her mine.

Have you not seen the stars retreat
When Sol salutes our hemisphere ?
So shrink the beauties, callèd great,
When sweet Rosela doth appear ;
   Were she as other women are,
    I should not love, nor yet despair.

Yet I could never wear a mind
Willing to stoop to common faces,
Nor confidence enough can find
To aim at one so full of graces :
   Fortune and Nature did agree
    No woman should be fit for me.

Merry Drollery, 1661.

THOMAS FLATMAN (1637-88)

C

THE ADVICE

Poor Celia once was very fair,
   A quick bewitching eye she had,
Most neatly looked her braided hair,
   Her dainty cheeks would make you mad,
Upon her lip did all the Graces play,
And on her breasts ten thousand Cupids lay.

Then many a doting lover came
  From seventeen till twenty-one,
Each told her of his mighty flame,
  But she, forsooth, affected none.
One was not handsome, t'other was not fine,
This of tobacco smelt, and that of wine.

But t'other day it was my fate
  To walk along that way alone,
I saw no coach before her gate,
  But at the door I heard her moan :
She dropped a tear, and sighing, seemed to say,
Young ladies, marry, marry while you may !

(1664)
Poems, 1674.

CI

FADING BEAUTY

As poor Aurelia sat alone
  Hard by a rivulet's flowery side,
  Envious of Nature's new-born pride,
Her slighted self she thus reflected on :

Alas, that Nature should revive
  Those flowers, which after winter's snow
  Spring fresh again, and brighter show,
But for our fairer sex so ill contrive.

Beauty, like theirs a short-lived thing,
  On us in vain she did bestow ;
  Beauty that only once can grow,
An Autumn has, but knows no second Spring.

Ibid.

CII

A WISH

Not to the hills where cedars move
Their cloudy heads ; not to the grove
Of myrtles in th' Elysian shade,
Nor Tempe which the poets made ;
Not on the spicy mountains play,
Or travel to Arabia,
I aim not at the careful throne,
Which Fortune's darlings sit upon ;
No, no, the best this fickle world can give
Has but a little, little time to live.

But let me soar, Oh let me fly
Beyond poor earth's benighted eye,
Beyond the pitch swift eagles tower,
Above the reach of human power ;
Above the clouds, above the way
Whence the sun darts his piercing ray,
Oh let me tread those courts that are
So bright, so pure, so blest, so fair,
As neither thou nor I must ever know
On earth : 'tis thither, thither would I go.

(1659)
Poems, 1674.

CIII

ANTHEM FOR THE EVENING

Sleep ! downy sleep ! come close my eyes,
Tired with beholding vanities !
Sweet slumbers come and chase away
The toils and follies of the day :

On your soft bosom will I lie,
Forget the world, and learn to die.
O Israel's watchful Shepherd ! spread
Tents of angels round my bed ;
Let not the spirits of the air,
While I slumber, me ensnare ;
But save Thy suppliant free from harms,
Clasped in Thine everlasting arms.
Clouds and thick darkness is Thy throne,
Thy wonderful pavilion :
Oh dart from thence a shining ray,
And then my midnight shall be day !
Thus when the morn in crimson drest,
Breaks through the windows of the East,
My hymns of thankful praises shall arise
Like incense or the morning sacrifice.

Ibid.

CIV

NUDUS REDIBO

Naked I came, when I began to be
A man among the sons of misery,
Tender, unarmed, helpless, and quite forlorn,
E'er since 'twas my misfortune to be born ;
And when the space of a few weary days
Shall be expired, then must I go my ways.
Naked shall I return, and nothing have,
Nothing wherewith to bribe my hungry grave.
Then what's the proudest monarch's pearly
        robe,
Or what's he, more than I, that ruled the globe ?
Since we must all without distinction die,
And slumber both stark naked, he and I.

(1660) *Ibid.*

CV

A THOUGHT OF DEATH

When on my sick bed I languish,
Full of sorrow, full of anguish;
  Fainting, gasping, trembling, crying,
  Panting, groaning, speechless, dying,
My soul just now about to take her flight
Into the regions of eternal night ;
    Oh tell me you,
  That have been long below,
    What shall I do ?
What shall I think, when cruel Death appears,
  That may extenuate my fears ?
Methinks I hear some gentle Spirit say,
  Be not fearful, come away !
Think with thyself that now thou shalt be free,
And find thy long-expected liberty ;
Better thou mayst, but worse thou canst not be
Than in this vale of tears and misery.
Like Caesar, with assurance then come on,
And unamazed attempt the laurel crown,
That lies on th' other side death's Rubicon.

Ibid.

CVI

A DOOMSDAY THOUGHT

ANNO 1659

Judgement ! two syllables can make
The haughtiest son of Adam shake.
'Tis coming, and 'twill surely come,
The dawning to that Day of Doom ;
Oh th' morning blush of that dread day,
When Heav'n and Earth shall steal away,

Shall in their pristine Chaos hide,
Rather than th' angry Judge abide.
'Tis not far off ; methinks I see
Among the stars some dimmer be ;
Some tremble, as their lamps did fear
A neighbouring extinguisher.
The greater luminaries fail,
Their glories by eclipses veil.
Knowing ere long their borrowed light
Must sink in th' universal night.
When I behold a mist arise,
Straight to the same astonished eyes
Th' ascending clouds do represent
A scene of th' smoking firmament.
Oft when I hear a blustering wind
With a tempestuous murmur joined,
I fancy, Nature in this blast
Practises how to breathe her last,
Or sighs for poor Man's misery,
Or pants for fair eternity.
  Go to the dull church-yard and see
Those hillocks of mortality,
Where proudest man is only found
By a small swelling in the ground.
What crowds of carcases are made
Slaves to the pickaxe and the spade !
Dig but a foot, or two, to make
A cold bed, for thy dead friend's sake,
'Tis odds but in that scantling room
Thou robbest another of his tomb,
Or in thy delving smitest upon
A shinbone, or a cranion.
  When th' prison's full, what next can be
But the grand gaol-delivery ?
The great assize, when the pale clay
Shall gape, and render up its prey ;
When from the dungeon of the grave
The meagre throng themselves shall heave,

Shake off their linen chains, and gaze
With wonder, when the world shall blaze.
Then climb the mountains, scale the rocks,
Force op'n the deep's eternal locks,
Beseech the clifts to lend an ear—
Obdurate they, and will not hear.
What ? ne'er a cavern, ne'er a grot,
To cover from the common lot ?
No quite forgotten hold, to lie
Obscured, and pass the reck'ning by ?
No—There's a quick all-piercing Eye
Can through the Earth's dark centre pry,
Search into th' bowels of the sea,
And comprehend Eternity.
　　What shall we do then, when the voice
Of the shrill trump with strong fierce noise
Shall pierce our ears, and summon all
To th' Universe' wide Judgement Hall ?
What shall we do ? we cannot hide,
Nor yet that scrutiny abide :
When enlarged conscience loudly speaks,
And all our bosom-secrets breaks ;
When flames surround, and greedy Hell
Gapes for a booty (who can dwell
With everlasting burnings ?), when
Irrevocable words shall pass on men ;
Poor naked men, who sometimes thought
These frights perhaps would come to nought !
What shall we do ? we cannot run
For refuge, or the strict Judge shun.
'Tis too late then to think what course to take ;
While we live here, we must provision make.

Ibid.

PHILIP AYRES (1638-1712)

CVII

EVER PRESENT

Her name is at my tongue, whene'er I speak,
  Her shape's before my eyes where'er I stir ;
Both day and night, as if her ghost did walk,
  And not she me, but I had murdered her.

Emblems of Love, 1680 (?)

CVIII

ON LYDIA DISTRACTED

A Sonnet

With hairs, which for the wind to play with,
      hung,
  With her torn garments, and with naked feet,
  Fair Lydia dancing went from street to street,
Singing with pleasant voice her foolish song.

On her she drew all eyes in ev'ry place,
  And them to pity by her pranks did move,
  Which turned with gazing longer into love
By the rare beauty of her charming face.

In all her frenzies, and her mimicries,
While she did Nature's richest gifts despise,
  There active love did subtly play his part.

Her antic postures made her look more gay,
Her ragged clothes her treasures did display,
  And with each motion she ensnared a heart.

Lyric Poems, 1687.

TO THE WINDS

Ye Winds that in your hasty flight,
  Just kiss the leaves, and then away,
The leaves that tremble with delight,
  And murmur at so short a stay :
    Stop here, and ere you further go,
    Give audience to a lover's woe.

Condoling Air, to you I speak,
  Since she is deaf to all my grief,
You see my heart will quickly break,
  If careless She gives no relief :
    I'm sure you're troubled at my pain,
    For when I sigh, you sigh again.

Go, gentle Air, fly to my dear,
  That thus with love inflames my breast,
And whisper softly in her ear,
  'Tis she that robs my soul of rest :
    Express, if possible, such moans,
    May imitate my dying groans.

Or with thy rougher breath make bold
  To toss the treasure of her hair,
Till thou dost all those curls unfold
  Which cunningly men's hearts ensnare ;
    Try all thy skill to break the net,
    That I, like thee, may freedom get.

Then let some thicker blasts arise,
  And with her face so sport, and play,
Till the bright rays of her fair eyes
  Be qualified, or ta'en away ;
    Make all those charms which men assail,
    Of lesser force, and less prevail.
Ibid.

CX

THE FLY

Out of Spanish from Don Francisco De Quevedo.

> Out of the wine-pot cried the Fly,
> Whilst the grave Frog sat croaking by :
> Than live a wat'ry life like thine,
> I'd rather choose to die in wine.

I never water could endure,
Though ne'er so crystalline and pure.
Water's a murmurer, and they
Design more mischief than they say,
Where rivers smoothest are and clear,
Oh there's the danger, there's the fear ;
But I'll not grieve to die in wine,
That name is sweet, that sound's divine.
    Thus from the wine-pot . . . .

Dull fish in water live, we know,
And such insipid souls as thou ;
While to the wine do nimbly fly,
Many such pretty birds as I :
With wine refreshed, as flowers with rain,
My blood is cleared, inspired my brain ;
That when the Tory boys do sing,
I buzz i' th' chorus for the king.
    Thus from the wine-pot . . . .

I'm more beloved than thou canst be,
Most creatures shun thy company ;
I go unbid to every feast,
Nor stay for grace, but fall o' th' best :
There while I quaff in choicest wine,
Thou dost with puddle-water dine,
Which makes thee such a croaking thing.
Learn to drink wine, thou fool, and sing.
    Thus from the wine-pot . . . .

In gardens I delight to stray,
And round the plants do sing and play :
Thy tune no mortal does avail,
Thou art the Dutchman's nightingale :
Would'st thou with wine but wet thy throat,
Sure thou would'st leave that dismal note ;
Lewd water spoils thy organs quite,
And wine alone can set them right.
    Thus from the wine-pot, ...

Thy comrades still are newts and frogs,
Thy dwelling saw-pits, holes and bogs :
In cities I, and courts am free,
An insect too of quality.
What pleasures, ah ! didst thou but know,
This heav'nly liquor can bestow :
To drink and drown thou'dst ne'er repine ;
The great Anacreon died by wine.

    Out of the wine pot cried the Fly,
    Whilst the grave Frog sat croaking by :
    Than live a wat'ry life like thine,
    I'd rather choose to die in wine.

Ibid.

THOMAS BETTERTON (1635-1710)

CXI

What shall I do to show how much I love her ?
    How many millions of sighs can suffice ?
That which wins other hearts, never can move
    her,
    Those common methods of love she'll despise.

I will love more than man e'er loved before me,
    Gaze on her all the day, melt all the night,
Till for her own sake at last she'll implore me
    To love her less, to preserve our delight.

Since gods themselves could not ever be loving,
    Men must have breathing recruits for new
        joys ;
I wish my love could be always improving,
    Though eager love, more than sorrow, destroys.

In fair Aurelia's arms leave me expiring
    To be embalmed by the sweets of her breath,
To the last moment I'll still be desiring :
    Never had hero so glorious a death.

The Prophetess, 1690.

SIR GEORGE ETHEREGE (1635-91)

CXII

BEAUTY NO ARMOUR AGAINST LOVE

Ladies ! though to your conquering eyes
Love owes his chiefest victories ;
And borrows those bright arms from you,
With which he does the world subdue :
Yet you yourselves are not above
The empire, nor the griefs, of Love.

Then rack not lovers with disdain,
Lest Love on you revenge their pain.
You are not free, because y'are fair ;
The Boy did not his mother spare.
Beauty's but an offensive dart,
It is no armour for the heart.

The Comical Revenge, 1664.

CXIII

GATTY'S SONG

To little or no purpose I spent many days
In ranging the Park, the Exchange, and the
  Plays;
For ne'er in my rambles, till now, did I prove
So lucky to meet with the man I could love.
  Oh! how I am pleased when I think on this
    man,
  That I find I must love, let me do what I can.

How long I shall love him, I can no more tell,
Than, had I a fever, when I should be well.
My passion shall kill me before I will show it,
And yet I would give all the world he did know
  it :
  But oh, how I sigh when I think, should he
    woo me,
  I cannot deny what I know would undo me.
She Would if She Could, 1668.

CXIV

THE FAIR BUT CRUEL GIRL

The nymph that undoes me, is fair and unkind;
No less than a wonder by Nature designed.
She's the grief of my heart, the joy of my eye;
And the cause of a flame that never can die.

Her mouth, from whence wit still obligingly
  flows,
Has the beautiful blush, and the smell, of the
  rose.
Love and Destiny both attend on her will;
She wounds with a look; with a frown, she can
  kill.

The desperate lover can hope no redress ;
Where beauty and rigour are both in excess.
In Sylvia they meet, so unhappy am I ;
Who sees her, must love ; and who loves her,
    must die.

Westminster Drollery, ii, 1671.
A Collection of Poems, 1672.

CXV

TO A LADY, ASKING HIM HOW LONG HE WOULD LOVE HER

  It is not, Celia, in our power
    To say how long our love will last ;
It may be we within this hour
    May lose those joys we now do taste :
The blessed, that immortal be,
From change in love are only free.

  Then, since we mortal lovers are,
    Ask not how long our love will last ;
But, while it does, let us take care
    Each minute be with pleasure passed.
Were it not madness to deny
To live, because we're sure to die ?

A Collection of Poems, 1672.

CXVI

TO A VERY YOUNG LADY

  Sweetest bud of beauty ! may
No untimely frost decay
Th' early glories, which we trace
Blooming in thy matchless face.
But kindly opening, like the rose,
Fresh beauties every day disclose ;

Such as by Nature are not shown
In all the blossoms she has blown :
And then what conquest shall you make
Who hearts already daily take ?
Scorched, in the morning, with thy beams,
How shall we bear those sad extremes
Which must attend thy threat'ning eyes,
When thou shalt to thy noon arise ?

A Collection of Poems, 1672.

CXVII

Ye happy swains, whose hearts are free
　From Love's imperial chain,
Take warning and be taught by me,
　T' avoid th' enchanting pain.
Fatal the wolves to trembling flocks,
　Fierce winds to blossoms prove,
To careless seamen, hidden rocks,
　To human quiet, Love.

Fly the fair sex if bliss you prize ;
　The snake's beneath the flower !
Who ever gazed on beauteous eyes,
　That tasted quiet more ?
How faithless is the lovers' joy,
　How constant is their care :
The kind, with falsehood do destroy,
　The cruel, with despair !

Miscellany (Mrs. Behn), 1685.

CXVIII

Tell me no more, I am deceived
　While Sylvia seems so kind,
And takes such care to be believed ;
　The cheat I fear to find.

To flatter me, should falsehood lie
 Concealed in her soft youth,
A thousand times, I'd rather die
 Than see the unhappy truth !

My love all malice shall outbrave ;
 Let fops in libels rail,
If she the appearances will save
 No scandal will prevail.
She makes me think I have her heart :
 How much for that is due ?
Though she but act the tender part,
 The joy she gives is true.

A Duke and no Duke (Tate), 1685.

CXIX

Fair Iris ! all our time is spent
 In trifling, whilst we dally.
The lovers who're indifferent
 Commit the grossest folly.
Ah ! stint not then the flowing pleasure
To such a wretched scanty measure.
Since boundless passion, boundless joys will
 prove ;
Excess can only justify our love.

Excess, in other things so bad,
 In Love's the justest measure.
No other reason's to be had
 In that seraphic pleasure.
From growing love, bright Nymphs, your faces
Receive ten thousand sweeter graces.
My Iris, then, that you may be divine.
Let your soft flame spread, night and day, like
 mine.

Chorus Poetarum, 1694.

CHARLES SACKVILLE, EARL OF DORSET (1638-1706)

CXX

WRITTEN AT SEA,
IN THE FIRST DUTCH WAR

To all you ladies now at land,
  We men at sea do write ;
But first I hope you'll understand
  How hard 'tis to indite :
The Muses now, and Neptune too,
We must implore, to write to you.

For though the Muses should be kind,
  And fill our empty brain ;
Yet when rough Neptune calls the wind
  To rouse the azure main,
Our paper, ink, and pen, and we
Roll up and down our ship at sea.

Then, if we write not by each post,
  Think not we are unkind,
Nor yet conclude that we are lost
  By Dutch or else by wind ;
Our tears we'll send a speedier way :
The tide shall bring them twice a day.

With wonder and amaze the king
  Will vow his seas grow bold ;
Because the tides more water bring
  Than they were wont of old :
But you must tell him that our cares
Send floods of grief to Whitehall Stairs.

To pass the tedious hours away,
  We throw the merry main ;
Or else at serious ombre play :
  But why should we in vain

Each other's ruin thus pursue ?
We were undone when we left you.

If foggy Opdam did but know
   Our sad and dismal story,
The Dutch would scorn so weak a foe,
   And leave the port of Goree ;
For what resistance can they find
From men that left their hearts behind ?

Let wind and weather do their worst,
   Be you to us but kind ;
Let Frenchmen vapour, Dutchmen curse,
   No sorrow shall we find :
'Tis then no matter how things go,
Nor who's our friend, nor who's our foe.

In justice, you cannot refuse
   To think of our distress,
Since we in hope of honour lose
   Our certain happiness ;
All our designs are but to prove
Ourselves more worthy of your love.

Alas ! our tears tempestuous grow
   And cast our hopes away ;
While you unmindful of our woe,
   Sit careless at a play :
And now permit some happier man
To kiss your busk, and wag your fan.

When any mournful tune you hear,
   That dies in every note
As if it sighed for each man's care
   For being so remote,
Think then how oft our love we made
To you, while all those tunes were played.

And now we have told all our love,
   And also all our tears,
We hope our declarations move
   Some pity for our cares ;
Let's hear of no unconstancy,
We have too much of that at sea.

1664.

CXXI

BONNY BLACK BESS

Methinks the poor town has been troubled too
      long
With Phyllis and Chloris in every song,
By fools who at once can both love and despair,
And will never leave calling them cruel and fair ;
Which justly provokes me in rhyme to express
The truth that I know of bonny Black Bess.

This Bess of my heart, this Bess of my soul,
Has a skin white as milk and hair black as coal ;
She's plump, yet with ease you may span round
      her waist,
But her round swelling thighs can scarce be
      embraced :
Her belly is soft, not a word of the rest,
But I know what I think when I drink to the
      best.

The ploughman and squire, the arranter clown,
At home she subdued in her paragon gown ;
But now she adorns the boxes and pit,
And the proudest town-gallants are forced to
      submit ;
All hearts fall a-leaping wherever she comes,
And beat day and night, like my Lord Craven's
      drums.

I dare not permit her to come to Whitehall,
For she'd outshine the ladies, paint, jewels, and
    all ;
If a lord should but whisper his love in the
    crowd,
She'd sell him a bargain, and laugh out aloud ;
Then the Queen overhearing what Betty did say,
Would send Mr. Roper to take her away.

But to these that have had my dear Bess in their
    arms,
She's gentle, and knows how to soften her
    charms ;
And to every beauty can add a new grace,
Having learned how to lisp and to trip in her
    pace,
And, with head on one side and a languishing
    eye,
To kill us by looking as if she would die.

Methinks the Poor Town, 1673.

CXXII

THE ADVICE

Phyllis, for shame, let us improve
    A thousand several ways
These few short minutes, stolen by love
    From many tedious days.

Whilst you want courage to despise
    The censure of the grave,
For all the tyrants in your eyes,
    Your heart is but a slave.

My love is full of noble pride,
    And never will submit
To let that fop, Discretion, ride
    In triumph over Wit.

False friends I have, as well as you,
    That daily counsel me
Vain frivolous trifles to pursue,
    And leave off loving thee.

When I the least belief bestow
    On what such fools advise,
May I be dull enough to grow
    Most miserably wise.

Westminster Drollery, i, 1671.

CXXIII

As he lay in the plain, his arm under his head,
And his flock feeding by, the fond Celadon said,
" If Love's a sweet passion, why does it torment ?
If a bitter (said he) whence are lovers content ?
Since I suffer with pleasure, why should I
        complain ?
Or grieve at my fate, when I know 'tis in vain ?
Yet so pleasing the pain is, so soft is the dart,
That at once it both wounds me, and tickles my
        heart :
To my self I sigh often without knowing why,
And when absent from Phillis, methinks I could
        die ;
But oh ! what a pleasure still follows my pain,
When kind Fortune does help me to see her
        again.
In her eyes, the bright stars that foretell what's
        to come
By soft stealth now and then I examine my
        doom.
I press her hand gently, look languishing down,
And by passionate silence I make my love
        known.

But oh ! how I'm bless'd when so kind she does
    prove,
By some willing mistake to discover her love ;
When in striving to hide, she reveals all her
    flame,
And our eyes tell each other what neither dare
    name."

A Collection of Poems, 1672.

CXXIV

At the sight of my Phillis, from every part
A spring-tide of joy does flow up to my heart,
Which quickens each pulse, and swells ev'ry
    vein :
But all my delights are still mingled with pain.

So strange a distemper sure love cannot bring ;
To my knowledge, love was a much quieter
    thing,
So gentle and tame, that he never was known,
So much as to wake me, when I lay alone.

But the boy is much grown and so alter'd of late,
He's become a more furious passion than hate ;
Since by Phillis restor'd to the empire of hearts,
He has new strung his bow, and sharpen'd his
    darts :
And strictly the rights of his crown to main-
    tain,
He breaks ev'ry heart, and turns ev'ry brain.

My madness, alas ! I too plainly discover ;
For he is at least as much madman as lover,
Who, for one cruel beauty, is ready to quit
All the nymphs of the stage, and those of the
    pit :

The joys of Hyde-Park, and the Mall's dear
    delight,
To live sober all day, and chaste all the night.
Covent Garden Drollery, 1672.

CXXV

May the ambitious ever find
    Reward in crowds and noise,
Whilst gentle love does fill my mind
    With silent real joys.

May fools and knaves grow rich and great,
    And the world think 'em wise,
Whilst I lie dying at her feet,
    And all that world despise.

Let conquering kings new trophies raise,
    And melt in court delights :
Her eyes shall give me brighter days,
    Her arms much softer nights.

MS. 1681.

CXXVI

Dorinda's sparkling wit and eyes,
    Uniting, cast too fierce a light,
Which blazes high, but quickly dies,
    Pains not the heart, but hurts the sight.

Love is a calmer, gentler joy,
    Smooth are his looks and soft his pace ;
Her Cupid is a black-guard boy
    That runs his link full in your face.

A New Miscellany, 1701.

CXXVII

AN EPITAPH

Here lies little . . . a yard deep and more,
That never lay silent or quiet before,
Her head always working, her tongue always
      prating,
And the pulse of her heart continually beating,
To the utmost extremes of loving and hating.
Her reason and humour were always at strife ;
And yet she perform'd all the duties of life :
An excellent friend, and a pretty good wife.
So indulgent a lover, that no man could say
Whether Patty or Minta did rule or obey ;
For the government chang'd some ten times a
      day.
At the hour of her birth, some lucky star gave
      her
Wit and beauty enough to have lasted for ever ;
But fortune, still froward when nature is kind,
A narrow estate maliciously join'd,
To a vast genius, and a noble mind.

Her body was built of that superfine clay,
That is apt to grow brittle for want of allay :
And, when, without shew, it was apt to decay,
It began by degrees to moulder away.
Her soul, then, too busy on some foreign
      affair,
Of its own pretty dwelling took so little care,
That the tenement fell for want of repair.

  Far be from hence the fool or the knave,
But let all that pretend to be witty or brave,
Whether gen'rous friend or amorous slave,
Contribute some tears to water her grave.

Miscellany Poems, v, 1704.

E

SIR CHARLES SEDLEY (1639-1701)

CXXVIII

TO CLORIS

Cloris, I cannot say your eyes
Did my unwary heart surprise ;
Nor will I swear it was your face,
Your shape, or any nameless grace :
For you are so entirely fair
To love a part injustice were ;
No drowning man can know which drop
Of water his last breath did stop ;
So when the stars in Heaven appear,
And join to make the night look clear,
The light we no one's bounty call,
But the obliging gift of all.
He that does lips or hands adore,
Deserves them only, and no more ;
But I love all, and every part,
And nothing less can ease my heart.
Cupid that lover weakly strikes,
Who can express what 'tis he likes.

CXXIX

CONSTANCY

Fear not, my dear, a flame can never die
That is once kindled by so bright an eye ;
View but thy self, and measure thence my love ;
Think what a passion such a form must move ;
For though thy beauty first allur'd my sight,
Now I consider it but as the light
That led me to the treasury of thy mind,
Whose inward virtue in that feature shin'd.

That knot, be confident, will ever last,
Which Fancy tied, and Reason has made fast,
So fast that time, although it may disarm
Thy lovely face, my faith can never harm ;
And Age deluded, when it comes, will find
My love removed, and to thy soul assign'd.

CXXX

THE PLATONIC

Fair Amaranta, wert thou not to blame,
To blow the fire, and wonder at the flame ?
I did converse, 'tis true, so far was mine,
But that I lov'd and hoped was wholly thine ;
Not hoped as others do, for a return,
But that I might without offending burn.
I thought those eyes which every hour enslave
Could not remember all the wounds they gave :
Forgotten in the crowd I wished to lie,
And of your coldness, not your anger, die.
Yet since you know I love, 'tis now no time
Longer to hide, let me excuse the crime ;
Seeing what laws I to my passion give,
Perhaps you may consent that it should live.
First then, it never shall a hope advance
Of waiting on you but by seeming chance :
I at a distance will adore your eyes,
As awful Persians do the eastern skies ;
I never will presume to think of sex,
Nor with gross thoughts my deathless love
    perplex ;
I tread a pleasant path without design,
And to thy care my happiness resign.
From Heaven itself thy beauty cannot be
A freer gift, than is my love to thee.

CXXXI

Not Celia, that I juster am
  Or better than the rest,
For I would change each hour like them,
  Were not my heart at rest.

But I am tied to very thee,
  By every thought I have,
Thy face I only care to see,
  Thy heart I only crave.

All that in woman is adored,
  In thy dear self I find,
For the whole sex can but afford
  The handsome and the kind.

Why then should I seek farther store,
  And still make love anew ;
When change itself can give no more,
  'Tis easy to be true.

CXXXII

Love still has something of the sea,
  From whence his Mother rose ;
No time his slaves from doubt can free,
  Nor give their thoughts repose ;

They are becalm'd in clearest days,
  And in rough weather tossed ;
They wither under cold delays,
  Or are in tempests lost.

One while they seem to touch the port,
  Then straight into the main
Some angry wind in cruel sport
  The vessel drives again.

At first disdain and pride they fear,
   Which if they chance to 'scape,
Rivals and falsehood soon appear
   In a more dreadful shape.

By such degrees to joy they come,
   And are so long withstood,
So slowly they receive the sum,
   It hardly does them good.

'Tis cruel to prolong a pain,
   And to defer a joy
Believe me, gentle Celemene,
   Offends the winged Boy.

An hundred thousand oaths your fears
   Perhaps would not remove ;
And if I gaz'd a thousand years
   I could no deeper love.

CXXXIII

Phillis, you have enough enjoy'd
   The pleasures of disdain ;
Methinks your pride should now be cloy'd,
   And grow itself again :
Open to love your long-shut breast,
And entertain its sweetest guest.

Love heals the wounds that beauty gives,
   And can ill usage slight ;
He laughs at all that Fate contrives,
   Full of his own delight ;
We in his chains are happier far
Than kings themselves without 'em are.

Leave then to tame philosophy
   The joys of quietness ;
With me into love's empire fly
   And taste my happiness ;

Where even tears and sighs can show
Pleasures the cruel never know.

CXXXIV

Fair Aminta, art thou mad,
    To let the world in me
Envy joys I never had,
    And censure them in thee ?

Fill'd with grief for what is past,
    Let us at length be wise,
And to love's true enjoyments haste,
    Since we have paid the price.

Love does easy souls despise
    Who lose themselves for toys,
And escape for those devise
    Who taste his utmost joys.

Love should, like the year be crown'd
    With sweet variety :
Hope should in the spring abound,
    Kind fears, and jealousy ;

In the summer flowers should rise,
    And in the autumn fruit.
His spring doth else but mock our eyes,
    And in a scoff salute.

CXXXV

Hears not my Phillis, how the birds
    Their feather'd mates salute ?
They tell their passion in their words :
    Must I alone be mute ?
Phillis, without frown or smile,
Sat and knotted all the while.

The God of Love in thy bright eyes
   Does like a tyrant reign ;
But in thy heart a child he lies,
   Without his dart or flame.
Phillis, without frown or smile,
Sat and knotted all the while.

So many months in silence past,
   And yet in raging love,
Might well deserve one word at last
   My passion should approve.
Phillis, without frown or smile,
Sat and knotted all the while.

Must then your faithful swain expire,
   And not one look obtain,
Which he, to soothe his fond desire,
   Might pleasingly explain ?
Phillis, without frown or smile,
Sat and knotted all the while.

CXXXVI

Phillis is my only joy,
   Faithless as the winds or seas ;
Sometimes coming, sometimes coy,
   Yet she never fails to please ;
     If with a frown
     I am cast down,
     Phillis smiling,
     And beguiling,
Makes me happier than before.

Tho', alas, too late I find
   Nothing can her fancy fix,
Yet the moment she is kind
   I forgive her all her tricks ;

Which, tho' I see,
I can't get free ;
She deceiving,
I believing ;
What need lovers wish for more ?

CXXXVII

Phillis, men say that all my vows
  Are to thy fortune paid ;
Alas, my heart he little knows
  Who thinks my love a trade.

Were I of all these woods the lord,
  One berry from thy hand
More real pleasure would afford
  Than all my large command.

My humble love has learnt to live
  On what the nicest maid,
Without a conscious blush, may give
  Beneath the myrtle shade.

CXXXVIII

Ah Cloris ! that I now could sit
  As unconcern'd as when
Your infant beauty could beget
  No pleasure, nor no pain.

When I the dawn used to admire,
  And prais'd the coming day ;
I little thought the growing fire
  Must take my rest away.

Your charms in harmless childhood lay,
  Like metals in the mine ;
Age from no face took more away,
  Than youth conceal'd in thine.

But as your charms insensibly
   To their perfection pressed,
Fond love as unperceiv'd did fly
   And in my bosom rest.

My passion with your beauty grew,
   And Cupid at my heart,
Still as his mother favour'd you,
   Threw a new flaming dart.

Each gloried in their wanton part :
   To make a lover he
Employed the utmost of his art,
   To make a beauty she.

Though now I slowly bend to love
   Uncertain of my fate,
If your fair self my chains approve,
   I shall my freedom hate.

Lovers, like dying men, may well
   At first disorder'd be,
Since none alive can truly tell
   What fortune they must see.

ANONYMOUS

CXXXIX

What care I though the world reprove
My bold, my over-daring love :
Ignoble minds themselves exempt
From interest in a brave attempt.

The eagle soaring to behold
The sun arrayed in flames of gold
Regards not though she burns her wings,
Since that rich sight such pleasure brings.

So feel I now my smiling thought
To such a resolution brought
That it contemns all grief and smart,
Since I so high have placed my heart.

And if I die, some worthy spirits
To future times shall sing my merits,
That easily did my life despise,
Yet ne'er forsook my enterprise.

Then shine, bright sun, and let me see
The glory of thy majesty :
I wish to die, so I may have
Thy look my death, thine eye my grave.

Westminster Drollery, i, 1671.

CXL

A SONG AT THE KING'S HOUSE

Cloris, let my passion ever
    Be to you as I design :
Flames so noble, that you never
    Saw the like till you knew mine.

Not a breath of feigned passion
    From my lips shall reach your ears ;
Nor this love that's now in fashion,
    Made of modish sighs and tears.

In my breast a room so fitting
    For your heart I will prepare,
That you'll never think of quitting,
    Were you once but harboured there.

The rent's not great that I require
    From your heart, mine to repay :
Fortitude's all I desire
    To keep your lodging from decay.

Fairest Saint, then be not cruel,
   Nor to love me count it sin ;
Since a smile from you is fuel
   For to keep this fire in.

When I am forced by death or age
   From your flames for to retire,
All true lovers I'll engage
   Still my passion to admire.

Ibid.

CXLI

All the flatteries of fate
   And the glories of state
Are nothing so sweet as what love doth create :
   If love you deny
   'Tis time I should die ;
Kind death's a reprieve when you threaten to
     hate.

In some shady grove
   Will I wander and rove,
With Philomel and the disconsolate dove :
   With a down-hanging wing
   Will I mournfully sing
The tragic events of unfortunate love.

With our plaints we'll conspire
   For to heighten love's fire,
Still vanquishing life, till at last we expire :
   But when we are dead,
   In a cold leafy bed,
Be interred with the dirge of this desolate choir.

Ibid.

CXLII

I pass all my hours in a shady old grove,
And I live not the day that I see not my Love.
I survey every walk now my Phyllis is gone,
And sigh when I think we were there all alone.
 Oh, then 'tis, oh, then I think there's no such
  hell
 Like loving, like loving too well.

But each shade and each conscious bower when
  I find,
Where I once have been happy and she has been
  kind,
And I see the print left of her shape in the green,
And imagine the pleasure may yet come again ;
 Oh, then 'tis, oh, then I think no joy's above
 The pleasures, the pleasures of love.

While alone to myself I repeat all her charms,
She I love may be locked in another man's arms :
She may laugh at my cares, and so false she may
  be
To say all the kind things she before said to me.
 Oh, then 'tis, oh, then I think there's no such
  hell
 Like loving, like loving too well.

But when I consider the truth of her heart,
Such an innocent passion, so kind, without art,
I fear I have wronged her, and hope she may be
So full of true love to be jealous of me.
 Oh, then 'tis, oh, then I think no joy's above
 The pleasures, the pleasures of love.

KING CHARLES II (?)

Ibid.

CXLIII

A lover I am, and a lover I'll be,
And hope from my love I shall never be free :
Let wisdom be blamed in the grave woman-
    hater,
Yet never to love, is a sin of ill nature :
But he who loves well, and whose passion is
    strong,
Shall never be wretched, but ever be young.

With hopes and with fears, like a ship in the
    ocean,
Our hearts are kept dancing and ever in motion ;
When our passion is palled, and our fancy would
    fail
A little kind quarrel supplies a fresh gale :
But when the doubt's cleared and the jealousy's
    gone,
How we kiss and embrace, and can never have
    done !

Ibid.

CXLIV

A SONG

Let Fortune and Phillis frown if they please,
    I'll no more on their deities call,
Nor trouble the Fates, but give myself ease,
    And be happy in spite of 'em all ;
I will have my Phillis, if I once go about her ;
Or if I have not, I'll live better without her.

If she prove virtuous, obliging and kind,
    Perhaps I'll vouchsafe for to love her ;
But if pride or inconstancy in her I find,
    I'd have her to know I'm above her ;

For at length I have learned, now my fetters are
    gone,
To love if I please, or to let it alone.

Westminster Drollery, ii, 1672.

CXLV

THE RURAL DANCE ABOUT THE
MAYPOLE

Come, lasses and lads,
Take leave of your dads,
And away to the maypole hie !
    For every he
    Has got him a she,
With a minstrel standing by :
For Willy has gotten his Jill, and Johnny has
    got his Joan,
To jig it, jig it, jig it, jig it, jig it up and down.

' Strike up ! ' says Wat,
' Agreed ! ' says Kate,
' And I prithee, fiddler, play ! '
    ' Content ! ' says Hodge,
    And so says Madge,
' For this is a holiday,'
Then every man did put his hat off to his lass,
And every girl did curchy, curchy, curchy on the
    grass.

' Begin ! ' says Hal,
' Ay, ay ! ' says Mall,
' We'll lead up Packington's Pound ' ;
    ' No, no ! ' says Noll,
    And so says Doll,
We'll first have Sellenger's Round.'
Then every man began to foot it round about,
And every girl did jet it, jet it, jet it in and out.

' You're out ! ' says Dick,
' 'Tis a lie ! ' says Nick,
' The fiddler played it false !
' 'Tis true ! ' says Hugh,
And so says Sue,
And so says nimble Alice.
The fiddler then began to play the tune again,
And every girl did trip it, trip it, trip it to the
men.

' Let's kiss ! ' says Jane,
' Content ! ' says Nan,
And so says every she :
' How many ? ' says Batt,
' Why, three,' says Matt,
' For that's a maiden's fee ; '
But they instead of three, did give 'em half a
score ;
And they in kindness gave 'em, gave 'em, gave
'em as many more.

Then, after an hour,
They went to a bower,
And played for ale and cakes,
And kisses too
Until they were due,
The lasses kept the stakes :
The girls did then begin to quarrel with the men,
And bid 'em take their kisses back, and give 'em
their own again.

Yet there they sate
Until it was late,
And tired the fiddler quite,
With singing and playing,
Without any paying,
From morning until night.

They told the fiddler then, they'd pay him for his
    play ;
And each a two-pence, two-pence, two-pence
    gave him, and went away.

Ibid.

CXLVI

THE MOON'S LOVE

The Moon, in her pride, once glancèd aside
    Her eyes and espied the Day,
As unto his bed, in waistcoat of red,
    Fair Phœbus him led the way ;
Such changes of thought in her chastity
    wrought,
    That thus she besought the boy :
      ' Oh tarry and marry the starry Diana
      That will be thy gem and joy !

' I will be as bright at noon as at night,
    If that may delight the Day ;
Come hither and join thy glories with mine,
    Together we'll shine for aye :
The night shall be noon, and every moon
    As pleasant as June or May ;
      Oh tarry and marry the starry Diana
      That will be thy gem and joy !

' Enamoured of none, I live chaste and alone,
    Though courted of one, some say ;
And true if it were, so frivolous fear
    Let never my dear dismay ;
I'll change my opinion, and turn my old
    minion,
    The sleepy Endymion, away ;
      Oh tarry and marry the starry Diana
      That will be thy gem and joy ! '

And but that the night should have wanted
  her light,
  Or lovers in sight should play,
Or Phœbus should shame to bestow such a
  dame
  (With a dower of his flame) on a boy,
Or day should appear eternally here,
  And night otherwhere, the Day
    Had tarried and married the starry'd
      Diana,
      And she been his gem and joy.

Ibid.

CXLVII

ONE AND HIS MISTRESS A-DYING

Shall we die, both thou and I,
  And leave the world behind us ?
Come, I say, and let's away,
  For nobody here doth mind us.

Why do we gape ? we cannot 'scape
  The doom that is assigned us ;
When we are in grave, although we rave,
  There nobody needs to bind us.

The clerk shall sing, the sexton ring,
  And old wives they shall wind us ;
The priest shall lay our bones in clay
  And nobody there shall find us.

Farewell wits, and folly's fits,
  And griefs that often pined us !
When we are dead we'll take no heed
  What nobody says behind us.

Merry nights and false delights
　Adieu, ye did but blind us ;
We must to mould, both young and old,
　Till nobody's left behind us.

Ibid.

CXLVIII

Give o'er, foolish heart, and make haste to
　despair,
For Daphne regards not thy vows nor thy
　prayer :
When I plead for thy passion, thy pains to
　prolong
She courts her guitar, and replies with a song.
　No more shall true lovers such beauties adore ;
　　Were the gods so severe, men would worship
　　　no more.

No more will I wait like a slave at the door,
I'll spend the cold nights at the window no
　more :
My lungs in long sighs no more I'll exhale,
Since your pride is to make me grow sullen and
　pale.
　No more shall Amintas your pity implore,
　　Were the gods so ingrate, men would worship
　　　no more.

No more shall your frowns or free humour
　persuade
To court the fair idol my fancy has made :
When your saints so neglected their follies give
　o'er
Your deity's lost, and your beauty's no more.
　No more shall true lovers such beauties adore ;
　　Were the gods so severe, men would worship
　　　no more.

How weak are the vows of a lover in pain,
When flattered by hope, or oppressed with
    disdain :
No sooner my Daphne's bright eyes I review
But all is forgot, and I vow all anew.
    No more, fairest nymph, I will murmur no
        more,
    Did the gods seem so fair, men would ever
        adore.

Ibid.

CXLIX

How charming are those pleasant pains
Which the successful lover gains !
Oh how the longing spirit flies,
On scorching sighs, from dying eyes,
Whose intermixing rays impart,
Love's welcome message to the heart !

Then how the active pulse grows warm,
To every sense gives the alarm ;
But oh, the raptures and the qualms
When love unites the melting palms !
What ecstasies, what hopes and fears,
What pretty talk and amorous tears !

To these a thousand vows succeed,
Oh then, O Heavens ! the secret deed
When sense and soul are bathed in bliss !
Think, dear Arminda, think on this,
And curse those hours we did not prove
The ravishing delights of love.

Covent Garden Drollery, 1672.

CL

Phillis, the time is come that we must sever,
Long we have lingered 'twixt kindness and strife,
And though we have promised ourselves to love
 ever
Yet there's a fate in love, as well as life :
So many jealousies daily we try,
Sometimes we freeze, and sometimes we fry,
That love in colds, or in fevers will die.

Both by our selves, and others tormented,
Still in suspense betwixt Heaven and Hell,
Ever desiring, and never contented,
Either not loving, or loving too well ;
Parting we still are in each other's powers,
Our love's a weather of sunshine and showers :
Its days are bitter, though sweet are its hours.

Why should we Fate any longer importune,
Since to each other unhappy we prove ?
Like losing gamesters, we tempt our ill fortune :
Both might be luckier in a new love.
This were the way should our reason bear sway ;
But when we so pleasing a passion destroy,
We may be more happy, but less should enjoy.

Ibid.

CLI

When first my free heart was surprised by desire,
So soft was the wound and so gentle the fire,
My sighs were so sweet and so pleasant the smart
I pitied the slave that had ne'er lost his heart.
He thinks himself happy and free, but alas !
He is far from the Heaven that lovers possess.

In Nature was nothing that I could compare
With the beauty of Phillis, I thought her so fair ;
A wit so divine all her sayings did fill,
A goddess she seemed, and I mentioned her still
With a zeal more inflamed and a passion more
    true
Than a martyr in flames for religion can show.

More virtues and graces I found in her mind
Than the Schools can invent, or the Gods e'er
    designed ;
She seemed to be mine by each glance of her eye,
If mortals might aim at a blessing so high.
Each day with new favours, new hope did she
    give,
But alas, what is wished we too soon do believe.

With awful respect while I loved and admired,
But feared to attempt what so much I desired.
How soon were my hopes and my heaven
    destroyed :
A shepherd, more daring, fell on and enjoyed,
Yet in spite of ill fate and the pains I endure
I will find a new Phillis to give me a cure.

Ibid.

CLII

Peace, Cupid ! Take thy bow in hand,
  I' th' gloomy shade in ambush stand
To watch a cruel nymph frequents this bower,
  Cold as the streams, but sweeter than each
    flower.
  There, there she is ! Direct thy dart
  Into that stony marble heart :
Draw, quickly draw ; and shew thy art.

Woe's me ! Thou art blind indeed, thou hast
    shot me !
While she 'scapes in the grove, and laughs at
    thee.

Methinks the Poor Town, 1673.

CLIII

Thou art so fair and cruel too
I am amazed what I shall do
    To compass my desire ;
Sometimes thy eyes do me invite,
But when I venture, kill me quite,
    Yet still increase my fire.

Oft have I tried my love to quell,
And thought its fury to repel
    Since I no hopes do find ;
But when I think of leaving thee
My heart so much doth torture me
    As 'twould rejoice, if kind.

I still must care, though hardly used
And never offer but refused :
    Can any suffer more ?
Be coy, be cruel, do thy worst;
Though for thy sake I am accursed,
    I must and will adore.

Ibid.

CLIV

Adieu, my Cordelia, my dearest, adieu,
No passion more slighted was ever more true,
No torment severer than this could you prove
To enjoin him to absence that's chained by your
    love.

Subdued by your charms, you enflamed my
    desire,
Till a spark from your eyes set my heart all on
    fire ;
Oh, cruelty shown, no offence but love known,
Exiled and outlawed by a hard heart of stone.

Ibid.

CLV

CHORUS

Many thousand follies are
The unhappy lover's share :
Doubtful pangs and wild desires,
Immoderate heat, unruly fires,
Tides of relenting and disdain,
Quickening rapture, joy and pain ;
But with these fantastic things
Love many true perfections brings.

Ibid.

CLVI

Fie, Chloris ! 'Tis silly to sigh thus in vain,
'Tis silly to pity the lovers you've slain ;
If still you continue your slaves to deride,
The compassion you feign will be taken for pride:
And sorrow for sin can never be true
In one that does daily commit it anew.

If, while you are fair, you resolve to be coy,
You may hourly repent, as you hourly destroy ;
Yet none will believe you, protest what you will,
That you grieve for the dead, if you daily do
    kill ;
And where are our hopes when we zealously woo,
If you vow to abhor what you constantly do ?

Then, Chloris, be kinder, and tell me my fate,
For the worst I can suffer's to die by your hate :
If thus you design, never fancy in vain
By your sighs and your tears to recall me again ;
Nor weep at my grave, for (I swear) if you do,
As you now laugh at me, I will then laugh at
    you.

Ibid.

CLVII

  Is Celadon unkind ? It cannot be.
    Or is he so unconstant grown
      To slight my vows, and break his own ?
  Forbid it, Heaven : no, it cannot be.
Then, my good Angel, whither is he fled ?
Tell me, Oh, tell me softly, is he dead ?
    Ah ! prophetic soul, forbear,
    Lest I languish in despair.
    No ! My heart, whene'er he dies,
    In the pain must sympathize.
    Since my soul and his are one,
    He cannot live, or die, alone.
Florella ! forbear to distrust, or repine,
Since his love, and his suff'rings, are equal with
    thine ;
And when he returns, if ever again,
We'll kiss away sorrow and laugh away pain.

Ibid.

CLVIII

Life of my Soul ! return, return,
Must I for ever sigh and mourn ?
The pains in thy absence that I do endure
Thou never shalt know, yet thou only canst cure ;

Then come away ! haste away ! Life is but
    short,
It cannot be longer without a support.

How does my gladded soul rejoice
To hear the music of his voice !
Then thanks, O Love ! to thy powerful charms
And welcome, dear Shepherd to Floria's arms ;
We'll banish all sorrow, and cast away fear :
'Twere a sin to be sad now my Celadon's here.

Ibid.

CLIX

TO A YOUNG LADY IN A GARDEN
The Rose's Speech

Fairest, if you roses seek,
Take the nearest like your cheek.
I, the damask, would presume
To tender you my sweet perfume ;
I am young, like you, a bud,
Peeping thorough my green hood,
Blushing only 'cause I see
Fresher roses grow on thee.
Crop me then and let me lie
In the sunshine of thine eye
Till full-blown ; then let me grow
In thy bosom, next thy snow,
That I may find, when my leaves fall,
In that sweet place a funeral.
Then, Celia, be you like the rose,
Who its season wisely chose ;
Do not keep your maiden flower
Beyond its time, its full ripe hour.
Like the rose, you need not offer ;
But when a worthy hand doth proffer,

Refuse not, Celia : on my life
You'll wear as fresh when you're a wife.
Let not your beauties untouch'd die,
Or withered and neglected lie ;
Rather let them thrive i' th' light
Of his am'rous eager sight,
That when at last they fall and spread
It may be sweetly on his bed.

Bristol Drollery, 1674.

CLX

How dull a thing this world would prove
If 'twere not for the joys of love :
For what pleasure can it bring
To see returns of the Spring,
And Summer in its chiefest pride,
If there were nought of love beside ?
To drink, to dance, to laugh and sing,
If love were not a guest within ?
To walk, to ride, to feast and sport,
The state and glories of a Court,
How lifeless do these all appear,
If love vouchsafe not to be there.
Let others glory in these things,
And think 'em happy as are Kings :
Than all their boastings, I say more
When I say, Celia, I adore.

Ibid.

CLXI

TO PHILLIS, March 5th, 1673

Give o'er, my dear Phillis, to whisper and smile
You betray my poor heart, and undo me the
while.

Yet whilst I look on you, so sweet and so nice,
For the pleasures I feel I'd refuse Paradise.
I die when I see you the length of a street,
But oh ! how you murder when nearer we meet.

'Tis then that my heart to your bosom straight
  flies
To be safe from the darts shot so thick from your
  eyes.
But when I think on, and do but compare
Amyntas unhappy and Phillis so fair,
Oh ! then my heart breaks and I die with
  despair.
While thus I choose rather alone to complain,
Than tell her I love, and am killed with disdain,

Thid.

CLXII

> Phillis, since you can ne'er be mine
>   (Not that less kind I'll prove)
> I wish in him that shall be thine,
>   All my extremes of love.
>
> In what a rapture then of bliss
>   Entranced he then will lie,
> Breathing his soul in every kiss
>   And every amorous sigh.
>
> When on that sacred night of love
>   Your bodies shall unite
> And every ravished sense shall prove
>   The excesses of delight
>
> Think, dearest, then on me forlorn
>   Waking and thoughtful lying,
> Thus cruelly from Phillis torn
>   For love and sorrow dying.

Ibid.

CLXIII

We are born, then cry
We know not for why ;
And all our lives long
Still but the same song.
Our lives are but short,
We're made Fortune's sport,
We spend them in care,
In hunting the hare,
In tossing the pot,
In venturing our lot
At dice, when we play
To pass time away.
We dress ourselves fine,
At noon we do dine,
We walk then abroad,
Or ride on the road ;
With women we dally,
Retreat and rally,
And then in the bed
We lay down our head.
And all this and more
We do o'er and o'er,
Till at last we all die,
And in the cold grave lie.

Then let us be merry,
Send down to the ferry
A bottle for him—
Old Charon the grim—
A bribe for our stay,
Till we must away.

Ibid.

APHRA BEHN (1640-89)

CLXIV

THE CAUTION

My Damon, if your heart be kind,
　Do not too long with beauty stay ;
For there are certain moments when the mind
　Is hurried by the force of charms away.
In Fate a minute critical there lies,
That waits on love, and takes you by surprise.

　A lover pleased with constancy,
　Lives still as if the maid he loved were by :
　　As if his actions were in view,
　　As if his steps she did pursue ;
　　Or that his very soul she knew.
Take heed ;　for though I am not present there,
My love, my Genius waits you everywhere.

The Lover's Watch, 1686.

CLXV

Oh ! how the hand the lover ought to prize
　'Bove any one peculiar grace,
While he is dying for the eyes
　And doting on the lovely face !
The unconsidering little knows,
How much he to this beauty owes.

That, when the lover absent is,
　Informs him of his mistress' heart ;
'Tis that which gives him all his bliss,
　When dear love-secrets 'twill impart,
That plights the faith the maid bestows ;
And that confirms the tim'rous vows.

'Tis that betrays the tenderness,
  Which the too bashful tongue denies :
'Tis that which does the heart confess,
  And spares the language of the eyes.
'Tis that which treasure gives so vast ;
Ev'n Iris 'twill to Damon give at last.

The Lady's Looking Glass, 1686.

CLXVI

LOVE ARMED

Love in fantastic triumph sat,
  Whilst bleeding hearts around him flow'd,
For whom fresh pains he did create,
  And strange tyrannic power he show'd.
From thy bright eyes he took his fire,
  Which round about in sport he hurl'd ;
But 'twas from mine he took desire,
  Enough t'undo the amorous world.

From me he took his sighs and tears,
  From thee his pride and cruelty ;
From me his languishments and fears,
  And every killing dart from thee :
Thus thou and I the God have arm'd,
  And set him up a deity ;
But my poor heart alone is harm'd,
  Whilst thine the victor is, and free.

Abdelazar, 1677.

CLXVII

THE DREAM

The grove was gloomy all around,
  Murm'ring the streams did pass,
Where fond Astrea laid her down
  Upon a bed of grass.

I slept and saw a piteous sight,
   Cupid aweeping lay,
Till both his little stars of light
   Had wept themselves away.

Methought I asked him why he cried,
   My pity led me on ;
All sighing the sad boy replied,
   " Alas I am undone.

" As I beneath yon myrtles lay,
   Down by Diana's springs,
Amyntas stole my bow away,
   And pinioned both my wings."

" Alas ! cried I, 'twas then thy darts
   Wherewith he wounded me :
Thou mighty Deity of Hearts,
   He stole his power from thee.

" Revenge thee, if a god thou be,
   Upon the amorous swain ;
I'll set thy wings at liberty,
   And thou shalt fly again.

" And for this service on my part,
   All I implore of thee,
Is that thou'lt wound Amyntas' heart,
   And make him die for me."

His silken fetters I untied,
   And the gay wings displayed ;
Which gently fanned, he mounts and cried,
   " Farewell, fond easy maid."

At this I blushed, and angry grew
   I should a god believe ;
And waking found my dream too true,
   Alas ! I was a slave.

Poems, 1684.

CLXVIII

O Love ! that stronger art than wine,
Pleasing delusion, witchery divine,
Wont to be priz'd above all wealth,
Disease that has more joys than health ;
Tho' we blaspheme thee in our pain,
And of thy tyranny complain,
We all are better'd by thy reign.

What reason never can bestow,
We to this useful passion owe.
Love wakes the dull from sluggish ease,
And learns a clown the art to please ;
Humbles the vain, kindles the cold,
Makes misers free, and cowards bold.
'Tis he reforms the sot from drink,
And teaches airy fops to think.

When full brute appetite is fed,
And chok'd the glutton lies, and dead ;
Thou new spirits dost dispense,
And 'fin'st the gross delights of sense.
Virtue's unconquerable aid,
That against nature can persuade,
And makes a roving mind retire
Within the bounds of just desire ;
Cheerer of age, youth's kind unrest,
And half the heaven of the blest.

The Lucky Chance, 1687, *Theatre of Music,* iv,
1687.

CLXIX

A thousand martyrs I have made,
    All sacrificed to my desire ;
A thousand beauties have betray'd,
    That languish in resistless fire.

The untam'd heart to hand I brought,
And fixed the wild and wandering thought.

I never vow'd nor sigh'd in vain,
   But both, tho' false, were well received.
The fair are pleased to give us pain,
   And what they wish is soon believed.
And tho' I talk'd of wounds and smart,
Love's pleasures only touched my heart.

Alone the glory and the spoil
   I always laughing bore away ;
The triumphs, without pain or toil,
   Without the hell, the heav'n of joy.
And while I thus at random rove
Despise the fools that whine for love

Lycidus, 1688.

EPHELIA

CLXX

TO PHYLOCLES, INVITING HIM TO FRIENDSHIP

Best of thy sex ! if sacred friendship can
Dwell in the bosom of inconstant man,
As cold and clear as ice, as snow unstained,
With love's loose crimes unsullied, unprofaned,

Or you a woman with that name dare trust,
And think to friendship's ties we can be just :
In a strict league together we'll combine,
And let our friendship's bright example shine.

We will forget the difference of sex,
Nor shall the world's rude censure us perplex.
Think me all man : my soul is masculine,
And capable of as great things as thine.

F

I can be generous, just and brave,
Secret and silent as the grave,
And if I cannot yield relief,
I'll sympathise in all thy grief.

I will not have a thought from thee I'll hide,
In all my actions thou shalt be my guide ;
In every joy of mine thou shalt have share,
And I will bear a part in all thy care.

Why do I vainly talk of what we'll do ?
We'll mix our souls, you shall be me, I you ;
And both so one it shall be hard to say
Which is Phylocles, which Ephelia.

Our ties shall be as strong as the chains of Fate,
Conquerors and kings our joys shall emulate ;
Forgotten friendship, held at first divine,
To its native purity we will refine.

Female Poems, 1679.

CLXXI

THE CHANGE OR MIRACLE

What miracles this childish God has wrought !
Things strange above belief ! Who would have
    thought
My temper could be to this tameness brought ?

I, who the wanton boy so long defied,
And his fantastic Godhead did deride,
And laughed at lovers with insulting pride,

Now pale and faint beneath his altar lie,
Own him a great and glorious Deity,
And want the pity that I did deny.

For my proud victor does my tears neglect,
Smiles at my sighs, treats me with disrespect :
And if I do complain, with frowns I'm checked.

Though all I sue for, be the empty bliss
Of a kind look, or at the most a kiss ;
Yet he's so cruel to deny me this.

Before my passion struck my reason blind,
Such generosity dwelt in my mind,
I cared for none, and yet to all was kind.

But now I tamely bend, and sue in vain
To one that takes delight to increase my pain
And proudly does me and my love disdain.

Ibid.

CLXXII

LOVE'S FIRST APPROACH

Strephon I saw, and started at the sight,
And interchangeably looked red and white ;
I felt my blood run swiftly to my heart,
And a chill trembling seize each outward part ;
My breath grew short, my pulse did quicker
        beat,
My heart did heave, as it would change its seat ;
A faint cold sweat o'er all my body spread,
A giddy megrim wheel'd about my head.
When for the reason of this change I sought,
I found my eyes had all the mischief wrought,
For they my fort to Strephon had betray'd,
And my weak heart his willing victim made ;
The traitors, conscious of the treason
They had committed 'gainst my reason,
Looked down with such a bashful guilty fear,
As made their fault to every eye appear.

Though the first fatal look too much had done,
The lawless wanderers would still gaze on,
Kind looks repeat, and glances steal, till they
Had looked my liberty and heart away.
Great Love, I yield ; send no more darts in vain,
I am already fond of my soft chain ;
Proud of my fetters, so pleased with my state
That I the very thought of freedom hate.
O mighty Love ! thy art and power join,
To make his frozen breast as warm as mine ;
But if thou try'st and canst not make him kind,
In love such pleasant, real sweets I find,
That, though attended with despair it be,
'Tis better still than a wild liberty.

Ibid.

CLXXIII

Know, Celadon, in vain you use
    These little arts to me :
Though Strephon did my heart refuse
    I cannot give it thee ;
His harsh refusal hath not brought
    Its value yet so low,
That what was worth that shepherd's thoughts
    I should on you bestow.

Nor can I love my Strephon less
    For his ungrateful pride,
Though Honour does, I must confess
    My guilty passion chide :
That lovely youth I still adore,
    Though now it be in vain ;
But yet of him I ask no more
    Than pity for my pain.

Ibid.

CLXXIV

You wrong me, Strephon, when you say
   I'm jealous or severe,
Did I not see you kiss and play
   With all you came a-near ?
Say, did I ever chide for this,
   Or cast one jealous eye
On the bold nymphs, that snatch'd my bliss
   While I stood wishing by.

Yet though I never disapproved
   This modish liberty,
I thought in them you only loved
   Change and variety :
I vainly thought my charms so strong,
   And you so much my slave,
No nymph had power to do me wrong,
   Or break the chains I gave.

But when you seriously address
   With all your winning charms
Unto a servile shepherdess,
   I'll throw you from my arms :
I'd rather choose you should make love
   To every face you see,
Than Mopsa's dull admirer prove
   And let her rival me.

Ibid.

CLXXV

To one that asked me why I loved J. G.

Why do I love ? go ask the glorious sun
Why every day it round the world doth run ;

Ask Thames and Tiber why they ebb and flow ;
Ask damask roses why in June they blow ;
Ask ice and hail the reason why they're cold ;
Decaying beauties, why they will grow old.
They'll tell thee, Fate, that everything doth
    move,
Enforces them to this, and me to love.
There is no reason for our love or hate,
'Tis irresistible as Death or Fate.
'Tis not his face : I've sense enough to see,
That is not good, though doted on by me ;
Nor is't his tongue, that has this conquest won,
For that at least is equalled by my own ;
His carriage can to none obliging be,
'Tis rude, affected, full of vanity,
Strangely ill-natur'd, peevish and unkind,
Unconstant, false, to jealousy inclin'd ;
His temper could not have so great a power,
'Tis mutable, and changes every hour ;
Those vigorous years that women so adore
Are past in him : he's twice my age and more ;
And yet I love this false, this worthless man,
With all the passion that a woman can ;
Doat on his imperfections, though I spy
Nothing to love ; I love, and know not why.
Since 'tis decreed in the dark book of Fate,
That I should love, and he should be ingrate.

Ibid.

WILLIAM WYCHERLEY (1640-1716)

CLXXVI

All over I'm in love with thee,
    As thou all over lovely art ;
There's not a part but pleases me
    Except thy proud, ungentle heart.

Your beauty's light is evident,
   Though where, or how, we cannot say ;
Thus unseen stars i' th' element,
   United, make the Milky Way.

Whoever loves your eyes alone,
   A kind look only should be his ;
And he whose lips but dwell upon
   The praise of yours, should lose his kiss.

I love each charm, each grace, alike,
   And to them all give all my heart :
Love did my breast too deeply strike
   For me to know or name the dart.

CLXXVII

I love variety, 'tis true,
   But for your sake, my dear, alone :
Variety I find in you,
   Who have all woman's charms in one.

Your humour varies like your look,
   Which you so daily change to me,
That if with change I were not took,
   Constant to you I could not be.

To please men more, you change your dress,
   And since all else, why not your mind ?
You would but please your lovers less,
   If you the same they still should find.

Then blame not my inconstancy,
   Which most my faith to you does prove :
Did I not love variety,
   Thee, fickle dear, how should I love ?

CLXXVIII

A DRINKING SONG

A merry cup ('faith) let us drink,
To be more wise, the less we think;
   Since thinking is a silly thing,
     Which brings us care,
     Fear and despair,
   To leave off thinking, we should sing.

We'll sing and drink eternally;
Who thinks too much, too soon will die;
   Too much thought is too little sense,
     He's sad, who thinks,
     He's glad, who drinks,
   He, who thinks least, is most a prince.

Wise Turks, that they may never think
Take opium, and wise Christians drink;
   Thought drains and dries the fertile brain,
     But moistening it
     Judgment and wit
   Will flourish and spring up again.

A merry cup then let us take,
That dreams asleep, nor cares awake,
   May break our rest, our peace destroy;
     When we drink deep
     Our sorrows sleep,
   Drowning our care, buoys up our joy.

The thinker is the greatest fool;
He without thought the greatest soul,
   Who lets the world jog on, as 'twill,
     Knowing that thought
     Is good for nought
   But minds to torture, men to kill.

Thus all we call philosophy,
Is not to think, if sense does lie
   In being but insensible
     Of pain and care;
     By which men are
More wise as less they know, think, feel.

CLXXIX

LOVE'S GOLDEN AGE

How happy was that age of old
When hearts were neither bought nor sold;
When each unmercenary she
For love expected nought but love;
And when the kind protesting he
His passion by his faith did prove;
When friends each other's words did take,
And honesty did all their bargains make.

Then look for look and kiss for kiss,
Was all was given her love, or his,
Or for exchange of hearts was paid
By the generous youthful swain
To the bright but artless maid,
His love to prove and hers to gain:
White Cupid, changed from what he was of old,
Now, like a negro slave, is bought and sold.

THOMAS RYMER (1641-1713)

CLXXX

A SERENADE

Phyllis appearing,
No star in the skies
So glorious does rise,
So warm to the heart, so gay to the eyes.

Fortune and fate
Their old malice forbearing,
On her influence wait :
But Fate who would value, when Phyllis is
    kind ?
Her eyes I adore : let Fortune be blind.

Curious Amusements, 1714.

CLXXXI

Late when Love I seemed to slight,
Phillis smiled, as well she might.
' Now,' said she, ' our throne may tremble,
Men our province now invade ;
Men take up our royal trade ;
Men, even men, do now dissemble :
In the dust our empire's laid.'

Tutored by the wise and grave,
Loath was I to be a slave :
Mistress sounded arbitrary,
So I chose, to hide my flame,
Friendship, a discreeter name.
But she scorns one jot to vary,
She will Love or nothing claim.

Be a lover, or pretend,
Rather than the warmest friend ;
Friendship of another kind is.
Swedish coin of gross allay,
A cart-load, will scarce defray :
Love, one grain, is worth the Indies,
Only Love is current pay.

Ibid.

CLXXXII

ON HER ABSENCE

Boast not your fresh unmingled sweets,
Boast not your noiseless sleepy nights
And such your country dear delights,
Since ye no longer feel the ray,
When all was dull, that made you gay,
And turned your darkness into day.

No doubt the town is nobly great,
No doubt the country purely sweet,
When that we there Clorinda meet ;
But all is desert, all despair :
For heaven itself I should not care
Unless I saw Clorinda there.

Ibid. (Written 1683).

CLXXXIII

TO ———

Let those with cost deck their ill-fashioned clay
Who only are with their fine feathers gay :
While you, despising false and borrowed light
Shine of yourself more gloriously bright.

Whatever Art can make, or Wit invent
Would be on you superfluously spent.
Your beauty needs no ornament or dress
And would be made by all additions less.

You still triumph, amidst your marriage toil,
And make the brightest virgin but your foil.
Still in its bloom you keep your maiden pride
And spite of all your children seem a bride.

Ibid.

THOMAS SHADWELL (1642-92)

CLXXXIV

LOVE OF FAME

... 'Tis an ambition above mortal state
And mind with glory never satiate,
Without which glory and ambition
No noble action ever yet was done :
So avidious and so covetous of Fame
As only for eternizing their name.
They, as the Phœnix life to's young does give,
Would be content to die, that that might live.
But now I'll tell what my opinion is
Of Fame (and pardon if I judge amiss)
Fame's but a shadow of great action,
And but the echo of't when we are gone,
Than whose trumpet no music is more sweet,
Nor none's alive more pleased with hearing it ;
But I don't know what pleasure I should have,
When I am dead, with music at my grave.

On the Duchess of Newcastle, Her Grace, 1676

CLXXXV

Nymphs and shepherds, come away,
In those groves let's sport and play,
Where each day is a holiday,
Sacred to ease and happy love,
To dancing, music, poetry ;
Your flocks may now securely rove
While you express your jollity.

We come, we come, no joy like this,
Now let us sing, rejoice and kiss ...
In these delightful fragrant groves,
Let's celebrate our happy loves ;

Let's pipe and dance and laugh and sing ;
Thus every happy living thing,
Revels in the cheerful spring.

The Libertine, 1676.

CLXXXVI

How wretched is the slave to love,
Who can no real pleasures prove ;
    For still they're mixed with pain :
When not obtained, restless is the desire,
Enjoyment puts out all the fire,
    And shows the love was vain.

It wanders to another soon,
Wanes and increases like the moon,
    And like her never rests :
Brings tides of pleasures now, and then of tears,
Makes ebbs and flows of joys and cares,
    In lovers' wavering breasts.

But spite of love I will be free,
And triumph in the liberty
    I without him enjoy ;
I' the worst of prisons I'll my body bind,
Rather than chain my free-born mind
    For such a foolish toy.

The Virtuoso, 1676.

JOHN RAWLET (1642-86)

CLXXXVII

MIDNIGHT MEDITATIONS

Look here, my soul, how sparkling and how
    bright
These stars do shine in this cold, frosty night.

From the sun's absence they advantage take
Their native lustre visible to make ;
Their beams set in array adorn the sky
As if they did night's black approach defy.
The cold which freezeth us, it does but clear
The air, and make their brightness more appear.
Let these fair stars be patterns unto thee
And teachers too, shewing what thou shouldst
    be,
When sacred Providence, the heavenly law
Made up of love and wisdom, shall withdraw
That pleasing sunshine of prosperity
Which from thy cradle hath attended thee,
And by its revolutions shall this state
Into affliction's dark, cold night translate ;
Or if thy body sickness should confine
To a dark room to languish there and pine
In pain, or malice should attempt thy fame,
And with black slanders strive to cloud thy
    name ;
Or, what's thought worse than either, shouldst
    thou be
Stark naked stripped and pinched by poverty ;
Or shouldst thou be for some great merit sent
To a dark prison or to banishment :
Then muster all thy powers up, O my Soul,
Whose shining may these clouds of night control,
And let a bright unspotted innocence
In sweet contentment, courage, patience,
Shed its mild beams, let hope and joy display
Lustres which turn night into lightsome day.

Poetic Miscellanies, 1687.

CLXXXVIII

AN ACCOUNT OF MY LIFE IN
THE NORTH

Bene qui latuit, bene vixit.

Since you, dear friend, wonder how here I live,
This homely verse a brief account shall give.
I live, if not in pleasure, yet at ease
Not in loud laughters, but in silent peace ;
And though I rarely meet with merriment
I more a stranger am to discontent.
Here's no excess, nor are things needful scant.
I seldom feast, but yet I never want.
No dainties here to luxury invite
Our food serves well the sober appetite,
Which need not be with poignant sauces dressed :
Our healthful hunger of all sauce is best.
Doctors we have none, nor much need them
    here ;
The doctors we more than diseases fear :
Our country folks think they sell death too
    dear.
Although I lie not on a rich down-bed,
Yet do sweet sleeps refresh my weary head.
No walks or gardens here, but yet the field
And fragrant meadows equal pleasures yield.
No lutes or viols entertain my ear,
But more melodious birds I daily hear :
Riches I have not, nor do riches need,
Whilst here at easy rates we clothe and feed.
I have no servants whom I may command,
Nor have I work that needs a servant's hand
I am not high enough to envied be,
Nor do I one whom I should envy see.
Here's no applause to make me proud or vain,
Nor do I meet with censures or disdain.

My people, if they are not wise and great,
Are not untractable through self-conceit :
No factious giddy heads that raise a schism
For fear of Popery or Arminianism ;
No saucy arrogant counsellors, such
That cry, This is too little, that too much ;
No such vile wretches who their preacher hate
'Cause he reviles sin at too smart a rate :
Wherefore I envy not flocks of more wealth,
Which give more trouble whilst they have less
    health.
If of companions I have no great store,
With my own mind I may converse the more ;
And from my old friends though I am confined,
Letters may keep us in each other's mind ;
Or if, while buried here, I lose their love,
I'll fix my mind on surer things above.
But need I friends, need I companions crave,
Whilst I as many friends as neighbours have ?
Or if I want the joy of bosom friends,
I 'scape the pain which still that joy attends :
For whilst they live our hearts oft ache with fear,
But break and bleed when of their death I hear.
And if I want the comfort of a wife
I have the pleasures of a single life.
If I no gallants here or beauties see,
From slavish love and courtship I am free.
What fine things else you in the South can name,
Our North can shew as good, if not the same :
Even as in winter you have shorter nights,
But summer us with longer days requites.
Thus if my want of joy makes life less sweet,
Death then will seem less bitter when we meet.
But what is this world's joy, 'tis innocence
And virtue that do truest joys dispense ;
If innocence and virtue with me dwell
They'll make a paradise of an hermit's cell.
Ibid.

JAMES WRIGHT (1643-1713)

CLXXXIX

OUT OF HORACE

What do I wish ? No more than what I have,
The same estate, and quiet to the grave :
That no succeeding hour the fates allow
My life's remains, may see me worse than now.
Plenty of books ; provision for the year ;
A settled mind, unswayed by hope or fear.
Life and estate are all I can invent
To ask of Heaven : I'll give myself content.

Miscellanea Sacra, 1692.

CXC

THE REBUILDING OF ST. PAUL'S

Once beauteous, and still reverend pile,
Mayst thou rise up the glory of this isle,
Much more majestic than thou wert erewhile.

Mayst thou a resurrection have,
Bright as thy Saints, from this thy mournful
  grave :
May a choir's beauty shine even in thy nave.

Mayst thou be built of such a lasting frame,
Such strength, shall laugh at any future flame,
And such a majesty shall awe the same.

But where shall then this generation be ?
And who shall live that miracle to see—
A beauty grown out of deformity ?

Three Poems of St. Paul's Cathedral, 1697.

JOHN MASON (1646-94)

CXCI

A SONG OF PRAISE FOR THE EVENING

Now from the altar of my heart
  Let incense flames arise.
Assist me, Lord, to offer up
  Mine evening sacrifice.

Awake, my love ; awake, my joy,
  Awake, my heart and tongue.
Sleep not when mercies loudly call :
  Break forth into a song.

Man's life's a book of history,
  The leaves thereof are days,
The letters mercies closely joined,
  The title is Thy praise.

This day God was my sun and shield,
  My Keeper and my Guide.
His care was on my frailty shown,
  His mercies multiplied.

Minutes and mercies multiplied
  Have made up all this day ;
Minutes came quick, but mercies were
  More fleet and free than they.

New time, new favours and new joys
  Do a new song require ;
Till I shall praise Thee as I would,
  Accept my heart's desire.

Lord of my time, whose hand hath set
  New time upon my score,
Then shall I praise for all my time,
  When time shall be no more.

Songs of Praise, 1683.

CXCII

A SONG OF PRAISE FOR FAMILY PROSPERITY

On all my flock both great and small,
    Thy sun doth sweetly shine ;
Thy fruitful drops do gently fall
    On every branch of mine.

Thy blessing made the loaves to grow,
    And multitudes were fed ;
My house is filled and feasted too,
    It is an house of bread.

How can I hear my children sing,
    And not sing unto Thee ?
Since they glad news from Heav'n do bring,
    My God must hear from me.

Ibid.

CXCIII

A GENERAL SONG OF PRAISE TO ALMIGHTY GOD

How shall I sing that Majesty
    Which Angels do admire ?
Let dust in dust and silence lie,
    Sing, sing ye heavenly choir.

Thousand of thousands stand around
    Thy Throne, O God, most High ;
Ten thousand times ten thousand sound
    Thy praise ; but who am I ?

Thy brightness unto them appears,
  Whilst I Thy footsteps trace;
A sound of God comes to my ears,
  But they behold Thy face.

They sing because Thou art their sun:
  Lord, send a beam on me,
For where Heav'n is but once begun
  There hallelujahs be.

Enlighten with faith's light my heart,
  Enflame it with love's fire,
Then shall I sing and bear a part,
  With that celestial choir.

I shall, I fear, be dark and cold,
  With all my fire and light:
Yet when Thou dost accept their gold,
  Lord, treasure up my mite.

How great a being, Lord, is Thine
  Which doth all beings keep!
Thy knowledge is the only line
  To sound so vast a deep.

Thou art a sea without a shore,
  A sun without a sphere,
Thy time is now and evermore,
  Thy place is everywhere.

How good art Thou whose goodness is
  Our parent, nurse, and guide;
Whose streams do water Paradise,
  And all the earth beside.

Thine upper and Thy nether springs
  Make both Thy worlds to thrive,
Under Thy warm and sheltering wings
  Thou keep'st two broods alive.

Ibid.

MARY MOLLINEUX (1648-95)

CXCIV

TO COUSIN M. S.

Sometimes (dear friend) this riseth in my
    heart:
Come, let's with Mary choose the better part,
Of which the meek shall not deprived be:
Her seat was low in deep humility
At holy Jesus' feet; when her desire
Was still to hear that voice which did inspire
Her heart with fervent love, she did not seek
Usurped power, but learned to be meek.
For certainly the humble-hearted shall
Exalted be, but pride portends a fall;
Whoever must be great, must first be low
And little, and a true subjection know
To that which teacheth lowliness of mind;
And to the truth their all must be resigned,
Before they can obtain that true content
And solid joy, that's firm and permanent.
Such then may say, No solace, joy nor love,
Like unto this, which freely from above
Distils and streams into the heart that's pure;
Here's treasure, pleasure, peace that will endure:
To this we ought to make our calling sure.

(1678)   *Fruits of Retirement,* 1702.

CXCV

CONTEMPLATION

My life, my love, my joy,
Who can enough admire
The sweet'ning influence
Of Shiloh's stream, from whence

Virtue abounds unto thy plants, whereby
The lily sprouts, free from the choking briers:
Thy trees do likewise bring forth fruit and
  flourish
To th' praise of Thee, who dost both prune and
  cherish.

  The time that is employ'd
  In holy meditation
  Of Thy prevailing love
  Engaging from above
The upright heart, (wherein it is enjoy'd)
In humble fear and sacred admiration,
Is best improv'd : for this indeed doth tend
To true content and peace, world without end.
(1678) *Ibid.*

CXCVI

SOLITUDE

How sweet is harmless solitude !
  What can its joys control ?
Tumults and noise may not intrude,
  To interrupt the soul,

That here enjoys itself, retired
  From earth's seducing charms ;
Leaving her pomp to be admired
  By such as court their harms.

While she, on contemplation's wings
  Soars far beyond the sky,
And feeds her thoughts on heavenly things
  Which in her bosom lie.

Great privileges here of old
  The wise men did obtain ;
And treasure far surpassing gold
  They digged for not in vain.

The tincture of philosophers
   Here happily they found ;
The music of the morning stars
   Here in their hearts did sound.

Ibid.

HENRY ALDRICH (1647-1710)

CXCVII

CHRIST CHURCH BELLS

Oh the bonny Christ Church bells :
   One, two, three, four, five, six,
   They sound so wondrous great,
     So woundy sweet,
   And they troll so merrily, merrily.
   Oh the first and second bell,
   That every day at four and ten
Cry, Come, come, come, come, come to prayers,
And the verger troops before the dean.
Tinkle, tinkle, ting, goes the small bell at nine
   To call the beerers home,
     But the devil a man
     Will leave his can
   Till he hears the mighty Tom.

The Musical Companion, (J. Playford), 1673.

CXCVIII

THE FIVE REASONS FOR DRINKING

If all be true that I do think,
There are five reasons we should drink :
Good wine ; a friend ; or being dry ;
Or lest we should be by and by ;
Or any other reason why.

The Banquet of Music (H. Playford), 1689.

THOMAS HEYRICK (1648 ?———)

CXCIX

ON AN INDIAN TOMINEIOS
THE LEAST OF BIRDS

I'm made in sport by Nature, when
  She's tired with the stupendous weight
Of forming elephants and beasts of state ;
  Rhinocerots, that love the fen ;
  The elks that scale the hills of snow,
And lions couching in their awful den ;
  These do work Nature hard, and then
  Her wearied hand in me doth show
What she can for her own diversion do.

Man is a little world ('tis said)
  And I in miniature am drawn,
A perfect creature, but in short-hand shown.
  The ruck in Madagascar bred,
  (If new discoveries truth do speak)
Whom greatest beasts and armed horsemen
    dread,
  Both him and me one artist made :
  Nature in this delight doth take,
That can so great and little monsters make.

The Indians me a sunbeam name,
  And I can be the child of one :
So small I am, my kind is hardly known.
  To some a sportive bird I seem,
  And some believe me but a fly ;
Tho' me a feathered fowl the best esteem :
  Whate'er I am, I'm Nature's gem,
  And like a sunbeam from the sky,
I can't be followed by the quickest eye.

I'm the true bird of Paradise,
  And heavenly dew's my only meat :
My mouth so small, 'twill nothing else admit.
  No scales know how my weight to poise,
  So light, I seem condensed air ;
And did at th' end of the Creation rise,
  When Nature wanted more supplies,
  When she could little matter spare,
But in return did make the work more rare.

Miscellany Poems, 1691.

JOHN WILMOT, EARL OF ROCHESTER,
(1647-80)

CC

From A DIALOGUE

DAPHNE

Tell me then the reason, why
Love from hearts in love does fly ?
Why the bird will build a nest,
Where he ne'er intends to rest ?

STREPHON

Love, like other little boys,
Cries for hearts, as they for toys ;
Which, when gained, in childish play,
Wantonly are thrown away.

DAPHNE

Still on wing, or on his knees,
Love does nothing by degrees :
Basely flying when most prized,
Meanly fawning when despised,
Flattering or insulting ever,
Generous and grateful never :
All his joys are fleeting dreams,
All his woes severe extremes.

CCI

Phillis, be gentler, I advise ;
  Make up for time misspent,
When beauty on its death-bed lies,
  'Tis high time to repent.

Such is the malice of your fate
  That makes you old so soon,
Your pleasure ever comes too late,
  How early e'er begun.

Think what a wretched thing is she
  Whose stars contrive in spite
The morning of her love should be
  Her fading beauty's night.

Then, if to make your ruin more,
  You'll peevishly be coy,
Die with the scandal of a whore,
  And never know the joy.

CCII

Give me leave to rail at you,
I ask nothing but my due,
To call you false and then to say
You shall not keep my heart a day :
But, alas ! against my will,
I must be your captive still.
Ah ! be kinder then ; for I
Cannot change, and would not die.

Kindness has resistless charms,
  All besides but weakly move ;
Fiercest anger it disarms,
  And clips the wings of flying love.

Beauty does the heart invade,
Kindness only can persuade ;
It gilds the lover's servile chain,
And makes the slaves grow pleased again.

CCIII

Insulting Beauty, you misspend
    Those frowns upon your slave ;
Your scorn against such rebels bend,
Who dare with confidence pretend
That other eyes their hearts defend
    From all the charms you have.

Your conquering eyes so partial are,
    Or mankind is so dull,
That while I languish in despair,
Many proud senseless hearts declare,
They find you not so killing fair
    To wish you merciful.

They an inglorious freedom boast ;
    I triumph in my chain.
Nor am I unrevenged, though lost,
Nor you unpunished, though unjust,
When I alone, who love you most,
    Am killed with your disdain.

CCIV

While on those lovely looks I gaze,
    To see a wretch pursuing,
In raptures of a blest amaze,
    His pleasing happy ruin ;
'Tis not for pity that I move ;
    His fate is too aspiring,
Whose heart, broke with a load of love,
    Dies wishing and admiring.

But if this murder you'd forego,
  Your slave from death removing ;
Let me your art of charming know,
  Or learn you mine of loving.
But, whether life or death betide,
  In love 'tis equal measure :
The victor lives with empty pride,
  The vanquished die with pleasure.

CCV

CONSTANCY

I cannot change, as others do,
  Though you unjustly scorn ;
Since that poor swain that sighs for you,
  For you alone was born.
No, Phyllis, no, your heart to move,
  A surer way I'll try,
  And to revenge my slighted love,
Will still love on, will still love on, and die.

When killed with grief Amyntas lies,
  And you to mind shall call
The sighs that now unpitied rise,
  The tears that vainly fall :
That welcome hour that ends this smart,
  Will then begin your pain,
  For such a faithful tender heart
Can never break, can never break in vain.

CCVI

LOVE AND LIVE

All my past life is mine no more,
  The flying hours are gone,
Like transitory dreams given o'er,
Whose images are kept in store,
  By memory alone.

The time that is to come, is not :
  How can it then be mine ?
The present moment's all my lot,
And that, as fast as it is got,
  Phyllis, is only thine.

Then talk not of inconstancy,
  False hearts, and broken vows ;
If I, by miracle, can be
This live-long minute true to thee,
  'Tis all that Heaven allows.

CCVII

Absent from thee I languish still ;
  Then ask me not when I return.
The straying fool 'twill plainly kill,
  To wish all day, all night to mourn.

Dear, from thine arms then let me fly,
  That my fantastic mind may prove
The torments it deserves to try,
  That tears my fixed heart from my Love.

When wearied with a world of woe
  To thy safe bosom I retire,
Where love, and peace, and truth does flow,
  May I contented there expire :

Lest once more wandering from that heaven,
  I fall on some base heart unblessed,
Faithless to thee, false, unforgiven,
  And lose my everlasting rest.

CCVIII

THE MISTRESS

An age in her embraces passed
    Would seem a winter's day
Where light and life with envious haste
    Are torn and snatched away.

But oh ! how slowly minutes roll,
    When absent from her eyes,
That fed my love, which is my soul ;
    It languishes and dies.

For then no more a soul but shade,
    It mournfully does move,
And haunts my breast, by absence made
    The living tomb of love.

You wiser men, despise me not,
    Whose love-sick fancy raves
On shades of souls, and heaven knows what ;
    Short ages live in graves :

Whene'er those wounding eyes, so full
    Of sweetness, you did see,
Had you not been profoundly dull,
    You had gone mad like me.

Nor censure us, you who perceive
    My best-belov'd and me
Sigh and lament, complain and grieve;
    You think we disagree.

Alas ! 'tis sacred jealousy,
    Love raised to an extreme :
The only proof 'twixt them and me,
    We love and do not dream.

Fantastic fancies fondly move
    And in frail joys believe,
Taking false pleasure for true love ;
    But pain can ne'er deceive.

Kind jealous doubts, tormenting fears,
    And anxious cares, when past,
Prove our heart's treasure fixed and dear,
    And make us blest at last.

CCIX

From HORACE

Conquered with soft and pleasing charms,
And never-failing vows of her return,
    Winter unlocks his frosty arms
    To free the joyful Spring ;
Which for fresh loves with youthful heat does
    burn ;
Warm south winds court her, and with fruitful
    showers
    Awake the drowsy flowers
    Who haste and all their sweetness bring
    To pay their yearly offering.

    No nipping white is seen,
But all the fields are clad in pleasant green,
    And only fragrant dews now fall :
    The ox forsakes his once warm stall
    To bask in the sun's much warmer beams ;
The plowman leaves his fire and his sleep,
Well pleased to whistle to his lab'ring teams ;
Whilst the glad shepherd pipes to his frisking
    sheep.
    Nay, tempted by the smiling sky
        Wrecked merchants quit the shore ;
    Resolving once again to try
    The wind and sea's almighty power ;
Choosing much rather to be dead than poor.

Since all the World's thus gay and free,
    Why should not we ?
Let's then accept our mother Nature's treat,
    And please ourselves with all that's sweet ;
        Let's to the shady bowers,
        Where, crowned with gaudy flowers,
We'll drink and laugh away the gliding hours.
Trust me, Thyrsis, the grim conqueror Death
With the same freedom snatches a king's breath,
    He huddles the poor fettered slave
        To his unknown grave.

Tho' we each day with cost repair,
He mocks our greatest skill and utmost care ;
    Nor loves the fair, nor fears the strong,
And he that lives the longest dies but young ;
    And once deprived of light,
    We're wrapped in mists of endless night.
Once come to those dark cells, of which we're
    told
So many strange romantic tales of old
(In things unknown invention's justly bold),
        No more shall mirth and wine
        Our loves and wit refine ;
    No more shall you your Phyllis have,
        Phyllis so long you've prized ;
    Nay she too in the grave
        Shall lie like us despised.

CCX

THE COMMONS' PETITION

TO KING CHARLES II

In all humanity, we crave
Our Sovereign may be our slave ;
And humbly beg, that he may be
Betrayed by us most loyally.

But if he please once to lay down
His Sceptre, Dignity, and Crown,
We'll make him, for the time to come,
The greatest Prince in Christendom.

THE KING'S ANSWER.

Charles, at this time, having no need,
Thanks you as much as if he did.

CCXI

UPON NOTHING

Nothing ! thou elder brother even to Shade,
Thou hadst a being ere the World was made,
And (well fixed) art alone, of ending not afraid.

Ere Time and Place were, Time and Place were
     not,
When primitive Nothing Something straight
     begot,
Then all proceeded from the great united—
     What.

Something, the general attribute of all,
Severed from thee, its sole original,
Into thy boundless self must undistinguished
     fall.

Yet Something did thy mighty power command,
And from thy fruitful emptiness's hand
Snatched men, beasts, birds, fire, air and land.

Matter, the wickedest offspring of thy race,
By Form assisted, flew from thy embrace,
And rebel Light obscured thy reverend dusky
     face.

G

With Form and Matter, Time and Place did join;
Body, thy foe, with them did leagues combine,
To spoil thy peaceful realm, and ruin all thy
　　line.

But turncoat Time assists the foe in vain,
And, bribed by thee, assists thy short-lived
　　reign,
And to thy hungry womb drives back thy slaves
　　again.

Though mysteries are barred from laic eyes.
And the divine alone with warrant pries
Into thy bosom, where the truth in private lies :

Yet this of thee the wise may freely say,
Thou from the virtuous nothing takest away,
And, to be part with thee, the wicked wisely
　　pray.

Great Negative, how vainly would the wise
Enquire, define, distinguish, teach, devise,
Didst thou not stand to point their dull philoso-
　　phies ?

Is, or *is not*, the two great ends of Fate,
And *true* or *false*, the subject of debate,
That perfect or destroy the vast designs of
　　Fate ;

When they have racked the politician's breast,
Within thy bosom must securely rest,
And, when reduced to thee, are least unsafe and
　　best.

But Nothing, why does Something still permit
That sacred monarchs should at council sit,
With persons highly thought, at best, for
　　nothing fit ?

Whilst weighty Something modestly abstains
From princes' coffers and from statesmen's
    brains,
And nothing there like stately Nothing reigns.

Nothing, who dwell'st with fools in grave dis-
    guise,
For whom they reverend shapes and forms devise.
Lawn sleeves, and furs, and gowns, when they
    like thee, look wise.

French truth, Dutch prowess, British policy,
Hibernian learning, Scotch civility,
Spaniards' dispatch, Danes' wit, are mainly seen
    in thee.

The great man's gratitude to his best friend,
Kings' promises, whores' vows, towards thee
    they bend,
Flow swiftly into thee, and in thee ever end.

CCXII

From ' A SATIRE AGAINST MANKIND '

Were I, who to my cost already am
One of those strange prodigious creatures, Man,
A spirit free to choose for my own share,
What sort of flesh and blood I pleased to wear,
I'd be a dog, a monkey, or a bear,
Or anything, but that vain animal,
Who is so proud of being rational.
The senses are too gross, and he'll contrive
A sixth to contradict the other five :
And before certain Instinct will prefer
Reason which fifty times for one does err,
Reason, an *Ignis Fatuus* of the mind,
Which leaves the light of nature, Sense, behind :

Pathless and dangerous wandering ways it takes
Through Error's fenny bogs and thorny brakes ;
Whilst the misguided follower climbs with pain
Mountains of whimsies, heaped in his own brain,
Stumbling from thought to thought, falls head-
    long down
Into Doubt's boundless sea, where, like to
    drown,
Books bear him up a while, and make him try
To swim with bladders of philosophy,
In hopes still to o'ertake the skipping light :
The vapour dances in his dazzled sight,
Till spent, it leaves him to eternal night.
Then Old Age and Experience, hand in hand,
Lead him to Death and make him understand,
After a search so painful, and so long,
That all his life he has been in the wrong.

JOHN SHEFFIELD, EARL OF
MULGRAVE
DUKE OF BUCKINGHAMSHIRE
(1648-1721)

CCXIII

LOVE'S SLAVERY

Grave fops my envy now beget,
    Who did my pity move ;
They by the right of wanting wit
    Are free from cares of love.

Turks honour fools, because they are
    By that defect secure
From slavery and toils of war,
    Which all the rest endure.

So I, who suffer cold neglect
   And wounds from Celia's eyes,
Begin extremely to respect
   These fools that seem so wise.

'Tis true they fondly set their hearts
   On things of no delight :
To pass all day for men of parts,
   They pass alone the night.

But Celia never breaks their rest ;
   Such servants she disdains ;
And so the fops are dully blest,
   While I endure her chains.

Works, 1726.

CCXIV

INCONSTANCY EXCUSED

I must confess I am untrue
   To Gloriana's eyes ;
But he that's smiled upon by you
   Must all the world despise.

In winter, fires of little worth
   Excite our dull desire ;
But when the sun breaks kindly forth,
   Those fainter flames expire.

Then blame me not for slighting now
   What I did once adore ;
Oh, do but this one change allow,
   And I can change no more :

Fixt by your never-failing charms,
   Till I with age decay,
Till languishing within your arms
   I sigh my soul away.

Ibid.

CCXV

DESPAIR

When in thy lonely bed
    My ghost its moan shall make,
With saddest signs that I am dead,
    And dead for thy dear sake,

Struck with that conscious blow
    Thy very soul will start ;
Pale as my shadow thou wilt grow,
    And cold as is thy heart.

Too late remorse will then
    Untimely pity show
To him, who of all mortal men
    Did most thy value know.

Yet, with this broken heart,
    I wish thou never be
Tormented with the thousandth part
    Of what I feel for thee.

Ibid.

CCXVI

THE RECONCILEMENT

Come, let us now resolve at last
    To live and love in quiet ;
We'll tie the knot so very fast,
    That time shall ne'er untie it.

The truest joys they seldom prove
    Who free from quarrels live ;
'Tis the most tender part of love
    Each other to forgive.

When least I seemed concerned, I took
  No pleasure, nor no rest ;
And when I feigned an angry look,
  Alas, I loved you best.

Own but the same to me, you'll find
  How blest will be our fate ;
Oh, to be happy, to be kind,
  Sure never is too late.

Ibid.

CCXVII

THE RELAPSE

Like children in a starry night,
  When I beheld those eyes before
I gazed with wonder and delight,
  Insensible of all their pow'r.

I played about the flame so long,
  At last I felt the scorching fire ;
My hopes were weak, my passion strong,
  And I lay dying with desire.

By all the helps of human art,
  I just recovered so much sense
As to avoid, with heavy heart,
  The fair but fatal influence.

But, since you shine away despair,
  And now my sighs no longer shun,
No Persian in his zealous prayer
  So much adores the rising sun.

If once again my vows displease,
  There never was so lost a lover ;
In love, that languishing disease,
  A sad relapse we ne'er recover.

Ibid.

CCXVIII

ON ONE WHO DIED DISCOVERING HER KINDNESS

Some vex their souls with jealous pain,
While others sigh for cold disdain ;
Love's various slaves we daily see ;
Yet happy all, compared with me.

Of all mankind I loved the best,
A nymph so far above the rest,
That we outshined the Blest above,
In beauty she, and I in love.

And therefore they who could not bear
To be outdone by mortals here
Among themselves have placed her now,
And left me wretched here below.

All other fate I could have borne,
And ev'n endured her very scorn ;
But oh ! thus all at once to find
That dread account, both dead, and kind,
What heart can hold ? If yet I live,
'Tis but to show how much I grieve.

Ibid.

CCXIX

ON MR. HOBBES AND HIS WRITINGS

Such is the mode of these censorious days,
The art is lost of knowing how to praise ;
Poets are envious now, and fools alone
Admire at wit, because themselves have none.

Yet whatsoe'er is by vain critics thought,
Praising is harder much than finding fault ;
In homely pieces ev'n the Dutch excel,
Italians only can draw beauty well . . . .
  While in dark ignorance we lay afraid
Of fancies, ghosts, and every empty shade,
Great Hobbes appeared, and by plain reason's
  light
Put such fantastic forms to shameful flight.
Fond is their fear, who think men needs must be
To vice enslaved, if from vain terrors free ;
The wise and good, morality will guide ;
And superstition all the world beside.
  In other authors tho' the thought be good,
'Tis not sometimes so eas'ly understood ;
That jewel oft unpolished has remained,
Some words should be left out, and some
  explained ;
So that in search of sense we either stray
Or else grow weary in so rough a way.
But here sweet eloquence does always smile,
In such a choice, yet unaffected style,
As must both knowledge and delight impart,
The force of reason, with the flowers of art ;
Clear as a beautiful transparent skin,
Which never hides the blood, yet holds it in :
Like a delicious stream it ever ran,
As smooth as woman, but as strong as man.
  Bacon himself, whose universal wit
Does admiration through the world beget,
Scarce more his age's ornament is thought,
Or greater credit to his country brought.
  While Fame is young, too weak to fly away,
Malice pursues her, like some bird of prey ;
But once on wing, then all the quarrels cease ;
Envy herself is glad to be at peace,
Gives over, wearied with so high a flight,
Above her reach, and scarce within her sight.

Hobbes to this happy pitch arrived at last,
Might have looked down with pride on dangers
    past.
But such the frailty is of human kind,
Men toil for fame, which no man lives to find ;
Long ripening under-ground this China lies ;
Fame bears no fruit, till the vain planter dies.

Ibid.

ROBERT WOLSELEY (1649-97)

CCXX

SONG

Say, nymph divine, for whom I burn,
    In absence is your heart at ease ?
Have you no joy for his return,
    Whom nothing but your sight can please ?

Who every moment pines away,
    And with a restless passion dies,
If he but pass one tedious day
    Unblessed of those all-charming eyes.

To serve you is my care and pride ;
    To please you, all this world can give ;
Dead to all human things beside,
    In that loved breast alone I live.

You night and day my thoughts employ,
    You only my desires can move ;
To have a taste for meaner joy,
    Is an ungrateful wrong to love.

Examen Miscellaneum, 1702.

THOMAS DUFFETT

CCXXI

ON A ROSE TAKEN FROM FRANCELIA'S BREAST

Poor hapless emblem of Amyntor's heart,
  Thy blooming beauty's overcast ;
Deep shades of grief seem to o'erspread each
    part,
  Yet still thy fragrant sweets do last.

Thou wert not, when my dearest nymph is kind,
  In all thy pride so blest as I,
She gone, my wounded heart thy fate does find,
  So does it droop, and so will die.

What joyful blushes did thy leaves adorn,
  How gay, how proudly didst thou swell,
When in Francelia's charming bosom worn,
  That Paradise where Gods would dwell.

Oh had my heart thy happy place possest,
  It never had from thence been torn,
But like a Phœnix in her spicy nest,
  It still should live and ever burn.

No wonder thy perfume so near thy death
  Still lasts, though thy vermilion's gone :
Thy sweets were borrowed from her sweeter
    breath,
  Thy fading colour was thy own.

See how my burning sighs thy leaves have dried,
  Where I have sucked thy stolen sweets :
So does the amorous youth caress his bride,
  And print hot kisses in her lips.

Hadst thou ungathered fall'n among the rest
   Lost and forgotten thou hadst been,
Thou hadst not flourished in Francelia's breast
   Nor been the subject of my pen.

Amber dissolved and beaten spices smell,
   That gold is valued most that's proved ;
Coy beauty's lost, but lasting fame will tell
   Their praise that love and are beloved.

New Poems, 1676.

CCXXII

   Liberty, Liberty !
Reason and Love are at war,
No more on wild Passion I'll wait,
Or cringe to an upstart Despair
The creature of idle conceit :
Draw up, my thoughts, let Shame the fight begin,
Charge to the heart, oh let not Hope get in,
'Tis Love's hero, if that appear in his defence,
A thousand thousand reasons cannot force him
   thence.

   Victory, Victory !
Love the usurper is fled,
His flames and his arrows are spent,
The toys by which fools are misled
To adore what themselves do invent.
The thing appears that did support his cause,
How pale she looks that to my heart gave laws !
The Nymph's vanish'd, set are the suns that
   made me blind,
And only woman, vain, weak woman's left
   behind.

Phillida, Phillida !
What's of my Goddess become ?
Oh where is the shape and the mien,
Whose presence has oft struck me dumb,
Whose beauty I thought all divine ?
As in the dark to one o'ercome by fear
Deformèd shapes and sprites seem to appear,
The fond lover strange wonders in his nymph
    does find,
When all the charms are in his own deluded
    mind.

Ibid.

CHARLES WEBBE

CCXXIII

More love or more disdain I crave ;
  Sweet, be not still indifferent :
Oh send me quickly to my grave,
  Or else afford me more content.
Or love or hate me more or less,
For love abhors all lukewarmness.

Give me a tempest if 'twill drive
  Me to the place where I would be ;
Or if you'll have me still alive,
  Confess you will be kind to me.
Give hopes of bliss or dig my grave :
More love or more disdain I crave.

New Airs and Dialogues, 1678.

CCXXIV

Sweet, be no longer sad,
  Prithee be wise !
Recall that quickness once you had
  In those fair eyes :

Methinks they're heavy grown
As they were not your own,
And had forgot hearts to surprise.

Tell me, oh, tell me now,
Where have you sent
The roses, in your cheeks did grow ?
Where's the content
You once enjoyed ? Say where
Those pleasing charms now are
Which daily did my heart torment ?

Ibid.

RICHARD LEIGH (1649-   )

CCXXV

SLEEPING ON HER COUCH

Thus lovely Sleep did first appear,
Ere yet it was with Death allied,
When the first fair one, like her here,
Lay down, and for a little died.

Ere happy souls knew how to die
And trod the rougher paths to bliss,
Transported in an ecstasy
They breathed out such smooth ways as this.

Her hand bears gently up her head,
And like a pillow, raised does keep ;
But softer than her couch is spread,
Though that be softer than her sleep.

Alas, that death-like Sleep or Night
Should power have to close those eyes,
Which once vied with the fairest light
Or what gay colours thence did rise.

Ah ! that lost beams thus long have shined
　To them with darkness overspread,
Unseen as day breaks to the blind
　Or the sun rises to the dead.

That sun in all his eastern pride
　Did never see a shape so rare,
Nor Night within its black arms hide
　A silent beauty half so fair.

Poems, 1675.

CCXXVI

BEAUTY OF CHANGE

Roses in their first ~~vermeil dress appear,~~
　Lilies their ancient beauties display,
And violets the same blue mantles wear
　They wore on their creation's great show-
　　day.

But tulips each new year their robes have new,
　Fertile in colours with the fertile spring ;
All shades pursuing still, save only blue,
　The season's changes, marked in theirs, they
　　bring.

These that like freckled beauties now appear,
　Their freckles gone, boast clearer white and
　　red :
Their colours changing with the changing year,
　They with new smiles and blushes dye their
　　bed.

Those which sprung from their mother's painted
　　womb
　In naked yellow, show a tawny skin ;
In new successions fairer yet will come,
　And white, as in their naked smocks be seen.

The widow, in her royal purple veiled,
    That hangs her head till her short mourning's
        done,
When she her time of widowhood has wailed,
    Light colours and striped Indian silks puts on.

Could living fair ones, living tulips, so
    As they resemblances in beauty hold,
Like resemblances in their changes show
    Changing more lovely still as they grow old,

Could lovers' beauties, like the florist's, bloom,
    And ever blow afresh, they would not grieve
That those impairing years which are to come,
    Take from their loves what they to flowers
        give.

Ibid.

CCXXVII

MAGNIFICENCE UNDER GROUND

In that deep gulf, where all past times are
    thrown,
Where waning moons and setting suns are gone ;
There months and days, extinguishing their
    light,
Are lost and buried in eternal night :
Our fathers' ages and our youth there cast,
Our yesterdays and their thousand years
    past . . .

Ibid.

CCXXVIII

THE ECHO

Where do these voices stray
Which lose in woods their way ?
Erring each step anew,
While they false paths pursue.
Through many windings led,
Some crookedly proceed :
Some to the ear turn back
Asking which way to take,
Wandering without a guide
They holloa from each side,
And call and answer all
To one another's call,

Whence may these sounds proceed,
From woods, or from the dead ?
Sure, souls here once forlorn,
The living make their scorn.
And shepherds that lived here,
Now ceasing to appear,
Mock thus in scorn the fair
That would not grant their prayer ;
While nymphs their voices learn
And mock them in return :
Or if at least the sound
Does from the woods rebound,
The woods of them complain
Who shepherds' vows disdain.
Woods and rocks answer all
To the wronged lover's call,
How deaf soe'er and hard,
They their complaints regard ;
Which nymphs with scorn repay,
More deaf, more hard, than they.

Ibid.

ANONYMOUS

CCXXIX

Amintas, to my grief I see,
With what neglect you look on me,
How much to love you are inclined,
Yet slight this heart, for you designed.
So have I seen some wretched slave,
Whose fortune should have made him crave,
Despise the wealth he had in store
And toil at every mine for more.

Caelia shall now turn miser too,
But 'tis to lay up love for you :
To lay up all her tears and sighs
And all her looks, with dying eyes :
That when by some inconstant maid,
You find your pains and heart betrayed,
She may put on those powerful charms
To bring you back to her own arms.

Choice Airs, ii (*J. Playford*), 1679.

CCXXX

Smiling Phillis has an air
   So engaging all men love her,
But her hidden beauties are
   Wonders I dare not discover ;
So bewitching, that in vain
   I endeavour to forget her ;
Still she brings me back again,
   And I daily love her better.

Kindness springs within her eyes,
   And from thence is always flowing ;
Every minute does surprise
   With fresh beauties still a-blowing ;

Were she but as true as fair,
　　Never man had such a treasure ;
But I die with jealous care
　　In the midst of all my pleasure.

Free and easy without pride
　　Is her language and her fashion,
Setting gentle love aside,
　　She's unmoved with any passion ;
When she says I have her heart,
　　Though I ought not to believe her,
She so kindly plays her part
　　I could be deceived for ever.

Ibid.

CCXXXI

Pastora's beauties when unblown,
　　Ere yet the tender bud did cleave,
To my more early love were known ;
　　Their fatal power I did perceive.
How often in the dead of night,
　　When all the world lay hushed in sleep,
Have I thought this my chief delight,
　　To sigh for you, for you to weep.

Upon my heart whose leaves of white
　　No letter yet did ever stain,
Fate, whom none can control, did write
　　' The fair Pastora here must reign :
Her eyes, those darling suns, shall prove
　　Thy love to be of noblest race ;
Which took its flight so far above
　　All human things, on her to gaze.'

How can you then a love despise,
　　A love that was infused by you ?
You gave breath to its infant sighs,
　　And all its griefs that did ensue :

The power you have to wound, I feel :
How long shall I of that complain ?
Now show the power you have to heal,
And take away the torturing pain.

Choice Airs, iii (*J. Playford*), 1681.

CCXXXII

BESS OF BEDLAM

From silent shades, and the Elysian groves
Where sad departed spirits mourn their loves,
From crystal streams, and from that country
    where
Jove crowns the fields with flowers all the year,
Poor senseless Bess, clothed in her rags and folly
Is come to cure her love-sick melancholy.

Bright Cynthia kept her revels late,
While Mab, the fairy queen, did dance,
And Oberon did sit in state,
When Mars at Venus ran his lance.

In yonder cowslip lies my dear,
Entombed in liquid gems of dew ;
Each day I'll water it with a tear,
Its fading blossom to renew.

For since my love is dead,
And all my joys are gone,
Poor Bess for his sake
A garland will make ;
My music shall be a groan.

I'll lay me down and die
Within some hollow tree ;
The raven and cat
The owl and bat
Shall warble forth my elegy.

Did you but see my love as he passed by you?
His two flaming eyes, if he come nigh you,
They will burn up your hearts.
Ladies, beware ye
Lest he should dart a glance that may ensnare
    ye.

Hark! Hark! I hear old Charon bawl:
His boat he will no longer stay,
And Furies lash their whips and call
' Come, come away! Come, come away! '

Poor Bess will return to the place whence she
    came;
Since the world is so mad, she can hope for no
    cure.
For love's grown a bubble, a shadow, a name,
Which fools do admire and wise men endure.

Cold and hungry am I grown,
Ambrosia will I feed upon,
Drink nectar still and sing
' Who is content
Doth all sorrow prevent '
And Bess in her straw
Whilst free from the law,
In her thoughts is as great as a King.

Choice Airs, iv (*J. Playford*), 1683.

CCXXXIII

A thousand several ways I tried,
    To hide my passion from your view:
Conscious that I should be denied
    Because I cannot merit you.

Absence, the last and worst of all,
    Did so increase my wretched pain,
That I returned, rather to fall
    By the swift fate of your disdain.

Choice Airs, v (*J. Playford*), 1684.

ROBERT GOULD (1650-1709)

CCXXXIV

Fair, and soft, and gay, and young,
All charm, she played, she danced, she sung !
There was no way to 'scape the dart,
No care could guard the lover's heart.
' Ah ! why,' cried I, and dropped a tear
(Adoring, yet despairing e'er
To have her to myself alone)
' Was so much sweetness made for one ? '

But growing bolder, in her ear
I in soft numbers told my care :
She heard, and raised me from her feet,
And seemed to glow with equal heat.
Like heaven's, too mighty to express,
My joys could but be known by guess.
' Ah, fool ! ' said I, ' what have I done,
To wish her made for more than one ? '

But long she had not been in view,
Before her eyes their beams withdrew ;
Ere I had reckoned half her charms,
She sank into another's arms.
But she, that once could faithless be,
Will favour him no more than me :
He, too, will find he is undone,
And that she was not made for one.

Works, 1709.

CCXXXV

THE UNWILLING INCONSTANT

Though she's so much for beauty famed
That Age is with her smiles inflamed,
Yet by some more resistless art,
That does unseen its force impart
You raze her image from my heart
Which nothing, nothing else but Death could
    part.

Oh tell me quickly, charming Maid,
By what new witchcraft I'm betrayed ?
Since she I've sworn to love is true,
Not only that, but beauteous too,
I should a strange injustice do,
To give the heart, so justly hers, to you.

Try then, thou who without control
Hast shot thy form into my soul,
Whose eyes still conquer with a view,
Oh try (though 'twill be hard to do)
Yet try to make me hate thee too ;
I care not if I'm wretched, so I'm true.

Ibid.

CCXXXVI

THE WANDERER FIXED

Ere I thy charming visage saw,
Each lesser beauty gave me law ;
This with her sweetness, that her pride,
And I for either could have died.
But when I first your eyes did view
Straight to my heart their lightning flew,
Deposed e'en all and set up you :

Before the magic of your air,
(So fine your shape, your face so fair)
Their fainter charms did disappear,
And were no longer what they were.

So of the stars that gild the sky
They've reverence paid from every eye ;
Not one but claims our lasting praise,
Not one but should our wonder raise,
Not one but what's all heavenly bright,
A constant shining globe of light
Able alone to rule the night :
Yet though so bright and glorious, they
All in a moment's time decay,
Grow dim and seem to die away,
When once Aurora opens day.

Ibid.

CCXXXVII

NO LIFE IF NO LOVE

Caelia is chaste, yet her bright eyes
    Are motives to desire ;
Each look, each motion, does surprise
    And lasting love inspire.
Her smiles would make the wretch rejoice
    Expiring just before,
And oh, to hear her charming voice
    Is Heaven—or something more !

And thus adorned, where'er she turns
    Fresh conquests on her wait ;
The trembling restless lover burns,
    Nor can resist his fate.

And as he did its hopeless distance see,
Sighed deep, and cried, ' How far is peace from
   me ! '

The Poet's complaint of his Muse.

NATHANIEL LEE (1653-92)

CCXLI

Hail to the myrtle shade,
All hail to the nymphs of the fields ;
Kings would not here invade
Those pleasures that virtue yields.
Beauty here opens her arms,
To soften the languishing mind ;
And Phillis unlocks her charms :
Ah Phillis ! oh why so kind ?

Phillis, thou soul of love,
Thou joy of the neighbouring swains ;
Phillis that crowns the grove,
And Phillis that gilds the plains,
Phillis, that ne'er had the skill
To paint, to patch, and be fine,
Yet Phillis whose eyes can kill
Whom Nature hath made divine.

Phillis, whose charming song
Makes labour and pains a delight ;
Phillis that makes the day young,
And shortens the live-long night.
Phillis, whose lips like May,
Still laugh at the sweets they bring ;
Where love never knows decay,
But sets with eternal Spring.

Theodosius, 1680.

CCXLII

EPITHALAMIUM

Blush not redder than the morning,
Though the virgins gave you warning ;
Sigh not at the chance befell ye
Though they smile and dare not tell ye.

Maids, like turtles, love the cooing,
Bill and murmur in their wooing.
Thus like you, they start and tremble
And their troubled joys dissemble.

Grasp the pleasure while 'tis coming ;
Though your beauties now are blooming,
Time at last your joys will sever,
And they'll part, they'll part for ever.

Caesar Borgia, 1680.

JOHN OLDHAM (1653-83)

CCXLIII

To the Memory of Mr. Charles Morwent.

Nor didst thou those mean spirits more approve,
Who virtue only for its dowry love ;
Unbribed thou didst her sterling self espouse,
Nor wouldst a better mistress choose.
Thou couldst affection to her bare idea pay,
The first that e'er caressed her the Platonic way.
  To see her in her own attractions dressed
      Did all thy love arrest,
  Nor lacked there new efforts to storm thy
    breast.

Thy generous loyalty
Would ne'er a mercenary be,
But chose to serve her still without a livery.
  Yet wast thou not of recompense debarred,
  But countedst honesty its own reward ;
  Thou didst not wish a greater bliss to accrue,
For to be good to thee was to be happy too ;
    That secret triumph of thy mind,
  Which always thou in doing well didst find,
Were Heaven enough, were there no other
    Heaven designed.

What virtues few possess but by retail,
  In gross could thee their owner call ;
They all did in thy single circle fall.
Thou wast a living system where were wrote
All those high morals which in books are sought.
    Thy practice did more virtues share
Than heretofore the learned Porch e'er knew,
Or in the Stagirite's scant ethics grew.
Devout thou wast as holy hermits are,
Which share their time 'twixt ecstasy and
    prayer ;
Modest as infant roses in their bloom,
  Which in a blush their lives consume ;
  So chaste, the dead are only more,
Who lie divorced from objects, and from power ;
  So pure, that if blest saints could be
Taught innocence, they'd gladly learn of thee.
Thy virtue's height in Heaven alone could grow,
Nor to aught else would for accession owe :
It only now 's more perfect than it was below.

  Hence, though at once thy soul lived here and
    there,
  Yet Heaven alone its thoughts did share ;
  It owned no home but in the active sphere.
Its motions always did to that bright centre roll,
  And seemed to inform thee only on parole.

Look how the needle does to its dear North
   incline,
  As, were't not fixed, 'twould to that region
    climb ;
        Or mark what hidden force
    Bids the flame upwards take its course,
    And makes it with that swiftness rise
  As if 'twere winged by the air through which
    it flies.
Such a strong virtue did thy inclinations bend
  And made them still to the blest mansions
    tend.
  That mighty slave, whom the proud victor's
    rage
    Shut prisoner in a golden cage,
    Condemned to glorious vassalage,
    Ne'er longed for dear enlargement more,
Nor his gay bondage with less patience bore,
Than this great spirit brooked its tedious stay,
    While fettered here in brittle clay,
    And wished to disengage and fly away.
  It vexed and chafed, and still desired to be
Released to the sweet freedom of Eternity.

1675.

JACOB ALLESTRY (1653-86)

CCXLIV

WHAT ART THOU, LOVE ?

What art thou, Love ? whence are those charms.
  That thus thou bear'st an universal rule.
For thee the soldier quits his arms,
  The king turns slave, the wise man fool.

In vain we chase thee from the field,
  And with cool thoughts resist thy yoke :

Next tide of blood, alas ! we yield,
  And all those high resolves are broke.

Can we e'er hope thou shouldst be true,
  Whom we have found so often base ?
Cozened and cheated, still we view
  And fawn upon the treacherous face.

In vain our nature we accuse,
  And dote, because she says we must :
This for a brute were an excuse,
  Whose very soul and life is lust.

To get our likeness ! what is that ?
  Our likeness is but misery ;
Why should I toil to propagate
  Another thing as vile as I ?

From hands divine our spirits came,
  And gods, that made us, did inspire
Something more noble in our frame,
  Above the dregs of earthly fire.

Examen Poeticum, 1693.

MATTHEW COPPINGER

CCXLV

TO VESPER

Sweet Vesper, bring the night,
  Why dost thou thus delay,
To rob me of delight ?
  Too long has been thy stay,
  Make haste away,
And check the lazy dawning of the day.

And Phœbus tell from me,
  That he his rays lay by,
Nor so discourteous be
  As once to mount the sky,
  Or once come nigh
With one small beam, to wake my love and I

How soon the Sun makes haste
  Unto his Thetis' bed
Longing to be embraced
  And cool his radiant head,
  Which now looks red :
Such longing hopes have lovers ever fed

How soon my prayer is heard,
  Cynthia's bright horns appear :
No, 'tis my love prepar'd
  Her lover for to cheer ;
  In all her sphere
Her borrowed lustre never shines so clear.

Poems, 1682.

CCXLVI

A SONG

I will not tell her that she's fair,
  For that she knows as well as I,
And that her virtues equal are
  Unto the glories of her eye.

And that I love her well, she knows,
  For who can view that heavenly face,
Not paying that respect he owes
  To beauty bearing such a grace ?

But this I'll tell and tell her true :
  She takes upon her too much state ;

For, by the Gods, it would undo
   A king to love at such a rate,

Let common beauties boast the power
   Of some uncommon excellence,
And thank Dame Nature for the dower
   Of that decoying, charming sense ;

Adorn themselves with pearls and gold,
   In rubies and rich diamonds shine,
In choicest silks that may be sold
   And all to make such ladies fine.

These are like some rich monument,
   Raised all of carved and costly stone,
Painted and gilt for ornament ;
   But full within of dead men's bones.

Such common ways my Delia scorns,
   Her lovely soul is too sublime ;
She's not complete that clothes adorn,
   Or does in aught but nature shine.

Ibid.

TOM DURFEY (1653-1723)

CCXLVII

Chloe's a Nymph in flowery groves,
   A Nereid in the streams,
Saint-like she in the temple moves,
   A woman in my dreams.

Love steals artillery from her eyes,
   The Graces point her charms,
Orpheus is rivalled in her voice,
   And Venus in her arms.

H

Never so happily in one
   Did heaven and earth combine ;
And yet 'tis flesh and blood alone
   That makes her so divine.

CCXLVIII

THE PERFECTION

We all to conquering beauty bow,
   Its pleasing power admire ;
But I ne'er knew a face till now
   That like yours could inspire.
Now I may say I met with one
   Amazes all mankind,
And, like men gazing on the sun,
   With too much light am blind.

Soft as the tender moving sighs
   When longing lovers meet,
Like the divining prophets wise,
   And as blown roses sweet ;
Modest, yet gay, reserved, yet free ;
   Each happy night a bride ;
A mien of stately majesty,
   And yet no spark of pride.

CCXLIX

DIRGE

Sleep, sleep, poor youth ! Sleep, sleep in peace,
   Relieved from love and mortal care ;
Whilst we, that pine in life's disease,
   Uncertain blessed, less happy are.
Couched in the dark and silent grave
   No ills of Fate thou now canst fear.
In vain would tyrant power enslave,
   Or scornful beauty be severe.

Wars, that do fatal storms disperse,
   Far from thy happy mansion keep.
Earthquakes, that shake the Universe,
   Can't rock thee into sounder sleep.
With all the charms of peace possessed,
   Secure from life's tormentor pain,
Sleep, and indulge thyself with rest,
   Nor dream thou e'er shall rise again.

Past is the fear of future doubt,
   The sun is from the dial gone,
The sands are sunk, the glass is out,
   The folly of the farce is done.

Don Quixote, i, 1694.

NAHUM TATE (1652-1715)

CCL

LAURA'S WALK

The sun far sunk in his descent
   Laid now his tyrant rays aside,
When Laura to the garden went
   To triumph over nature's pride.

The rose-buds blushed with deeper dye,
   Envying lilies paler grew ;
The violets drooped with fear to spy
   On Laura's veins a richer blue.

She stooped and gathered as she went,
   But whilst she slaughtered, sweetly smiled ;
As angels, though for ruin sent,
   Appear with looks serene and mild.

But now, grown weary with her toil,
    A garland for her brow she frames;
Thus with proud trophies made of the spoil,
    Her conquest o'er the Spring proclaims.

Poems, 1684.   (1st ed., 1677)

CCLI

THE PENANCE

Nymph Fanaret, the gentlest maid
That ever happy swain obeyed,
(For what offence I cannot say)
A day and night, and half a day,
Banished her shepherd from her sight ;
His fault for certain was not slight,
Or sure this tender judge had ne'er
Imposed a penance so severe.
And lest she should anon revoke
What in her warmer rage she spoke,
She bound the sentence with an oath,
Protested by her faith and troth,
Nought should compound for his offence
But the full time of abstinence.
Yet when his penance-glass were run,
His hours of castigation done,
Should he defer one moment's space
To come and be restored to grace,
With sparkling threat'ning eyes she swore
That failing would incense her more
Than all his trespasses before.

Ibid.

CCLII

THE AMORIST

See where enamoured Thirsis lies,
    And cannot cease to gaze
On his Larissa's sparkling eyes,
    But takes delight to see those comets blaze
Whose lustre still is fatal to the swain
    O'er whom they reign,
For by their influence the poor shepherd dies
    Or (more to be lamented) lives in pain.

Ibid.

CCLIII

THE BANQUET

Dispatch, and to the myrtle grove convey
Whatever with the natural palate suits,
The dairy's store, with salads, roots, and fruits ;
I mean to play the epicure to-day.
Let nought be wanting to complete
    Our bloodless treat ;
But bloodless let it be, for I've decreed
The grape alone for this repast shall bleed.
Sit, worthy friends.   But e'er we feed,
Let Love b' expelled the company ;
Let no man's mirth here interrupted be
With thought of any scornful little She !
Fall to, my friends.   Trust me, the cheer is good !
Ah ! (if our bliss we understood)
How should we bless th' indulgent Fates,
Indulgent Fates that with content have stored
    Our rural board,
A rarity ne'er found amongst the cates
Of most voluptuous potentates.

Poems, 1677.

THE ROUND

How vain a thing is Man whom toys delight
And shadows fright !
Variety of impertinence
Might give our dotage some pretence ;
But to a circle bound
We toil in a dull round :
We sit, move, eat and drink,
We dress, undress, discourse and think,
By the same passions hurried on,
Imposing or imposed upon ;
We pass the time in sport or toil
We plough the seas or safer soil.
Thus all that we project and do,
We did it many a year ago,
We travel still a beaten way
And yet how eager rise we to pursue
Th' affairs of each returning day,
As if its entertainments were all new.

Poems, 1684.

PSALM XLII

As pants the hart for cooling streams
 When heated in the chase,
So longs my soul, my God, for Thee
 And Thy refreshing grace.

For Thee, my God, the living God,
 My thirsty soul doth pine ;
Oh when shall I behold Thy face,
 Thou majesty divine ?

Why restless, why cast down, my soul ?
  Hope still, and thou shalt sing
The praise of Him who is thy God,
  Thy health's eternal spring.

New Version of the Psalms, 1696 (with Nicholas Brady).

CCLVI

SONG OF THE ANGELS AT THE NATIVITY OF OUR BLESSED SAVIOUR

While shepherds watched their flocks by night
  All seated on the ground,
The angel of the Lord came down,
  And glory shone around.

' Fear not,' said he, for mighty dread
  Had seized their troubled mind,
' Glad tidings of great joy I bring
  To you and all mankind.

' To you, in David's town, this day
  Is born of David's line
The Saviour, who is Christ the Lord ;
  And this shall be the sign :

' The heavenly Babe you there shall find
  To human view displayed,
All meanly wrapt in swathing bands,
  And in a manger laid.'

Thus spake the seraph ; and forthwith
  Appeared a shining throng
Of angels praising God, and thus
  Addressed their joyful song :

' All glory be to God on high,
  And to the earth be peace ;
Good will henceforth from Heaven to men
  Begin, and never cease ! '

Supplement to the New Version, 1700.

ANONYMOUS

CCLVII

EIRENE'S SONG

O my Philander, ope your breast,
  I can no longer keep my heart.
Why do you call it from its nest,
  With such a soft resistless art ?

It sighs and looks itself away,
  Dissolving with each word I speak.
Oh, take it, take it ! If you stay,
  You will have nothing left to take.

There will be no injustice done,
  Though you have fired its native house,
If you will lodge it in your own,
  Where it can only find repose.

And there I'll rest, secure from harm,
  Let angry winds roar as they will.
That tongue can ev'ry tempest charm ;
  Those eyes, the blackest cloud dispel.

Poems by Several Hands (Tate), 1685.

CCLVIII

PHILANDER AND EIRENE

. . . . Eirene's eyes had purified the air,
He breathed in the clear sunshine of his fair :
Eirene could the dross and dregs remove,
Extracting the pure spirit of his love ;
And that was all divine, and would not mix
With the gross inclinations of his sex.
Thus angel-like the youth and virgin loved,
And pleasure to the highest pitch improved.

The circling year rolled in its usual round
And still their eyes fixed on each other found ;
The circling year did various seasons bring,
But their young love was always in the Spring ;
It never altered, but from bliss to bliss,
No angry sky blasted their happiness ;
For whilst Eirene smiled, his heaven was clear,
And she would always smile when he was near.

Ibid.

CCLIX

THE CONVERT

When first I saw Lucinda's face,
And viewed the dazzling glories there
She seemed of a diviner race
Than that which Nature planted here.

With sacred homage down I fell
Wondering whence such a form could spring :
Tell me, I cried, fair Vision, tell
The dread commands from heaven you bring.

For if past sins may be forgiven
By this bright evidence I know
The careful gods have made a Heaven
That made such angels for it too.

Ibid.

JOHN NORRIS (1657-1711)

CCLX

THE MEDITATION

It must be done, my soul, but 'tis a strange,
  A dismal and mysterious change,

H 2

When thou shalt leave this tenement of clay,
And to an unknown *somewhere* wing away ;
When Time shall be Eternity, and thou
Shalt be thou know'st not what, and live thou
    know'st not how.

Amazing state ! No wonder that we dread
  To think of Death, or view the dead.
Thou'rt all wrapped up in clouds, as if to thee
Our very knowledge had antipathy.
Death could not a more sad retinue find,
Sickness and pain before, and darkness all
    behind.

Some courteous ghost, tell this great secrecy,
  What 'tis you are, and we must be.
You warn us of approaching death, and why
May we not know from you what 'tis to die ?
But you, having shot the gulf, delight to see
Succeeding souls plunge in with like uncertainty.

When life's close knot, by writ from Destiny,
  Disease shall cut, or Age untie ;
When after some delays, some dying strife,
The soul stands shivering on the ridge of life ;
With what a dreadful curiosity
Does she launch out into the sea of vast eternity...

Miscellanies, 1687.

CCLXI

HYMN TO DARKNESS

Hail, thou most sacred, venerable thing !
  What Muse is worthy thee to sing ?
Thee, from whose pregnant, universal womb
All things, even light, thy rival, first did come.

What dares he not attempt that sings of thee,
   Thou first and greatest mystery ?
Who can the secrets of thy essence tell,
Thou, like the light of God, art inaccessible.

Before great Love this monument did raise,
   This ample theatre of praise ;
Before the folding circles of the sky
Were tuned by Him who is all harmony ;
Before the morning stars their hymn began,
   Before the council held for man,
Before the birth of either time or place,
Thou reign'st unquestioned monarch in the
     empty space.

Thy native lot thou didst to light resign,
   But still half of the globe is thine,
Here with a quiet, but yet awful hand,
Like the best Emperors thou dost command.
To thee the stars above their brightness owe,
   And mortals their repose below ;
To thy protection Fear and Sorrow flee,
And those that weary are of light, find rest in
   thee.

Though Light and Glory be the Almighty's
   throne,
   Darkness is his pavilion ;
From that his radiant beauty, but from thee
He has his terror and his majesty.
Thus, when he first proclaimed his sacred law,
   And would his rebel subjects awe,
Like princes on some great solemnity
He appeared in's robes of state, and clad himself
   with thee.

The blest above do thy sweet umbrage prize,
   When, cloyed with light, they veil their eyes ;
The vision of the Deity is made
More sweet and beatific by thy shade ;

But we, poor tenants of this orb below,
   Don't here thy excellencies know
Till death our understandings does improve,
And then our wiser ghosts thy silent night-walks
    love.

But thee I now admire, thee would I choose
   For my religion, or my muse.
'Tis hard to tell whether thy reverend shade
Has more good votaries or poets made :
From thy dark caves were inspirations given,
   And from thick groves went vows to Heaven.
Hail, then, thou Muse's and Devotion's spring,
'Tis just we should adore, 'tis just we should thee
    sing.

Ibid.

CCLXII

SUPERSTITION

   I care not, though it be
By the preciser sort thought Popery ;
   We poets can a licence show
    For every thing we do :
Hear then, my little Saint, I'll pray to thee.

   If now thy happy mind,
Amidst its various joys can leisure find
   To attend to any thing so low
    As what I say or do,
Regard, and be what thou wast ever, kind.

   Let not the blest above
Engross thee quite, but sometimes hither rove :
   Fain would I thy sweet image see,
    And sit and talk with thee ;
Nor is it curiosity, but love.

Ah, what delight 'twould be,
Wouldst thou sometimes by stealth converse
　　with me !
　How should I thy sweet commerce prize,
　　And other joys despise !
Come then, I ne'er was yet denied by thee.

　　I would not long detain
Thy soul from bliss, nor keep thee here in pain ;
　Nor should thy fellow-saints e'er know
　　Of thy escape below ;
Before thou'rt missed, thou shouldst return
　　again.

　　Sure, Heaven must needs thy love
As well as other qualities improve ;
　Come then, and recreate my sight
　　With rays of thy pure light ;
'Twill cheer my eyes more than the lamps above.

　　But if Fate's so severe
As to confine thee to thy blissful sphere,
　(And by thy absence I shall know
　　Whether thy state be so),
Live happy, but be mindful of me there.
Ibid.

CCLXIII

THE ASPIRATION

　How long, great God, how long must I
　　Immured in this dark prison lie,
Where, at the grates and avenues of sense,
My soul must watch to have intelligence ;
Where but faint gleams of Thee salute my sight,
Like doubtful moonshine in a cloudy night ?
　　When shall I leave this magic sphere,
　　And be all mind, all eye, all ear ?

How cold this clime ! and yet my sense
   Perceives even here Thy influence.
Even here Thy strong magnetic charms I feel,
And pant and tremble like the amorous steel.
To lower good, and beauties less divine,
Sometimes my erroneous needle does decline ;
   But yet, so strong the sympathy,
   It turns, and points again to Thee.

I long to see this excellence
   Which at such distance strikes my sense.
My impatient soul struggles to disengage
Her wings from the confinement of her cage.
Wouldst Thou, great Love, this prisoner once
    set free,
How would she hasten to be linked to thee !
   She'd for no Angel's conduct stay,
   But fly, and love on all the way.

Ibid.

CCLXIV

THE PROSPECT

What a strange moment will that be,
My soul, how full of curiosity,
When, winged and ready for thy eternal flight
(Though th' utmost edges of thy tottering clay
   Hovering and wishing longer stay)
Thou shalt advance, and have Eternity in sight !
When just about to try that unknown sea,
   What a strange moment will that be !

But yet how much more strange that state
When loosened from th' embrace of this close
    mate
Thou shalt at once be plunged in liberty,

And move as swift and active as a ray
  Shot from the lucid spring of day !
Thou who just now was clogged with dull
    mortality,
How wilt thou bear the mighty change, how
    know
  Whether thou'rt then the same or no ?

  Then to strange mansions of the air
And stranger company must thou repair ;
What a new scene of things will then appear !
This world thou by degrees wast taught to know
  Which lessened thy surprise below,
But knowledge all at once will overflow thee
    there.
That world as the first man did this, thou'lt see,
  Ripe-grown in full maturity.

  There with bright splendours must thou
    dwell,
And be, what only those pure forms can tell.
There must thou live a while, gaze and admire,
Till the great Angel's trump this fabric shake,
  And all the slumbering dead awake ;
Then to thy old, forgotten state must thou
    retire :
This union then will seem as strange, or more,
  Than thy new liberty before.

  Now for the greatest change prepare,
To see the only Great, the only Fair.
Veil now thy feeble eyes, gaze and be blest ;
Here all thy turns and revolutions cease,
  Here's all serenity and peace :
Thou'rt to the centre come, the native seat of
    rest.
There's now no further change nor need there be ;
  When One shall be variety.

Ibid.

ANONYMOUS

CCLXV

THE FEMALE WITS

Men with much toil and time and pain,
  At length at Fame arrive,
While we a nearer way obtain
  The palms for which they strive.

We scorn to climb by reason's rules
  To the loud name of wit,
And count them silly, modest fools,
  Who to that test submit.

Our sparkling way a method knows
  More airy and refined,
And should dull reason interpose,
  Our lofty flight 'twould bind.

Then let us on and still believe ;
  A good bold faith will do,
If we ourselves can well deceive,
  The world will follow too.

What matter though the witty few
  Our emptiness do find,
They for their int'rest will be true,
  'Cause we are brisk and kind.

BY A LADY OF QUALITY.

Miscellany Poems (Behn), 1685.

CCLXVI

THE ADVICE

She that would gain a constant lover
　　Must at a distance keep the slave,
Not by a look her heart discover,
　　Men should but guess the thoughts we have.

Whilst they're in doubt their flame increases,
　　And all attendance they will pay ;
When we're possess'd their transport ceases,
　　And vows, like vapours, fleet away.

LADY E— M—.

Miscellany (Behn), 1687.

CCLXVII

. . . Oh then let my Cloe know
When her youth is faded so,
And a race of nymphs appears,
Gay and sprightly in their years,
Proud and wanton in their loves,
While the shepherds of the groves
Strive with presents who shall share
Most the favours of the fair ;
And herself she does behold
Like Aurelia now grown old :
Sighing to herself she'll say,
' I was once adored as they ! '
Yet with pleasure think that she
Loved and was beloved by me . . .

Ibid.

CCLXVIII

Break, break, sad heart, unload thy grief,
   Give, give thy sorrow way,
Seek out thy only last relief,
   And thy hard stars obey.
Those stars that doom thee to revere
   What does themselves outshine,
And placed her too in such a sphere
   That she can ne'er be mine.

Because Endymion once did move
   Night's goddess to come down,
And listen to his tale of love,
   Aim not thou idly at the moon.
Be it thy pleasure and thy pride
   That racked on stretched desire,
Thou canst thy fiercest torments hide
   And silently expire.

Ibid.

CCLXIX

Reason at last has got the day,
   To Sylvia's yoke no more I bow;
The harder 'twas to break away
   The sweeter is my freedom now:
Yet I resolve the scornful nymph to see
And tell her I'm as unconcerned as she.

But why should I a visit make
   To her whose charms I did admire,
Unless my soul her part does take
   Unknowing of its amorous fire?
Alas! my flames are greater than before,
For he loves most who thinks he loves no more.

Ibid.

COLONEL SACKVILLE

CCLXX

I never saw a face till now
    That could my passion move.
I liked, and ventured many a vow ;
    But durst not think of love.

Till beauty, charming every sense,
    An easy conquest made ;
And shewed the vainness of defence,
    When Phyllis does invade.

But oh, her colder heart denies
    The thoughts her looks inspire ;
And while, in ice, that frozen lies,
    Her eyes dart only fire.

Betwixt extremes, I am undone,
    Like plants too northward set,
Burnt by too violent a sun,
    Or chilled for want of heat.

Theatre of Music, i, 1685.

CCLXXI

    vain, Clemene, you bestow
    The promised empire of your heart
If you refuse to let me know
    The wealthy charms of every part.

My passion with your kindness grew,
    Though beauty gave the first desire ;
But beauty only to pursue
    Is following a wand'ring fire.

As hills in perspective suppress
  The free enquiry of the sight,
Restraint makes every pleasure less
  And takes from love the full delight.

Faint kisses may in part supply
  Those eager longings of my soul ;
But oh ! I'm lost if you deny
  A quick possession of the whole.

Banquet of Music, vi, 1692.

JOHN HOWE (1657-1722)

CCLXXII

In Cloris, all soft charms agree,
Enchanting humour, powerful wit,
Beauty from affectation free,
And for eternal empire fit :
Where'er she goes love waits her eyes,
The women envy, men adore ;
Though did she less the triumph prize,
She would deserve the conquest more.

But vanity so much prevails,
She begs what else none can deny her,
And with inviting treacherous smiles
Gives hopes, which e'en prevent desire,
Catches at every trifling heart,
Grows warm with every glimmering flame.
The common prey so deads her dart
It scarce can pierce a noble game.

I could lie ages at her feet,
Adore her, careless of my pain,
With tender vows her rigour meet,
Despair, love on, and not complain ;

My passion, from all change secure
No favours raise, no frown controls :
I any torment can endure,
But hoping with a crowd of fools.
Choice Airs, v, 1685.

HENRY CROMWELL (1658-1728)

CCLXXIII

A beauteous face, fine shape, engaging air,
With all the graces that adorn the fair,
If these could fail their so-accustomed parts,
And not secure the conquest of our hearts,
Sylvia has yet a vast reserve in store.
At sight, we love ; but hearing, must adore.

There falls continual music from her tongue :
The wit of Sappho, with her artful song.
From sirens thus we lose the power to fly ;
We listen to the charm, and stay to die.
Ah, lovely nymph, I yield, I am undone :
Your voice has finished what your eyes begun.
Miscellany Poems (Gildon), 1692.

RICHARD DUKE (1658-1711)

CCLXXIV

TO CELIA

Fly swift, ye hours, ye sluggish minutes fly,
Bring back my love, or let her lover die.
Make haste, O sun, and to my eyes once more
My Celia brighter than thyself restore.
In spite of thee, 'tis night when she's away,
Her eyes alone can the glad beams display,
That make my sky look clear, and guide my day.

Oh, when will she lift up her sacred light,
And chase away the flying shades of night ?
With her how fast the flowing hours run on !
But oh, how long they stay when she is gone !
So slowly Time when clogg'd with grief does
    move ;
So swift when borne upon the wings of love.
Hardly three days, they tell me, yet are past,
Yet 'tis an age since I beheld her last.
O my auspicious star make haste to rise,
To charm our hearts and bless our longing eyes !

Miscellany Poems (*Dryden*), 1684.

CCLXXV

Through mournful shades, and solitary groves,
Fanned with the sighs of unsuccessful loves,
    Wild with despairs, young Thyrsis strays ;
Thinks over all Amyra's heavenly charms,
Thinks he now sees her in another's arms,
Then at some willow's root himself he lays,
    The loveliest, most unhappy swain,
And thus to the wild woods he does complain.

' How art thou changed, O Thyrsis ! since the
    time
    When thou couldst love, and hope, without a
    crime !
    When Nature's pride, and Earth's delight
(As through her shady evening grove she past,
And a new day did all around her cast)
Could see, nor be offended at the sight,
The melting, sighing, wishing swain,
That now must never hope to wish again.

Riches and titles, why should they prevail
Where duty, love, and adoration fail ?

Lovely Amyra, shouldst thou prize
The empty noise that a fine title makes,
Or the vile trash that with the vulgar takes,
Before a heart that bleeds for thee, and dies ?
    Unkind ! but pity the poor swain
Your rigour kills, nor triumph o'er the slain ! '

Examen Poeticum, 1693.

CCLXXVI

CELIA'S SOLILOQUY

Mistress of all my senses can invite,
Free as the air, and unconfined as light ;
Queen of a thousand slaves that fawn and bow
And with submissive fear my power allow,
Should I exchange this noble state of life
To gain the vile detested name of Wife ?
Should I my native liberty betray,
Call him my lord, who at my footstool lay ?
No : thanks, kind Heaven, that hast my soul
        employed
With my great sex's useful virtue, pride :
That generous pride, that noble just disdain,
That scorns the slave that would presume to
        reign.
Let the raw amorous scribbler of the times
Call me his Celia in insipid rhymes ;
I hate and scorn you all, proud that I am
T' revenge my sex's injuries on man.
Compared to all the plagues in marriage dwell,
It were preferment to lead apes in Hell.

Poems, 1717.

ANONYMOUS

CCLXXVII

Farewell, all joys, when he is gone
That filled each hour with pleasure ;
To waves and wind
Not half so kind,
I must resign this treasure.
Whilst I with pensive look and tears
This cruel absence mourn,
With moving sighs and panting fears
Court them for his return.

That happy moment, when it comes
Will satisfaction give :
Though I endure
I'm then most sure
In lasting love to live.
In my Alexis' godlike mind,
None can destroy that bliss ;
He must be faithful, true and kind,
And I for ever his.

Theatre of Music, i (*H. Playford*), 1685.

CCLXXVIII

Cupid, the slyest rogue alive
One day was plundering of a hive,
But as with too too eager haste,
He strove the liquid sweet to taste,
A bee surprised the heedless boy,
Pricked him, and dashed the expected joy.

The urchin, when he felt the smart
Of the envenomed angry dart,

He kicked, he flung, he spurned the ground,
He blew and then he chafed the wound ;
He blew and chafed the wound in vain :
The rubbing still increased the pain.

Straight to his mother's lap he hies,
With swelling cheeks and blubbered eyes :
Cries she ' What does my Cupid ail ? '
When thus he told his mournful tale.
' A little bird they call a bee
With yellow wings, see, Mother, see,
How it has gored and wounded me ! '

' And are not you,' replied his mother,
' For all the world just such another,
Just such another peevish thing,
Like in bulk and like in sting ?
For when you aim a poisonous dart
Against some poor unwary heart,
How little is the archer found,
And yet how wide, how deep the wound ! '

Theatre of Music, ii (*H. Playford*), 1685.

CCLXXIX

When, lovely Phillis, thou art kind,
Nought but raptures fill my mind ;
'Tis then I think thee so divine,
To excel the mighty power of wine ;
But when thou insult'st and laugh'st at my pain,
I wash thee away with sparkling champagne ;
So bravely contemn both the Boy and his
    Mother,
And drive out one God by the power of another.

When pity in thy looks I see,
I frailly quit my friends for thee ;

Persuasive Love so charms me then,
My freedom I'd not wish again.
But when thou art cruel and heed'st not my care,
Straightway with a bumper I vanish despair,
So bravely contemn both the Boy and his
    Mother,
And drive out one God by the power of another.

Ibid. 1685.

CCLXXX

How sweet is the air and refreshing
Comes over the neighbouring plains.
This ever was counted a blessing
'Mongst other enjoyments of swains ;
It sweetens our humours, which glide in our
    veins
Like streams in the channels, and softens our
    strains.
While we sing by a fountain surrounded with hills,
And the gentle nymph Echo does keep up the
    trills.

Sometimes in a grove, as delighting,
We sit by our sweetings in bowers,
Fine roundelays to them reciting
Whilst making us garlands of flowers.
As loving as turtles, we pass the soft hours,
No shepherd is sullen nor shepherdess lowers.
While we sing by a fountain surrounded with
    hills,
And the gentle nymph Echo does keep up the
    trills.

Then Laura, leave off your despising
Those freedoms the village allows,
Town-gallants with finest devising
Can't make you so happy a spouse.

Like shoots in the spring our passion still grows,
Our flocks are not blither, which wantonly
   browse.
While we sing by a fountain surrounded with
   hills,
And the gentle nymph Echo does keep up the
   trills.

Theatre of Music, iv (*H. Playford*), 1687.

CCLXXXI

When thou dost dance the spheres do play,
By night stars' torches, sun by day ;
Each step so loth to wrong thy birth,
Afraid to hurt thy mother Earth ;
    The tender blades of grass when thou
    Dost dance upon them do not bow.

The falling dew too doth thee woo,
When tripp'st on it scarce wets thy shoe :
Then, lady like, doth change thy mind
And dances on the wavering wind :
    The thinner air strives thine to meet
    To tread it with thy gentle feet.

MS., 1687.

CCLXXXII

  Whilst I gaze on Chloe trembling,
    Till her eyes my fate declare,
  If she smiles, I fear dissembling,
    When she frowns, I straight despair ;
  Jealous of some rival's favour,
    If a wandering look she give,
  Fain would I desire to leave her
    But can sooner cease to live.

Happy they, whom inclination
   Warms but with a gentle heat,
Never flies up to a passion;
   Love's a torment, if too great.
When the storm is once blown over,
   Soon the ocean quiet grows,
But a faithful constant lover
   Seldom is in true repose.

Banquet of Music, iii (*H. Playford*), 1689.

CCLXXXIII

How happy's that lover, who, after long years
Of wishing and doubting, despairing and sorrow,
Shall hear his kind mistress say, ' Shake off thy
   tears,
And prepare to be happy to-morrow.'

Jove of Io possessed, or on Danaë's breast,
Was ne'er half so happy, or really blessed,
As Sylvio would be, might he laugh, love and
   say,
' Let the sun rise in state, for to-morrow's the
   day.'

Banquet of Music, iv (*H. Playford*), 1690.

CCLXXXIV

Celinda, think not by disdain
To vanquish my desire,
By telling me I sigh in vain
And feed a hopeless fire.
Despair itself too weak does prove
Your beauty to disarm :
By Fate I was ordained to love
As you were born to charm.

Ibid.

A CATCH

I gave her cakes and I gave her ale
And I gave her sack and sherry :
I kissed her once, I kissed her twice
And we were wondrous merry.
I gave her beads and bracelets fine
And I gave her gold, down derry,
I thought she was afeard, till she stroked my
  beard
And we were wondrous merry.
Merry my hearts, merry my cocks, merry my
  sprights,
Merry, merry, merry, hey down derry,
I kissed her once, I kissed her twice
And we were wondrous merry.
Ibid.

I once had virtue, wealth and fame,
Now I'm a ruined sinner :
I lost them all at love's sweet game,
Yet think myself a winner.
While that dear lovely youth to gain
My heart was still pursuing,
I'm rich enough, nor dare complain
Of such a sweet undoing.

Banquet of Music, v (*H. Playford*), 1691.

FAIRY SONG

When the cock begins to crow
Cock-a-doodle-doo :

When the embers leave to glow
And the owl cries to-whit to-who :
When crickets do sing and mice roam about,
When midnight bells ring to call the devout ;
When the lazy lie stretching, and think 'tis no
    harm,
Their zeal is so cold and their beds are so warm ;
When the long lazy slut
Has not made the parlour clean,
No water on the hearth is put
But all things in disorder seen ;
Then we trip it round the room,
And make, like bees, a drowsy hum ;
Be she Betty, Nan or Sue
We make her of another hue,
And pinch her, pinch her black and blue.

(1690).

Orpheus Britannicus, ii, 1711.

MARY CHUDLEIGH, LADY CHUDLEIGH
(1656-1710)

CCLXXXVIII

SOLITUDE

When all alone in some belov'd retreat,
Remote from noise, from business and from
    strife,
Those constant cursed attendants of the great,
I freely can with my own thoughts converse,
    And clothe them in ignoble verse,
'Tis then I taste the most delicious feast of life :
There, uncontroll'd, I can my self survey,
    And from observers free,
    My intellectual pow'rs display,
And all th' opening scenes of beauteous Nature
    see :

Form bright ideas, and enrich my mind,
Enlarge my knowledge, and each error find ;
Inspect each action, ev'ry word dissect,
And on the failure of my life reflect.
Then from my self, to books, I turn my sight,
And there, with silent wonder and delight,
Gaze on th' instructive venerable dead,
Those that in virtue's school were early bred,
And since by rules of honour always led ;
Who its strict laws with nicest care obey'd,
And were by calm unbiass'd reason sway'd.
Their great examples elevate my mind,
And I the force of all their precepts find ;
By them inspir'd above dull earth I soar,
And scorn those trifles which I priz'd before.

Poems, 1703.

CCLXXXIX

Why, Damon, why, why, why, so pressing ?
The heart you beg's not worth possessing.
Each look, each word, each smile's affected ;
And inward charms are quite neglected.
Then scorn her ! scorn her ! foolish swain ;
And sigh no more, no more in vain !

Beauty's worthless, fading, flying ;
Who would, for trifles, think of dying ?
Who, for a face, a shape, would languish,
And tell the brooks and groves his anguish,
Till She, till She thinks fit to prize him ;
And all, and all beside, despise him ?

Fix, fix your thoughts on what's inviting,
On what will never bear the slighting.

Wit and Virtue claim your duty ;
They're much more worth than Gold and
    Beauty.
To them, to them, your heart resign ;
And you'll no more, no more repine.

Ibid.

JANE BARKER

CCXC

A VIRGIN LIFE

Since, O ye Powers, ye have bestowed on me
So great a kindness for virginity,
Suffer me not to fall into the powers
Of men's almost omnipotent amours ;
But in this happy life let me remain
Fearless of twenty-five and all its train
Of slights or scorns, or being called Old Maid,
Those goblins which so many have betrayed :
Like harmless kids that are pursued by men,
For safety run into a lion's den.

Poetical Recreations, 1688.

CCXCI

IN COMMENDATION OF THE FEMALE SEX

In vain would Man his mighty patent show,
That reason makes him lord of all below ;
If Woman did not moderate his rule
He'd be a tyrant, or a softly fool ;
For ere Love's documents inform his breast
He's but a thoughtless kind of household beast.

Houses, alas, there no such thing would be,
He'd live beneath the umbrage of a tree,
Or else usurp some free-born native's cave,
And so inhabit, whilst alive, a grave ;
Or o'er the world this lordly brute would rove
Were he not taught and civilized by love.

Ibid.

CCXCII

TO HER LOVER'S COMPLAINT

If you complain your flames are hot,
  'Tis 'cause they are impure,
For strongest spirits scorch us not,
  Their flames we can endure.

Love, like zeal, should be divine,
  And ardent as the same :
Like stars, which in cold weather shine,
  Or like a lambent flame.

It should be like the morning rays
  Which quickens, but not burns ;
Or th' innocence of children's plays,
  Or lamps in ancient urns.

Ibid.

CCXCIII

PARTING WITH ———-

Although thou now putt'st me in doubt,
  By going I know not where,
Yet know my soul will beat about
Nor rest till she have found thee out,
  And tend upon thee there.

I

Look to your actions then, for she
　　So strict a watch will keep,
That if you give one thought from me,
She'll swear it is flat felony
　　Though't be when you're asleep.

But if a sigh or glance or smile
　　Should to my rival 'scape,
She'll cry out *Robbery* and *Spoil* :
But if a kiss thy lips should soil,
　　Then *Murder*, and *A rape*.

All this a metaphor may seem,
　　Or mad philosophy,
To the unthinking world, who deem
That but a fancy or a dream,
　　Which souls do really hear and see.

Ibid.

MRS. TAYLOR

CCXCIV

Ye virgin powers, defend my heart
　　From amorous looks and smiles,
From saucy love or nicer art
　　Which most our sex beguiles ;
From sighs and vows, from awful fears
　　That do to pity move ;
From speaking silence and from tears,
　　Those springs that water love.
But if through passion I grow blind,
　　Let honour be my guide,
And when frail nature seems inclined,
　　Then fix a guard of pride.
A heart whose flames are seen, though pure,
　　Needs every virtue's aid,

And she who thinks herself secure,
   The soonest is betrayed.

Miscellany (Behn), 1685.

CCXCV

Strephon hath fashion, wit, and youth,
   With all things else that please ;
He nothing wants but love and truth
   To ruin me with ease.

But he is flint, and bears the art
   To kindle fierce desire,
Whose power enflames another's heart,
   And he ne'er feels the fire.

Oh how it does my soul perplex,
   When I his charms recall,
To think he should despise our sex ;
   Or, what's worse, love 'em all.

So that my heart, like Noah's dove,
   In vain has sought for rest,
Finding no hope to fix my love,
   Returns into my breast.

Ibid.

MRS. LOVELACE (?)

CCXCVI

TO STREPHON

I strove in vain ! Here, take my heart !
   But do not think your thanks are due.
For I had first tried ev'ry art,
   Th' invading passion to subdue.

For succour fled to wit and pride,
  But both, alas, their aid denied.
And reason too her weakness has confessed,
Unable to dislodge th' imperious guest.

How swiftly does the poison spread !
  How soon't has seized each noble part :
Wildly it rages in my head ;
  Like tides of fire, consumes my heart.
Yet think not, that you conqueror are
By the wise conduct of the war.
There was a traitor took your part within,
And gave you, Strephon, what you could not
  win.

The Gentleman's Journal, 1693.

CCXCVII

SONG BY A LADY

Ah cruel Strephon, now give o'er
  To swear 'tis me you love ;
Since absence you still covet more
  Than saints the joys above.
Else sure the sighs, the grief, the tears,
  From which I ne'er am free
Would bring you back to my relief,
  And change my destiny.

While you in deserts take delight
  Poor Saraphena dies ;
For nothing's pleasing to her sight
  But her loved Strephon's eyes :
Then leave, ah, leave your hawks and hounds,
  And quick return to me ;
Since every absent minute wounds
  The soul that lives by thee.

Ibid.

ANNE WHARTON (1659-85)

CCXCVIII

Spite of thy godhead, powerful Love,
  I will my torments hide ;
But what avail if life must prove
  A sacrifice to pride ?

Pride, thou'rt become my goddess now,
  To thee I'll altars rear,
To thee each morning pay my vow
  And offer every tear.

But oh, I fear, should Philemon
  Once take thy injured part,
I should soon cast that idol down,
  And offer him my heart.

Vinculum Societatis, i, 1687.

CCXCIX

How hardly I conceal'd my tears !
  How oft did I complain !
When many tedious days my fears
  Told me I lov'd in vain.

But now my joys as wild are grown,
  And hard to be conceal'd :
Sorrow may make a silent moan,
  But joy will be reveal'd.

I tell it to the bleating flocks,
  To every stream and tree,
And bless the hollow murmuring rocks
  For echoing back to me.

Thus you may see with how much joy
 We what we wish, believe ;
'Tis hard such passion to destroy,
 But easy to deceive.

A Collection of Poems, 1693.

CCC

VERSES ON THE SNUFF OF A CANDLE,
MADE IN SICKNESS

See there the taper's dim and doleful light
 In gloomy waves silently rolls about,
And represents to my dim weary sight
 My light of life almost as near burnt out.

Ah Health ! best part and substance of our joy,
 (For without thee 'tis nothing but a shade)
Why dost thou partially thyself employ,
 Whilst thy proud foes as partially invade ?

What we, who ne'er enjoy, so fondly seek,
 Those who possess thee still, almost despise ;
To gain immortal glory, raise the weak,
 Taught by their former want thy worth to
 prize.

Dear, melancholy Muse ! my constant guide,
 Charm this coy health back to my fainting
 heart,
Or I'll accuse thee of vain-glorious pride,
 And swear thou dost but feign the moving art.

But why do I upbraid thee, gentle Muse,
 Who for all sorrows mak'st me some amends ?
Alas ! our sickly minds sometimes abuse
 Our best physicians and our dearest friends,

Miscellany Poems (Dryden), 1684.

ANNE KILLIGREW (1660-85)

CCCI

ON DEATH

Tell me, thou safest end of all our woe,
Why wretched mortals do avoid thee so :
Thou gentle drier of the afflicted's tears,
Thou noble ender to the coward's fears ;
Thou sweet repose to lover's sad despair ;
Thou calm t'ambition's rough tempestuous care.

If in regard of bliss thou wert a curse,
And than the joys of paradise art worse :
Yet after Man from his first station fell,
And God from Eden, Adam did expel,
Thou wert no more an evil, but relief,
The balm and cure to every human grief.
Through thee, what Man has forfeited before
He now enjoys, and ne'er can lose it more :
No subtle serpents in the grave betray,
Worms on the body there, not soul do prey ;
No vice there tempts, no terrors there affright,
No coz'ning sin affords a false delight ;
No vain contentions do that peace annoy,
No fierce alarums break the lasting joy.

Ah, since from thee so many blessings flow,
Such real good as life can never know,
Come when thou wilt, in thy affrighting'st dress,
Thy shape shall never make thy welcome less.
Thou mayst to joy, but ne'er to fear give birth,
Thou best, as well as certain'st thing on earth.
Fly thee ? May travellers then fly their rest,
And hungry infants fly the proffered breast ?
No, those that faint and tremble at thy name,
Fly from their good on a mistaken fame :

Thus childish fear did Israel of old
From plenty and the Promised Land withhold :
They fancied giants, and refused to go,
When Canaan did with milk and honey flow.

Poems, 1686.

CCCII

ON THE SOFT AND GENTLE MOTIONS
OF EUDORA

Divine Thalia, strike th' harmonious lute,
But with a stroke so gentle as may suit
The silent gliding of the hours
Or yet the calmer growth of flowers,
Th' ascending or the falling dew,
Which none can see, though all find true.
For thus alone
Can be shewn
How downy, how smooth,
Eudora doth move,
How silken her actions appear,
The air of her face
Of a gentler grace
Than those that do stroke the ear ;
Her address so sweet
So modestly meet
That 'tis not the loud though tuneable string
Can shew forth so soft, so noiseless a thing !
Oh this to express, from thy hand must fall,
Than music's self, something more musical.

Ibid

ANNE FINCH, COUNTESS OF WINCHILSEA (1661-1720)

CCCIII

Love, thou art best of human joys,
　　Our chiefest happiness below ;
All other pleasures are but toys,
Music without thee is but noise,
　　And beauty but an empty show.

Heav'n, who knew best what man would move
　　And raise his thoughts above the brute,
Said, ' Let him be and let him love ;
That must alone his soul improve,
　　Howe'er philosophers dispute.'

Miscellany Poems, 1713.

CCCIV

From *ALL IS VANITY*

Trail all your pikes, dispirit every drum,
March in a slow procession from afar,
Ye silent, ye dejected men of war.
Be still the hautboys, and the flute be dumb !
Display no more, in vain, the lofty banner ;
For see where on the bier before ye lies
The pale, the fall'n, the untimely sacrifice
To your mistaken shrine, to your false idol
　　Honour.

Ibid.

I 2

AN EPILOGUE

To Jane Shore

There is a season, which too fast approaches,
And every list'ning beauty nearly touches ;
When handsome ladies, falling to decay,
Pass thro' new epithets to smooth the way :
From *fair* and *young* transportedly confessed,
Dwindle to *fine, well fashioned,* and *well dressed.*
Thence as their fortitude's extremest proof,
To *well as yet* ; from *well* to *well enough* ;
Till having on such weak foundation stood,
Deplorably at last they sink to *good.*
Abandoned then, 'tis time to be retired,
And seen no more, when not, alas ! admired.
By men indeed a better fate is known,
The pretty fellow, that has youth outgrown,
Who nothing knew, but how his clothes did sit,
Transforms to a *Free-thinker* and a *Wit* ;
At operas becomes a skilled musician ;
Ends in a partyman and politician ;
Maintains some figure, while he keeps his breath,
And is a fop of consequence till death.

Myra Reynolds—*The Poems of Anne, Countess
    of Winchilsea.*   Reprinted by permission of
The University of Chicago Press.

AN INVITATION TO DAPHNIS

*To leave his study and usual employments—
    mathematics, painting, etc., and to take the
    pleasures of the fields with Ardelia.*

When such a day blessed the Arcadian plain,
Warm without sun, and shady without rain,

Fanned by an air, that scarcely bent the flowers,
Or waved the woodbines on the summer bowers,
The nymphs disordered beauty could not fear,
Nor ruffling winds uncurled the shepherds' hair;
On the fresh grass they trod their measures light,
And a long evening made, from noon to night.
Come then my Daphnis, from those cares descend
Which better may the winter season spend.
   Come, and the pleasures of the fields survey,
    And through the groves with your Ardelia
      stray.

Reading the softest poetry refuse,
To view the subjects of each rural muse ;
Nor let the busy compasses go round,
When fairy circles better mark the ground ;
Rich colours on the vellum cease to lay,
When ev'ry lawn much nobler can display,
When on the dazzling poppy may be seen
A glowing red, exceeding your carmine,
And for the blue that o'er the sea is borne,
A brighter rises in our standing corn.
   Come then, my Daphnis, and the fields survey,
    And through the groves with your Ardelia
      stray.

Come and attend, how as we walk along
Each cheerful bird shall treat us with a song,
Not such as fops compose, where wit nor art,
Nor plainer nature, ever bear a part ;
The crystal springs shall murmur as we pass,
But not like courtiers, sinking to disgrace ;
Nor shall the louder rivers in their fall,
Like unpaid sailors or hoarse pleaders brawl ;
But all shall form a concert to delight,
And all to peace, and all to love invite.
   Come then, my Daphnis, and the fields survey,
    And through the groves with your Ardelia
      stray.

As Baucis and Philemon spent their lives,
Of husbands he, the happiest she of wives,
When through the painted meads their way
    they sought,
Harmless in act, and unperplexed in thought,
Let us, my Daphnis, rural joys pursue,
And courts or camps not ev'n in fancy view.
    So let us through the groves, my Daphnis
      stray,
    And so the pleasures of the fields survey.

Myra Reynolds—*The Poems of Anne, Countess
    of Winchilsea*.   Reprinted by permission of
    The University of Chicago Press.

CCCVII

A NOCTURNAL REVERIE

In such a night, when every louder wind
Is to its distant cavern safe confined ;
And only gentle Zephyr fans his wings,
And lonely Philomel still waking sings ;
Or from some tree, famed for the owl's delight,
She, holloing clear, directs the wanderer right :
In such a night, when passing clouds give place,
Or thinly veil the heavens' mysterious face ;
When in some river, overhung with green,
The waving moon and trembling leaves are seen ;
When freshened grass now bears itself upright,
And makes cool banks to pleasing rest invite,
Whence springs the woodbine and the bramble-
    rose,
And where the sleepy cowslip sheltered grows ;
Whilst now a paler hue the foxglove takes,
Yet chequers still with red the dusky brakes ;
When scattered glow-worms, but in twilight
    fine,
Show trivial beauties, watch their hour to shine,

Whilst Salisbury stands the test of every light,
In perfect charm, and perfect virtue bright ;
When odours, which declined repelling day,
Through temperate air uninterrupted stray ;
When darkened groves their softest shadows
     wear,
And falling waters we distinctly hear ;
When through the gloom more venerable shows
Some ancient fabric, awful in repose,
While sunburnt hills their swarthy looks conceal,
And swelling haycocks thicken up the vale ;
When the loosed horse now, as his pasture leads,
Comes slowly grazing through th' adjoining
     meads,
Whose stealing pace, and lengthen'd shade we
     fear,
Till torn up forage in his teeth we hear ;
When nibbling sheep at large pursue their food,
And unmolested kine rechew the cud ;
When curlews cry beneath the village walls,
And to her straggling brood the partridge calls;
Their shortliv'd jubilee the creatures keep,
Which but endures, whilst tyrant man does
     sleep ;
When a sedate content the spirit feels,
And no fierce light disturbs, whilst it reveals ;
But silent musings urge the mind to seek
Something, too high for syllables to speak ;
Till the free soul to a compos'dness charmed,
Finding the elements of rage disarmed,
O'er all below a solemn quiet grown,
Joys in th' inferior world, and thinks it like her
     own :
In such a night let me abroad remain,
Till morning breaks, and all's confused again,
Our cares, our toils, our clamours are renewed,
Or pleasures, seldom reached, again pursued.

Miscellany Poems, 1713.

JOHN, LORD CUTTS
(1661-1707)

CCCVIII

IN PRAISE OF HUNTING

Leaving the Town and Phillis.

Tell me no more of Venus and her Boy,
His flaming darts, and her transporting joy:
With dreams of pleasure they delude our mind,
Which pass more swiftly than the fleeting wind.
The bright, the chaste Diana I'll adore,
She'll free my heart from Love's insulting
    power ;
Through pleasing groves, and o'er the healthful
    plain,
She leads the innocent and happy swain.
Then farewell, guilty crowds and empty noise ;
I leave you for more pure and lasting joys ;
In stately woods gilded with morning rays,
I'll teach the echoes great Diana's praise.

Poetical Exercises, 1687.

CCCIX

THE INNOCENT GAZER

Lovely Lucinda, blame not me,
    If on your beauteous looks I gaze ;
How can I help it, when I see
    Something so charming in your face ?

That like a bright, unclouded sky,
    When in the air the sun-beams play,
It ravishes my wond'ring eye,
    And warms me with a pleasing ray.

An air so settled, so serene,
   And yet so gay, and easy too,
On all our plains I have not seen
   In any other nymph but you.

But Fate forbids me to design
   The mighty conquest of your breast ;
And I had rather torture mine,
   Than rob you of one minute's rest.

Ibid.

CCCX

Only tell her that I love,
   Leave the rest to her and Fate.
Some kind planet from above,
May perhaps her pity move ;
   Lovers on their stars must wait.
Only tell her that I love.

Why, oh, why should I despair ?
   Mercy's pictur'd in her eye ;
If she once vouchsafe to hear,
Welcome Hope, and farewell Fear.
   She's too good to let me die ;
Why, oh, why should I despair ?

Ibid.

WILLIAM CLELAND (1661-89)

CCCXI

HALLO ! MY FANCY

In conceit like Phaeton
I'll mount Phœbus' chair ;
Having ne'er a hat on

All my hair's a-burning
In my journeying,
Hurrying through the air ;
Fain would I hear his fiery horses neighing ;
And see how they on foamy bits are playing ;
All the stars and planets I will be surveying.
  Hallo ! my Fancy, whither wilt thou go ?

Oh from what ground of Nature
Doth the pelican,
That self-devouring creature
Prove so froward
And toward
Her vitals for to restrain !
And why the subtle fox, while in death-wounds
  is lying
Doth not lament his pangs, by howling and by
  crying :
And why the milk-white swan doth sing when
  she's a-dying.
  Hallo ! my Fancy, whither wilt thou go ?

Fain would I conclude this—
At least make an essay,
What similitude is
Why fowls of a feather,
Do flock and fly together,
And lambs know beasts of prey ;
How Nature's alchemists, these small laborious
  creatures,
Acknowledge still a prince in ordering their
  matters,
And suffers none to live, who slothing lose their
  features.
  Hallo ! my Fancy, whither wilt thou go ?

I'm rapt with admiration,
When I do ruminate
Men of one occupation,

How each one calls him brother,
Yet each envieth other,
And yet still imitate ;
Yea, I admire to see, some natives farther
 sundered
Than Antipodes to us, is it not to be wondered
In myriads ye'll find of one mind scarce an
 hundred.
 Hallo ! my Fancy, whither wilt thou go ?

What multitude of notions
Doth perturb my pate,
Considering the motions
How heavens they are preserved
And this world served
In moisture, light, and heat :
If one spirit sits the outmost circle turning,
Or if one turns another, continuing in journeying ;
If rapid circle's motion, be that which they call
 burning.
 Hallo ! my Fancy, whither wilt thou go ?

Fain also would I prove
This, by considering,
What that which you call love is ;
Whether it be a folly,
Or a melancholy,
Or some heroic thing ;
Fain would I have it proved, by one whom love
 hath wounded
And fully upon one their desire hath founded,
That nothing else could please them, tho' the
 World be rounded.
 Hallo ! my Fancy, whither wilt thou go ?

To know this world's centre,
Height, depth, breadth, and length,
Fain would I adventure,

To search the hid attractions
Of magnetic actions
And adamatick strength.
Fain would I know if in some lofty mountain,
Where the moon sojourns, if there be trees or
fountain,
If there be beasts of prey, or yet fields to hunt
in.
Hallo ! my Fancy, whither wilt thou go ?

Fain would I have it tried
By experiments
By none can be denied,
If in this bulk of Nature
There be voids less or greater
Or all remains complete.
Fain would I know if beasts have any reason ;
If falcons killing eagles do commit a treason ;
If fear of winter's want, makes swallow fly the
season.
Hallo ! my Fancy, whither wilt thou go ?

Hallo, my Fancy, Hallo !
Stay thou at home with me,
I can thee no longer follow,
Thou hast betrayed me
And bewrayed me,
It is too much for thee.
Stay, stay at home with me, leave off thy lofty
soaring ;
Stay thou at home with me, and on thy books be
poring,
For he that goes abroad, lays little up in storing ;
Thou's welcome home, my Fancy,
Welcome home to me !

Poems, 1697.

SIR SAMUEL GARTH (1661-1719)

CCCXII

To die, is landing on some silent shore,
Where billows never break, nor tempests roar :
Ere well we feel the friendly stroke, 'tis o'er.
The wise through thought th' insults of death
    defy ;
The fools, through blest insensibility.
'Tis what the guilty fear, the pious crave ;
Sought by the wretch, and vanquished by the
    brave.
It eases lovers, sets the captive free ;
And, though a tyrant, offers liberty.

The Dispensary, 1699.

JOHN SMITH

CCCXIII

THE ROSES

Go, lovely pair of roses, go,
This clad in scarlet, that in snow.
Go say to my ungentle fair,
    (If on your forms she deigns to gaze),
You dare not hope to rival her,
    Or match the glories of her face ;
But that you're humbly sent, to prove
A youth undone by beauty, and her love.

The sickly white in this pale rose
My wan and meagre looks disclose ;
But that which shines so fiercely bright,
    Whose head in painted flames aspires,
And blushes so with purple light
    It seems to send forth real fires,

Tell her, that rose's ruddy fires impart
The flames her eyes have kindled in my heart.

Poems, 1713.

BENJAMIN HAWKSHAW (-1738)

CCCXIV

THE DREAM

Methought I heard the charming Echo say
' Arise, my love, from hence, and come away ;
Though the waves roll, the mighty tempest's
    done,
And all's concluding with the setting sun ;
I'm come to lead thee to thy port again,
And place thee in the lost Jerusalem."
At this my feeble pulse with joy beat high
To see my ancient Paradise so nigh ;
Then swift I hoised up sail and bore away,
As swift as eagles when they find a prey ;
Here I presumed more solid joys to find,
But thoughts conveyed me back though 'gainst
    the wind.

Poems, 1693.

CCCXV

The lilies have more springs than one,
They rise and perish every year,
But when thy beauty's gone,
Alas, it never will again appear.

All pluck the roses whilst they may,
For if some ruder breath of wind
Should kiss their life away,
They leave no tokens of their place behind.

'Tis time then, Celia, to improve,
Because your life's more short than theirs,
To taste the joys of love
And with an hour's bliss to poise an age's cares.
Ibid.

CCCXVI

THE ADVICE

Chloe, be kind, I say;
Beauty has wings as well as time,
To suffer either pass away
Without advantage, is a crime.
See, Heaven itself with conscious smiles approves
The future union of our tender loves.

Then why, my dear, should you
So fatal to your beauties prove ?
Pay unto Nature what's her due,
And then you'll ne'er refuse my love ;
Take my advice, preserve that Vestal fire,
When it is doubled, it will ne'er expire.

Sweet Chloe, hear my call,
And think to live no more alone ;
Though man was born as lord of all,
Himself but oddly fills a throne ;
Eden was not composed of that or this,
Woman and Man made up the Paradise.
Ibid.

JOHN ELSUM

CCCXVII

An old man playing upon a cymbal, by Tintoret.

How quick the minstrel's fingers play !
As if he felt not a decay,
But all his hours were brisk and gay.

Methinks I hear his melody;
But if I hear not, sure I see
In ev'ry touch great harmony,
Notes high and low in order set
And in the bass the air of Tintoret.

*Epigrams upon the paintings of the most eminent
masters ancient and modern*, 1700

CCCXVIII

Vanity, by a Modern Master.

Her face young, airy, fleering, licked and patched,
The wanton'st giddy'st thing that e'er was
    hatched.
Her hair's in bushy puffs, and not in tresses,
Her garments flying both in flaunting dresses.
She struts and views her features in her glass,
And thinks them such as may for beauty pass.
Her tiffanies, and ribbons flung about,
Catch fluttering fops, and awe the gaping rout.
At her feet heaps of toys and trinkets lie,
And round her empty head gay bubbles fly.
Nothing more light, none more unfit to reign,
Yet none has greater sway nor greater train.
Ibid.

THOMAS CHEEK

CCCXIX

Love's a dream of mighty treasure
    Which in fancy we possess;
In the folly lies the pleasure,
    Wisdom ever makes it less.
When we think, by passion heated,
    We a goddess have in chase,
Like Ixion we are cheated,
    And a gaudy cloud embrace.

Only happy is the lover
    Whom his mistress well deceives;
Seeking nothing to discover,
    He contented lives at ease;
But the wretch that would be knowing
    What the fair one would disguise,
Labours for his own undoing,
    Changing happy to be wise.

Miscellany Poems (Gildon), 1692.

ANONYMOUS

CCCXX

Let other beauties boast in vain
    How they a heart ensnare,
Which they by artful means obtain,
    And but preserve with care;
Whilst Cloe with resistless power
    Does all mankind subdue,
As are her conquests every hour
    So are her charms still new.

Yet she for whom so many die,
    Neglecting does surprise,
As loath the utmost force to try
    Of her victorious eyes;
Her influence she does moderate,
    And some in pity spare,
That beauties of a lower rate
    May have a little share.

Ibid.

CCCXXI

All thoughts of freedom are too late.
    Not any new fair lady's art,
Nor both the Indias' wealth, nor Fate
    Itself can disengage my heart.

Not, which kind Heaven forbid, your hate,
    And that which follows, proud disdain,
My passion could at all abate,
    But only make it last with pain.

Thus all my quiet does depend
    On hopes t'obtain a smile from you,
That so my love, that knows no end,
    May last with equal pleasure too.

Ibid.   J. S.

COLONEL HEVENINGHAM

CCCXXII

If music be the food of love,
    Sing on, till I am filled with joy :
For then my list'ning soul you move
    To pleasures that can never cloy.
Your eyes, your mien, your tongue, declare
That you are music everywhere.

Pleasures invade both eye and ear ;
    So fierce the transports are, they wound.
And all my senses feasted are,
    Though yet the treat is only sound.
Sure, I must perish by your charms,
Unless you save me in your arms.

The Gentleman's Journal, 1692.

ANONYMOUS

CCCXXIII

You understand no tender vows
    Of fervent and eternal love ;
That lover will his labour lose,
Who does with sighs and tears propose
    Your heart to move.

But if he talk of settling land,
A house in town, and coach maintained,
    You understand.

You understand no charms in wit,
    In shape, in breeding, or in air ;
To any fops you will submit,
The nauseous clown, or fulsome cit,
    If rich they are.
Who guineas can, may you, command ;
Put gold, and then put in your hand,
    You understand.

Ibid.

CCCXXIV

'Tis done, Urania, I am free,
    And thanks to your disdain
Shake off that yoke of tyranny
    So many hearts retain.
I've broke the chain that kept me bound,
    I'm out of prison freed,
Thanks to your coldness, now my wounds
    Are too well healed to bleed.

Yet whom I loved I ne'er can hate,
    Much less can I despise ;
And though not love, respect shall wait
    Upon her beauteous eyes.
So strong the tie, so great the weight
    Was of my amorous chain,
That though now broke, th' impression yet
    For ever will remain.

Ibid.

CCCXXV

A RONDEAU

Ah ! who can the joys discover
Of a happy tender lover,
When the nymph no more refuses,
When at once he wins and loses ;
Secret be their mutual pleasure,
Secret as a fairy treasure ;
Silence adds to the possessing,
Silence best secures the blessing.
To her arms he headlong rushes,
Stifles all her frowns and blushes,
Still new beauties doth discover,
And almost enjoys all over.
Humid eyes, sighs, kisses, glances,
Close embraces, melting trances ;
Panting, grasping, trembling, firing,
Then ah then ! ah then ! ah then ! expiring.
Ibid.

CCCXXVI

Not your eyes, Melania, move me,
Nor your flowing charms or wit,
Nor your daily vows to love me
Make my easy soul submit.
Shape nor dress can never sway me,
Nor the softest looks betray me.

But your mind, my dear, subdues me
Where a thousand graces shine ;
Goodness, love and honour woos me,
And my passion's all divine :
Goodness as a boundless treasure
Yields the purest, sweetest pleasure.
Ibid. 1693.

DE LA SALE

CCCXXVII

All own the young Silvia is fatally fair,
　　All own the young Silvia is pretty ;
Confess her good nature, and easy soft air,
　　Nay more, that she's wanton and witty :
Yet all these keen arrows at Damon still cast
　　Could never his quiet destroy,
Till the cunning coquette shot me flying at last,
　　By a Je ne say, Je ne say quoy.

So though the young Silvia were not very fair,
　　Though she were but indifferently pretty,
Much wanting Aurelia's, or Celia's, soft air,
　　But not the dull sense of the city :
Yet still the dear creature would please without
　　　　doubt,
　　And give one abundance of joy,
Since all that is missing is plainly made out
　　By a Je ne say, Je ne say quoy.

Gentleman's Journal, 1694.

ANONYMOUS

CCCXXVIII

I loved fair Celia many years
Before she showed her art ;
Her beauty first, her humour next,
By turns engaged my heart.

And when to these her friendship joined,
Her charms were so entire
That without being dull and blind
I could none else admire.

Orpheus Britannicus, ii, 1702.

CCCXXIX

In vain she frowns, in vain she tries
The darts of her disdainful eyes ;
She still is charming, still is fair,
And I must love, though I despair :
Nor can I of my fate complain, or her disdain,
Who would not die, to be so sweetly slain ?

Like those who magic spells employ,
At distance wounds, and does destroy,
She kills with her severe disdain,
And absent I endure the pain :
But spare, oh spare, the cruel art ! The fatal dart
Stabs your own image in your lover's heart.

Pills to Purge Melancholy, 1699.

CCCXXX

THE SAINT AT ST. JAMES'S CHAPEL.

Last Sunday at St. James's prayers,
  The Prince and Princess by,
I dressed with all my whalebone airs
  Sat in a closet nigh.
I bowed my knees, I held my book,
  I read the answers o'er,
But was perverted by a look
  That pierced me from the door.

High thoughts of Heaven I came to use
  And blest devotion there,
Which gay young Strephon made me lose,
  And other raptures share.
He watched to lead me to my chair
  And bowed with portly grace,
But whispered love into my ear
  Too warm for that grave place.

' Love, Love,' cried he, ' by all adored
   My fervent heart has won.'
But I grown peevish at that word
   Desired he would be gone :
He went quite out of sight, whilst I
   A kinder answer meant;
Nor did I for my sins that day
   By half so much repent.

Ibid.

PETER ANTHONY MOTTEUX (1660-1718)

CCCXXXI

I love, but she alone shall know,
   Who is herself my treasure :
Vain lovers when their joys they show
   Call partners to their pleasure :
Let empty beaux the favour miss
   While they would have it known ;
That soul's too narrow for the bliss
   Who can't enjoy alone.

Then never let my love be told
   By way of modern toasting ;
The sweetest joy, like fairy gold,
   Is lost by selfish boasting.
Too rich to show what I profess,
   My treasure I'll conceal ;
I may my pains of love confess,
   But ne'er my joys reveal.

Muses' Mercury, 1707.

ANONYMOUS

CCCXXXII

THE GROVE

See how Damon's age appears ;
This grove declares his fading years :

For this he planted once, and ate
The maiden fruits of what he set.
Young it was then, like him ; but now,
Sapless, and old, is ev'ry bough.
Thus, my Lesbia, will it be,
In time to come, with thee and me.
Come then, in love and youthful play
Let's pass the smiling hours away,
Before this tender am'rous mark
Grow wide upon its fading bark ;
And show, like Damon's grove, that we
Are old and gray as well as he.

Examen Poeticum, 1693.

SIR HORATIO TOWNSHEND

CCCXXXIII

THE ENQUIRY AFTER HIS MISTRESS

" Thou shepherd, whose intentive eye
O'er ev'ry lamb is such a spy
No wily fox can make 'em less,
Where may I find my shepherdess ? "

A little pausing, then said he,
" How can that jewel stray from thee ?
In summer's heat, in winter's cold,
I thought thy breast had been her fold."

" That is indeed the constant place
Wherein my thoughts still see her face,
And print her image in my heart,
But yet my fond eyes crave a part."

With that he smiling said, " I might
Of Chloris partly have a sight,
And some of her perfections meet,
In ev'ry flower was fresh and sweet.

" The growing lilies bear her skin,
  The violets her blue veins within,
  The blushing rose new blown and spread
  Her sweeter cheeks, her lips the red.

The winds that wanton with the spring
Such odours as her breathing bring,
But the resemblance of her eyes
Was never found beneath the skies.

" Her charming voice who strives to hit
  His object must be higher yet ;
  For Heav'n and Earth, and all we see
  Dispers'd, collected is but she."

Amaz'd at this discourse, methought
Love and ambition in me wrought,
And made me covet to engross
A wealth would prove a public loss.

With that I sighed, ashamed to see
Such worth in her, such want in me ;
And closing both mine eyes, forbid
The world my sight, since she was hid.

Miscellany Poems, iv, 1694.

ANONYMOUS

CCCXXXIV

A SHORT VISIT

So the long absent winter sun,
  When of the cold we most complain,
Comes slow, but swift away does run ;
  Just shows the day, and sets again.

So the prime beauty of the spring,
  The virgin lily, works our eyes ;
No sooner blown, but the gay thing
  Steals from the admirer's sight, and dies.

The gaudy sweets o' the infant year,
   That ravish both the smell and view,
Do thus deceitfully appear,
   And fade as soon as smelt unto.

Aminta, though she be more fair
   Than untouched lilies, chaste as those,
Welcome as suns in winter are,
   And sweeter than the blowing rose :

Yet, when she brought, as late she did,
   All that a dying heart could ease,
And by her swift return forbid
   The joys to last, she's too like these.

Ah, tyrant beauty ! do you thus
   Increase our joy to make it less ?
And do you only show to us
   A heaven, without design to bless ?

This was unmercifully kind,
   And all our bliss too dear has cost :
For is it not a hell to find
   We had a paradise that's lost ?

Miscellany Poems, iv, 1694.

SAMUEL WESLEY (1662-1735)

CCCXXXV

THE BOYS AND THE BUBBLE

See where 'tis fallen among a ring of boys
Who from it blow them worlds of gaudy joys,
Fine soon-ripe bubbles, A la mode and gay,
Dressed in the glories of the blooming day,
Bright as court-madam, though they hardly be
Perhaps as tender or as frail as she.

Created both by breath, both upwards borne,
Proud in the beauties of the rainbow morn.
And thus, when sailing through the heavier skies
By breath 'twas made and lived, by breath it
    dies,
And that same blast on which itself it rears
Dashes the airy jewel into tears.

Maggots, 1685.

CCCXXXVI

THE LIAR

For naked truth let others write
And fairly prove that black's not white ;
Quarrel and scold, then scratch and bite
    Till they're with cuffing weary.
Give me a lie, tricked neat and gay
As fine as any hedge in May :
Most think so too, although they say
    Perhaps the clear contrary.

The Courtier first is counted rude
If he's with lying unendued,
Nay, when he's in his altitude
    He gives it oaths for clenching ;
The brisk and young sour truth despise
And kick her back to the old and wise ;
Wenching's the gallant's life, a lie's
    The very life of wenching.

Room for the Man of Parchment next,
Whose comments so perplex the text
And Truth's highroad so much perplexed
    One scarce can c'er get at it :
With his own practice not content
He'll either quote, or he'll invent,
He'll find or make a precedent,
    And gravely lie by statute.

K

Next the poor Scholar loaden comes
With packs of Sentences and Sums,
Scratches his head and bites his thumbs
 The truth is all his vigour ;
Like Lynceus' self, oh who but he
The essences of things can see ;
When he deceives but orderly
 And lies in Mood and Figure.

Who but the Poet ought to appear
I' th' end ? Who should bring up the rear
But he who without wit or fear
 Lays on his lies by clusters :
Never of sneaking truth afraid
He'll her with open arms invade,
And dreadful armies in the aid
 Of his own heroes musters.

Well, since on all sides 'tis confessed
A quiet life must needs be best,
Who'd think it hard to purchase rest
 By such a slight complying ?
Let him that will speak the truth for me,
Truth the worst incivility.
I'd rather in the fashion be
 Since all the world's for lying.

Ibid.

TOM BROWN (1663-1704)

CCCXXXVII

IN PRAISE OF THE BOTTLE

What a plague d'ye tell me of the Papist's
 design ?
Would to God you'd leave talking and drink off
 your wine,

Away with your glass, Sir, and drown all debate,
Let's be loyally merry, ne'er think of the state.
The King (Heavens bless him) knows best how
 to rule ;
And who troubles his head I think is but a fool.

Come, Sir, here's his health ! your brimmer
 advance,
We'll ingross all the claret and leave none for
 France.
'Tis by this we declare our loyal intent,
And by our carousing the customs augment.
Would all mind their drinking and proper
 vocation,
We should ha' none of this bustle and stir in the
 nation.

Let the hero of Poland, and monarch of France,
Strive by methods of fighting their crowns to
 advance ;
Let chapels in Lime-Street be built or destroyed,
And the Test and the Oath of Supremacy void ;
It shall ne'er trouble me : I'm none of those
 maggots
That have whimsical fancies of Smithfield and
 faggots.

Then banish all groundless suspicions away,
The King knows to govern, let us learn to obey,
Let every man mind his business and drinking,
When the head's full of wine, there's no room
 left for thinking.
'Tis nought but an empty and whimsical pate
That makes fools run giddy with notions of state.

1685.

WILLIAM KING (1663-1712)

CCCXXXVIII

You say you love ! Repeat again,
  Repeat the amazing sound ;
Repeat the ease of all my pain,
  The cure of every wound.

What you to thousands have denied,
  To me you freely give ;
Whilst I in humble silence died,
  Your mercy bids me live.

So upon Latmos' top each night
  Endymion sighing lay,
Gazed on the moon's transcendent light,
  Despaired, and durst not pray.

But divine Cynthia saw his grief,
  The effect of conquering charms ;
Unasked, the goddess brings relief,
  And falls into his arms.

Examen Poeticum, 1693.

CCCXXXIX

MULLY OF MOUNTOWN

Mountown ! thou sweet retreat from Dublin
    cares,
Be famous for thy apples and thy pears ;
For turnips, carrots, lettuce, beans and peas ;
For Peggy's butter, and for Peggy's cheese.
May clouds of pigeons round about thee fly,
But condescend sometimes to make a pie !
May fat geese gaggle with melodious voice,
And ne'er want gooseberries or apple-sauce !

Ducks in thy ponds, and chicken in thy pens,
And be thy turkeys numerous as thy hens.
May thy black pigs lie warm in little sty,
And have no thought to grieve them till they
    die.
Mountown ! the Muses' most delicious theme,
Oh ! may thy codlins ever swim in cream.
Thy rasp- and straw-berries in Bordeaux drown,
To add a redder tincture to their own !
Thy white-wine, sugar, milk, together club,
To make that gentle viand, syllabub.
Thy tarts to tarts, cheese-cakes to cheese-cakes
    join,
To spoil the relish of the flowing wine.
But to the fading palate bring relief,
By thy Westphalian ham, or Belgic beef ;
And, to complete thy blessings, in a word,
May still thy soil be generous as its lord.

Miscellanies, 1704.

TOP-KNOTS

'Tis no small art to give direction
How to suit knots to each complexion,
How to adorn the breast and head,
With blue, white, cherry, pink, or red.
As the morn rises, so that day
Wear purple, sky-colour, or grey :
Your black in Lent, your green in May,
Your filamot when leaves decay.
All colours in the summer shine ;
The nymphs should be like gardens fine.

The Art of Love. 1709.

GEORGE STEPNEY (1663-1707)

CCCXLI

TO THE EVENING STAR

Bright star ! by Venus fixed above,
To rule the happy realms of Love ;
Who in the dewy rear of day,
Dost other lights as far outshine
As Cynthia's silver glories thine ;
Known by superior beauty there,
As much as Pastorella here.
Exert, bright star, thy friendly light,
And guide me through the dusky night ;
Defrauded of her beams the moon
Shines dim and will be vanished soon.
I would not rob the shepherd's fold ;
I seek no miser's hoarded gold ;
To find a nymph I'm forced to stray
Who lately stole my heart away.

WILLIAM WALSH (1663-1708)

CCCXLII

TO HIS BOOK

Go, little book, and to the world impart
The faithful image of an amorous heart.
Those who love's dear deluding pains have
    known,
May in my fatal stories read their own.
Those who have lived from all its torments free,
May find the thing they never felt, by me :
Perhaps, advised, avoid the gilded bait,
And, warned by my example, shun my fate ;

While with calm joy, safe landed on the coast,
I view the waves on which I once was tossed.
Love is a medley of endearments, jars,
Suspicions, quarrels, reconcilements, wars,
Then peace again. Oh ! would it not be best
To chase the fatal poison from our breast ?
But, since so few can live from passion free,
Happy the man, and only happy he,
Who with such lucky stars begins his love,
That his cool judgment does his choice approve.
Ill-grounded passions quickly wear away ;
What's built upon esteem can ne'er decay.

Poems, 1692.

CCCXLIII

Of all the torments, all the cares,
   With which our lives are cursed,
Of all the plagues a lover bears,
   Sure rivals are the worst !
By partners, in each other kind,
   Afflictions easier grow ;
In love alone we hate to find
   Companions of our woe.

Sylvia, for all the pangs you see
   Are labouring in my breast,
I beg not you would favour me,
   Would you but slight the rest !
How great soe'er your rigours are,
   With them alone I'll cope ;
I can endure my own despair,
   But not another's hope.

Miscellany Poems, v, 1704.

PHYLLIS'S RESOLUTION

When slaves their liberty require,
　They hope no more to gain,
But you not only that desire,
　But ask the power to reign.

Think how unjust a suit you make,
　Then you will soon decline ;
Your freedom, when you please, pray take,
　But trespass not on mine.

No more in vain, Alcander, crave,
　I ne'er will grant the thing,
That he who once has been my slave
　Should ever be my king.

Ibid.

THE DESPAIRING LOVER

Distracted with care
For Phyllis the fair,
Since nothing could move her,
Poor Damon, her lover,
Resolves in despair
No longer to languish,
Nor bear so much anguish ;
But, mad with his love,
To a precipice goes,
Where a leap from above
Would soon finish his woes.

When in rage he came there,
Beholding how steep
The sides did appear,
And the bottom how deep ;

His torments projecting,
And sadly reflecting,
That a lover forsaken
A new love may get,
But a neck when once broken
Can never be set ;
And that he could die
Whenever he would,
But that he could live
But as long as he could :
How grievous soever
The torment might grow,
He scorned to endeavour
To finish it so,
But bold, unconcerned
At thoughts of the pain,
He calmly returned
To his cottage again.

Ibid.

CCCXLVI

SONNET : DEATH

What has this bugbear, Death, that's worth our
        care ?
    After a life in pain and sorrow past,
After deluding hope and dire despair,
    Death only gives us quiet at the last.

How strangely are our love and hate misplaced !
    Freedom we seek, and yet from freedom flee ;
Courting those tyrant-sins that chain us fast,
    And shunning Death, that only sets us free.

'Tis not a foolish fear of future pains,
(Why should they fear who keep their souls from
        stains ?)

That makes me dread thy terrors, Death, to
    see ;
'Tis not the loss of riches, or of fame,
Or the vain toys the vulgar pleasures name :
    'Tis nothing, Caelia, but the losing thee.

Poems, 1692.

CCCXLVII

DELIA

What lover in his mistress hopes to find
A form so lovely, with so bright a mind ?
Doris may boast a face divinely fair,
But wants thy shape, thy motions, and thy air.
Lucinda has thy shape, but not those eyes
That, while they did th' admiring world surprise,
Disclosed the secret lustre of the mind,
And seemed each lover's inmost thoughts to
    find.
Others, whose beauty yielding swains confess,
By indiscretion make their conquest less,
And want thy conduct and obliging wit
To fix those slaves who to their charms submit.
As some rich tyrant hoards an useless store
That would, well placed, enrich a thousand more,
So didst thou keep a crowd of charms retired
Would make a thousand other nymphs admired.
Gay, modest, artless, beautiful, and young,
Slow to resolve, in resolution strong ;
To all obliging, yet reserved to all ;
None could himself the favoured lover call :
That which alone could makes his hopes endure,
Was that he saw no other swain secure.
Whither, ah ! whither are those graces fled ?
Down to the dark, the melancholy shade !

Miscellany Poems, v, 1704.

MATTHEW PRIOR (1664-1721)

CCCXLVIII

THE GARLAND

The pride of every grove I chose,
  The violet sweet, the lily fair,
The dappled pink, and blushing rose,
  To deck my charming Cloe's hair.

At morn the nymph vouchsafed to place
  Upon her brow the various wreath ;
The flowers less blooming than her face,
  The scent less fragrant than her breath.

The flowers she wore along the day :
  And every nymph and shepherd said,
That in her hair they looked more gay
  Than glowing in their native bed.

Undressed at evening, when she found
  Their odours lost, their colours past,
She changed her look, and on the ground
  Her garland and her eye she cast.

That eye dropped sense distinct and clear,
  As any Muse's tongue could speak,
When from its lid a pearly tear
  Ran trickling down her beauteous cheek.

Dissembling what I knew too well,
  ' My love, my life,' said I, ' explain
This change of humour : prithee, tell :
  That falling tear, what does it mean ? '

She sighed ; she smiled ; and to the flowers
  Pointing, the lovely moralist said :
' See, friend, in some few fleeting hours,
  See yonder, what a change is made.

' Ah me ! the blooming pride of May,
    And that of beauty are but one :
At morn both flourish bright and gay,
    Both fade at evening, pale, and gone.

' At dawn poor Stella danced and sung ;
    The amorous youth around her bowed :
At night her fatal knell was rung ;
    I saw, and kissed her in her shroud.

' Such as she is, who died to-day,
    Such I, alas ! may be to-morrow ;
Go, Damon, bid thy muse display
    The justice of thy Cloe's sorrow.'

CCCXLIX

If wine and music have the power
    To ease the sickness of the soul,
Let Phœbus every string explore,
    And Bacchus fill the sprightly bowl.

Let them their friendly aid employ,
    To make my Cloe's absence light ;
And seek for pleasure, to destroy
    The sorrows of this live-long night.

But she to-morrow will return ;
    Venus, be thou to-morrow great ;
Thy myrtles strow, thy odours burn ;
    And meet thy fav'rite nymph in state.

Kind goddess, to no other powers
    Let us to-morrow's blessings own :
Thy darling loves shall guide the hours,
    And all the day be thine alone.

CCCL

PHILLIS'S AGE

How old may Phillis be, you ask,
   Whose beauty thus all hearts engages ?
To answer is no easy task :
   For she has really two ages.

Stiff in brocade, and pinched in stays,
   Her patches, paint, and jewels on,
All day let envy view her face,
   And Phillis is but twenty-one.

Paint, patches, jewels laid aside,
   At night astronomers agree
The evening has the day belied :
   And Phillis is some forty-three.

CCCLI

In vain you tell your parting lover
You wish fair winds may waft him over :
Alas ! what winds can happy prove
That bear me far from what I love ?
Alas ! what dangers on the main
Can equal those that I sustain,
From slighted vows, and cold disdain ?

Be gentle, and in pity choose
To wish the wildest tempests loose :
That thrown again upon the coast
Where first my shipwrecked heart was lost,
I may once more repeat my pain ;
Once more in dying notes complain
Of slighted vows, and cold disdain.

A LOVER'S ANGER

As Cloe came into the room t' other day,
I peevish began: "Where so long could you
    stay?
In your life-time you never regarded your hour:
You promised at two; and (pray look, child) 'tis
    four.
A lady's watch needs neither figures nor wheels:
'Tis enough, that 'tis loaded with baubles and
    seals.
A temper so heedless no mortal can bear—"
Thus far I went on with a resolute air.
"Lord bless me," said she, "Let a body but
    speak:
Here's an ugly hard rose-bud fall'n into my
    neck;
It has hurt me, and vexed me to such a degree—
See here! for you never believe me; pray see,
On the left side my breast what a mark it has
    made!"
So saying, her bosom she careless displayed:
That seat of delight I with wonder surveyed,
And forgot every word I designed to have said.

THE SECRETARY

Written at The Hague, MDCXCVI

While with labour assiduous due pleasures I mix,
And in one day atone for the business of six,
In a little Dutch chaise on a Saturday night,
On my left hand my Horace, a nymph on my
    right,

No memoir to compose, and no postboy to
    move,
That on Sunday may hinder the softness of love.
For her, neither visits, nor parties at tea,
Nor the long-winded cant of a dull refugee.
This night and the next shall be hers, shall be
    mine,
To good or ill fortune the third we resign :
Thus scorning the world, and superior to fate,
I drive on my car in processional state.
So with Phia through Athens Pisistratus rode ;
Men thought her Minerva, and him a new god.
But why should I stories of Athens rehearse,
Where people knew love, and were partial to
    verse ;
Since none can with justice my pleasures oppose,
In Holland half drowned in interest and prose ?
By Greece and past ages what need I be tried,
When The Hague and the present are both on my
    side ?
And is it enough for the joys of the day,
To think what Anacreon or Sappho would say ?
When good Vandergoes and his provident Vrow,
As they gaze on my triumph, do freely allow,
That search all the province, you'll find no man
    dar is
So blest as the Englishen Heer Secretar is.

CCCLIV

QUID SIT FUTURUM CRAS FUGE
QUAERERE

For what to-morrow shall disclose,
May spoil what you to-night propose :
England may change, or Cloe stray.
Love and life are for to-day.

DEMOCRITUS AND HERACLITUS

Democritus, dear droll, revisit earth,
And with our follies glut thy heightened mirth ;
Sad Heraclitus, serious wretch, return,
In louder grief our greater crimes to mourn.
Between you both I unconcerned stand by :
Hurt, can I laugh ? and honest, need I cry ?

WRITTEN IN THE BEGINNING OF MEZERAY'S HISTORY OF FRANCE

Whate'er thy countrymen have done
By law and wit, by sword and gun,
    In thee is faithfully recited ;
And all the living world that view
Thy work give thee the praises due,
    At once instructed and delighted.

Yet for the fame of all these deeds,
What beggar in the Invalides,
    With lameness broke, with blindness
        smitten,
Wished ever decently to die,
To have been either Mezeray,
    Or any monarch he has written ?

It strange, dear author, yet it true is,
That, down from Pharamond to Louis,
    All covet life, yet call it pain,
All feel the ill, yet shun the cure.
Can sense the paradox endure ?
    Resolve me, Cambray or Fontaine.

The man in graver tragic known
(Though his best part long since was done)
　　Still on the stage desires to tarry :
And he who played the Harlequin
After the jest still loads the scene,
　　Unwilling to retire, though weary.

ADRIANI MORIENTIS AD ANIMAM SUAM (IMITATED)

Poor little, pretty, fluttering thing,
　　Must we no longer live together ?
And dost thou prune thy trembling wing
　　To take thy flight thou know'st not whither ?

Thy humorous vein, thy pleasing folly
　　Lies all neglected, all forgot ;
And pensive, wavering, melancholy,
　　Thou dread'st and hop'st thou know'st not
　　　　what.

Come here, my sweet landlady, pray how d'ye
　　do ?
Where is Ciccly so cleanly, and Prudence, and
　　Sue ?
And where is the widow that dwelt here below ?
And the hostler that sung, about eight years ago ?

And where is your sister, so mild and so dear ?
Whose voice to her maids like a trumpet was
　　clear.
By my troth ! she replies, you grow younger, I
　　think.
And pray, Sir, what wine does the gentleman
　　drink ?

Why now let me die, Sir, or live upon trust,
If I know to which question to answer you first :
Why, things, since I saw you, most strangely have
    varied,
And the hostler is hanged, and the widow is
    married.

And Prue left a child for the parish to nurse ;
And Cicely went off with a gentleman's purse ;
And as to my sister, so mild and so dear,
She has lain in the churchyard full many a year.

CCCLIX

JINNY THE JUST

Released from the noise of the butcher and baker
Who, my old friends be thanked, did seldom
    forsake her,
And from the soft duns of my landlord the
    Quaker,

From chiding the footmen and watching the
    lasses,
From Nell that burned milk, and Tom that broke
    glasses
(Sad mischiefs through which a good housekeeper
    passes !)

From some real care, but more fancied vexation,
From a life party-coloured, half reason, half
    passion,
Here lies after all the best wench in the nation.

From the Rhine to the Po, from the Thames to
    the Rhone,
Joanna or Janneton, Jinny or Joan,
'Twas all one to her by what name she was known.

For the idiom of words very little she heeded ;
Provided the matter she drove at succeeded,
She took and gave languages just as she needed.

So for kitchen and market, for bargain and sale
She paid English or Dutch or French down on
the nail,
But in telling a story she sometimes did fail ;

Then begging excuse as she happened to
stammer
With respect to her betters, but none to her
grammar,
Her blush helped her out and her jargon became
her.

Her habit and mien she endeavoured to frame
To the different *goût* of the place where she came,
Her outside still changed, but her inside the
same.

At the Hague in her slippers and hair as the mode
is ;
At Paris all falbalowed fine as a goddess ;
And at censuring London in smock sleeves and
bodice.

She ordered affairs that few people could tell
In what part about her that mixture did dwell
Of vrow, or mistress, or mademoiselle.

For her surname and race let the heralds e'en
answer ;
Her own proper worth was enough to advance
her,
And he who liked her, little valued her grandsire.

But from what house soever her lineage may
come,
I wish my own Jinny but out of her tomb
Though all her relations were there in her room.

Of such terrible beauty she never could boast
As with absolute sway o'er all hearts rules the
    roast,
When J—— bawls out to the chair for a toast.

But of good household features her person was
    made,
Nor by faction cried up nor of censure afraid,
And her beauty was rather for use than parade.

Her blood so well mixed and flesh so well pasted,
That tho' her youth faded her comeliness lasted ;
The blue was wore off, but the plum was well
    tasted.

Less smooth than her skin and less white than
    her breast
Was this polished stone beneath which she lies
    pressed.
Stop, reader, and sigh while thou think'st on the
    rest.

With a just trim of virtue her soul was endued,
Not affectedly pious nor secretly lewd,
She cut even between the coquette and the
    prude.

Her will with her duty so equally stood,
That seldom opposed, she was commonly good,
And did pretty well, doing just what she would.

Declining all power, she found means to
    persuade,
Was then most regarded when most she obeyed,
The mistress, in truth, when she seemed but the
    maid.

Such care of her own proper actions she took,
That on other folks lives she had no time to look,
So censure and praise were struck out of her
    book.

Her thought still confined to its own little sphere,
She minded not who did excel or did err,
But just as the matter related to her.

Then, too, when her private tribunal was reared,
Her mercy so mixed with her judgment appeared
That her foes were condemned and her friends
    always cleared.

Her religion so well with her learning did suit,
That, in practice sincere, and in controverse
    mute,
She showed she knew better to live than
    dispute.

Some parts of the Bible by heart she recited,
And much in historical chapters delighted,
But in points about faith she was something
    short-sighted.

So notions and modes she referred to the schools,
And in matters of conscience adhered to two
    rules :
To advise with no bigots, and jest with no fools.

And scrupling but little, enough she believed ;
By charity ample small sins she retrieved ;
And when she had new clothes, she always
    received.

Thus still whilst her morning unseen fled away,
In ordering the linen and making the tea,
That she scarce could have time for the psalms
    of the day ;

And while after dinner the night came so soon,
That half she proposed very seldom was done,
With twenty God bless me's, how this day is
    gone ;

While she read and accounted and paid and
    abated,
Ate and drank, played and worked, laughed and
    cried, loved and hated,
As answered the end of her being created;

In the midst of her age came a cruel disease
Which neither her juleps nor receipts could
    appease,
So down dropped her clay, may her soul be at
    peace.

Retire from this sepulchre, all the profane,
You that love for debauch, or that marry for
    gain,
Retire lest ye trouble the manes of J——

But thou that know'st love above interest or lust,
Strew the myrtle and rose on this once-beloved
    dust,
And shed one pious tear upon Jinny the Just.

Tread soft on her grave, and do right to her
    honour,
Let neither rude hand nor ill tongue light upon
    her,
Do all the small favours that now can be done
    her.

And when what thou liked shall return to her
    clay,
(For so I'm persuaded she must do one day,
Whatever fantastic J—— Asgil may say).

When, as I have done now, thou shalt set up a
    stone
For something however distinguished or known,
May some pious friend the misfortune bemoan,
And make thy concern by reflection his own.
Longleat MSS.

SIR JOHN VANBRUGH (1664-1726)

CCCLX

(*AN ADVENTURE*)

A Band, a Bob-wig, and a Feather,
Attacked a lady's heart together :
The Band in a most learned plea,
Made up of deep philosophy,
Told her, if she would please to wed
A reverend beard, and take, instead
   Of vigorous youth,
   Old solemn truth
With books and morals into bed,
   How happy she would be.

The Bob, he talked of management,
What wondrous blessings Heaven sent
On care, and pains, and industry ;
And truly he must be so free,
To own he thought your airy beaux,
With powdered wigs, and dancing shoes,
Were good for nothing (mend his soul !)
But prate, and talk, and play the fool.
He said, 'twas wealth gave joy and mirth,
   And that to be the dearest wife
   Of one who laboured all his life
To make a mine of gold his own,
And not spend sixpence when he'd done,
   Was Heaven upon earth.

When these two blades had done, d'ye see,
The Feather (as it might be me)
Steps out, Sir, from behind the screen,
With such an air, and such a mien :
Look you, old gentleman ! in short,
He quickly spoiled the statesman's sport,

It proved such charming weather,
That, you must know, at the first beck,
The lady leaped about his neck,
    And off they went together.

Aesop, 1697.

CCCLXI

A FABLE

Once on a time a nightingale
    To changes prone,
Unconstant, fickle, whimsical,
    (A female one),
Who sung like others of her kind,
Hearing a well-taught linnet's airs,
Had other matters in her mind;
To imitate him she prepares.
Her fancy straight was on the wing:
    I fly, quoth she,
    As well as he;
    I don't know why
    I should not try,
As well as he to sing.
From that day forth she changed her note,
She spoiled her voice, she strained her throat;
She did as learned women do;
    Till every thing
    That heard her sing
Would run away from her, as I from you.

Ibid.

CCCLXII

Not an angel dwells above
Half so fair as her I love;

Heaven knows how she'll receive me ;
If she smiles, I'm blest indeed,
If she frowns, I'm quickly freed ;
    Heaven knows she ne'er can grieve me.

None can love her more than I,
Yet she ne'er shall make me die,
    If my flame can never warm her.
Lasting beauty I'll adore ;
I shall never love her more,
    Cruelty will so deform her

The Provoked Wife, 1697.

CCCLXIII

Fly, fly, you happy shepherds fly '
    Avoid Philira's charms ;
The rigour of her heart denies
    The heaven that's in her arms.
Ne'er hope to gaze, and then retire,
    Nor yielding, to be blest :
Nature, who formed her eyes of fire,
    Of ice composed her breast.

Yet, lovely maid, this once believe
    A slave whose zeal you move ;
The gods, alas, your youth deceive :
    Their heaven consists in love.
In spite of all the thanks you owe,
    You may reproach 'em this,
That where they did their form bestow,
    They have denied their bliss.

Ibid.

JOHN GLANVILL (1664-1735)

CCCLXIV

THE FOOLISH DELAY.   1688

No more this dallying and suspense,
Vain doubts and heedless negligence,
But think with just concern and fears
Of passing days and coming years.

Pleasures that to receive us wait,
If we pass by and will not bait
Are lost ; there's no returning back
That which we let alone to take.

That stage for ever is passed o'er ;
All we can do's to lose no more,
But make ourselves the best amends
With the remainder that attends.

Youth must with all its joys decay,
Nor can vain care prolong its stay ;
Spare ne'er so much, spend ne'er so fast,
'Tis all the selfsame thing at last.

What boots it to be covetous
Where avarice can no gain produce ?
What fool would that estate not use,
Which he howe'er must surely lose.

You fear to wear out Love too soon ;
And let profusely Time run on,
That uncontrolled pursues its race ;
Should pleasure not keep equal pace.

Fruition is a harmless thing,
Drinks fair of a recruiting spring,
Whets the renewing appetite,
Nor palls the relish of delight.

Enjoyment will not harm one grace,
One charm, one feature in the face,
Or bring at thirty, wrinkles there,
Would not till fifty else appear.

Will parts for being employed decay ?
Can you e'er kiss those lips away ?
Or will that marble snowy breast
The sooner fade for being pressed ?

No, 'tis a fond unjust presage
To think youth used advances age.
Be bold, and when the worst y'have done,
The cautious maid grows old as soon.

Does it more fast the flowers destroy,
When men the fragrant scent enjoy ?
Does summer hasten from our clime
Because we use its harvest-time ?

No, May would pass as swiftly by
Did all its sweets neglected lie ;
Should we the summer's fruit forbear
Yet winter still would be as near.

Since then youth too must quit its room,
And age, that dreadful winter, come,
Age, that dry, shrivelled, frozen thing,
Let's use our summer and our spring.

Poems, 1725.

CCCLXV

Can nothing, nothing move her
To save a hapless swain ?
Nor kindness for the lover,
Nor pity of the pain ?

See how she flies, denying
To hear me but complain,
Leaves me all faint and dying,
Helpless and vainly trying
To bring her back again.

Let nothing, nothing move her
To save a hapless swain,
Nor kindness for the lover,
Nor pity of the pain :
Yet seeking no restoring
No change his faith shall stain,
Nor will he cease adoring,
Nor sighing, nor imploring,
Though all shall be in vain.

But hopeless thus to languish
When he no more shall bear,
But pined with ceaseless anguish
Shall sink beneath his care :
Then she that did bereave him
Of life, shall mourn his fate,
Then wish she could retrieve him,
Then willing to relieve him ;
But then 'twill be too late.

Ibid.

CCCLXVI

TO LOVE

Love, thou chief good of human kind,
    How friendly is thy influence !
Thy passion sweetest soothes the mind,
    Thy pleasures highest treat the sense.

And yet we wrong thee and thy joy ;
    We waste thy day and lose thy night ;
Vain men deride thee as a toy,
    Poor women fly thee in a fright.

No matter, Love's the gentle prize,
   And such as know thee hold thee dear ;
They find thy pleasing follies wise,
   Thy loss is what alone they fear.

Some every day to thee converts ;
   And nobly thou hast this to boast,
No youth thy service e'er deserts,
   No nymph once gained was ever lost.

Ibid.

CCCLXVII

OF HIS MISTRESS

My mistress so bewitches me in love
No hours at rest from her enchantments move ;
When she is present, to all else I'm blind,
And absent still she's present to my mind ;
No crowd so great her image to exclude,
And from her spirit there's no solitude ;
None, none from her ; nor any do I crave,
'Tis solitude and She that I would have.

Ibid.

THOMAS FLETCHER (1664-1718)

CCCLXVIII

Oh, ecstasy divine ! I cannot hold !
Farewell, dull earth ! See where my ravished
   soul
Stands shivering on the edge of its slow clay !
With the next rising note 'twill fly away.
I faint, I faint. The powerful charm forbear !
Nay, but sing on : sure that will keep it here.
Whither fond soul, ah, whither wouldst thou
   fly ?
To Heav'n ? Can there be sweeter harmony ?

'Tis strange the charms of harmony which give
To all things life, should make me cease to live.
Yet is this death ?   If it be thus to die,
Death cannot be a curse ; or if it be,
Ye angry Powers, may't ever light on me.
Poems, 1692.

CCCLXIX

While you with music and with beauty charm,
      And every sense alarm,
All hearts their strange united power confess,
      Yet dare not wish it less.
Love finds to every heart an easy way,
      Or through the ear or eye.
        So fair your face
        So sweet your voice,
      You seem at once to be
      Both Orpheus and Eurydice.

See how the amorous, the happy air,
      More happy far than I,
Proud to be moulded into sounds by her,
      About her lips does play ;
Till kissed into a note it skips away,
      And prattles loud its joy.
        Ah, cruel fair,
        Your scorn forbear,
      Nor give that liberty
      To air, which is denied to me.
Ibid.

CCCLXX

From *ETERNITY, A PINDARIC ODE*

But how much better they
Who climbing to the same eternity,

Yet trod the paths of virtue and of honour,
Heroes who bravely died,
Their country's fall preventing by their own!
This was the purchase of their sufferings.
Ev'n dying, still they hoped
The loss of some few wretched years
Should be repaid with everlasting fame.
This from all nations drew
Young daring champions to th' Olympian
    plains;
For this the wrestler strove,
This was the racer's goal:
Not flowery garlands and one year's applause
They sought, but to be registered
In the records of fame and to be known for ever;
This they all sought, but ah! how few obtained.
Hiero, Theron and some happy few
Has Pindar saved
From the iron teeth of time:
And left their names richly embalm'd
In spicy verse
To be the envy of succeeding heroes.
And they shall live, but all the rest
Long since unremembered be
Lost in the grave and mixed with nameless
    things . . .

Ibid.

CCCLXXI

ON A LADY'S PICTURE

Believe, Posterity, believe it true
This from no fancied form the pencil drew;
No angel sat with lucid visions sent
To bless the eyes of some departing saint.
No, all the charms which on this picture dwell
(And ah what pity 'tis) were mortal all.

Thus much 'tis fit to let the picture speak
Lest this for some bright being they mistake
Of heavenly race ; and to mankind be lost
The greatest honour it could ever boast.

Ibid.

CCCLXXII

THE IMPATIENT

Enough, enough of this world's fruitless care
And even its pleasures I have suffered here ;
I'm weary of life's gross hypocrisy
With plenty starved, cloyed with variety.
Oh happy, happy state, when shall I be
From fancied good and real evil free !
When one short well-spent sigh shall me remove
From all the cheats mistaken mortals love :
When undeceived by fancied shadows, I
Shall very Beauty in its fountain see !
Oh happy, happy state ! Why do I stay ?
Move faster, Time, how slowly dost thou fly,
As if the weight of years had crippled thee !
Thou, Death's procurer, quickly bring me safe
Into the cold embraces of the grave ;
There shall I blest, at least shall quiet lie
Till the angelic summons from on high
Call me to bliss and real life away :
Then shall devouring flame with fury hurled
Revenge my quarrel on the injurious world ;
Then thou shalt cease, and Death himself shall
        die ;
And both together lost and buried lie,
He in eternal life and thou in vast eternity.

Ibid.

GEORGE GRANVILLE, LORD LANS-
DOWNE (1667-1735)

CCCLXXIII

EPIGRAMS

CLOE

Bright as the day, and like the morning fair,
Such Cloe is, and common as the air.

_____

*INSCRIPTION FOR A FIGURE REPRE-
SENTING THE GOD OF LOVE*

Whoe'er thou art, thy lord and master see;
Thou wast my slave, thou art, or thou shalt be.

_____

WRITTEN IN HER PRAYER-BOOK

In vain, Clarinda, night and day
For pity to the gods you pray ;
What arrogance on Heav'n to call
For that which you deny to all !

CCCLXXIV

CORINNA

Corinna, in the bloom of youth
    Was coy to every lover,
Regardless of the tenderest truth,
    No soft complaint could move her.

Mankind was hers, all at her feet
    Lay prostrate and adoring,
The witty, handsome, rich and great,
    In vain alike imploring.

L

But now grown old, she would repair
  Her loss of time and pleasure,
With willing eyes and wanton air
  Inviting every gazer.

But love's a summer flower, that dies
  With the first weather's changing ;
The lover, like the swallow, flies
  From sun to sun, still ranging.

Myra, let this example move
  Your foolish heart to reason ;
Youth is the proper time for love,
  And age is virtue's season.

CCCLXXV

CLOE

Impatient with desire, at last
  I ventured to lay forms aside ;
'Twas I was modest, not she chaste ;
  Cloe, so gently pressed, complied.

With idle awe, an amorous fool,
  I gazed upon her eyes with fear ;
Say, Love, how came your slave so dull,
  To read no better there ?

Thus to ourselves the greatest foes,
  Although the nymph be well inclined ;
For want of courage to propose,
  By our own folly she's unkind.

CCCLXXVI

TO MYRA

Loving at first sight

No warning of th' approaching flame ;
Swiftly, like sudden death, it came ;

Like travellers by lightning killed,
I burnt the moment I beheld.

In whom so many charms are placed,
Is with a mind as nobly graced ;
The case so shining to behold
Is filled with richest gems and gold.

To what my eyes admired before
I add a thousand graces more ;
And fancy blows into a flame
The spark that from her beauty came.

The object thus improved by thought,
By my own image I am caught ;
Pygmalion so, with fatal art,
Polished the form that stung his heart.

CCCLXXVII

I'll tell her the next time, said I :
In vain ! in vain ! for when I try,
Upon my timorous tongue the trembling accents
    die.
Alas ! a thousand thousand fears
Still overawe when she appears.
My breath is spent in sighs, my eyes are drowned
    in tears.

JONATHAN SWIFT (1667-1745)

CCCLXXVIII

TO MRS. BIDDY FLOYD

Or the receipt to form a beauty

When Cupid did his grandsire Jove entreat
To form some beauty by a new receipt,

Jove sent and found far in a country scene
Truth, innocence, good nature, look serene,
From which ingredients first the dextrous boy
Picked the demure, the awkward, and the coy;
The Graces from the court did next provide
Breeding, and wit, and air, and decent pride;
These Venus cleansed from every spurious grain
Of nice, coquette, affected, pert, and vain.
Jove mixed up all, and his best clay employ'd,
Then call'd the happy composition, FLOYD.

CCCLXXIX

A DESCRIPTION OF THE MORNING

Now hardly here and there an hackney coach
Appearing, showed the ruddy morn's approach.
Now Betty from her master's bed had flown,
And softly stole to discompose her own.
The slipshod 'prentice from his master's door
Had pared the dirt, and sprinkled round the floor.
Now Moll had whirled her mop with dextrous
    airs,
Prepared to scrub the entry and the stairs.
The youth with broomy stumps began to trace
The kennel's edge, where wheels had worn the
    place.
The small-coal-man was heard with cadence
    deep,
Till drowned in shriller notes of chimney-sweep.
Duns at his lordship's gate began to meet;
And brick-dust Moll had screamed through half
    the street.
The turnkey now his flock returning sees,
Duly let out a-nights to steal for fees.
The watchful bailiffs take their silent stands;
And school-boys lag with satchels in their hands.

The Tatler, 1709.

CCCLXXX

THE DAY OF JUDGMENT

With a whirl of thought oppressed,
I sunk from reverie to rest.
An horrid vision seized my head:
I saw the graves give up their dead,
Jove, armed with terrors, burst the skies,
And thunder roars, and lightning flies.
Amazed, confused, its fate unknown,
The world stands trembling at his throne.
While each pale sinner hung his head,
Jove nodding, shook the Heavens, and said :
' Offending race of human-kind,
By nature, reason, learning, blind ;
You who, through frailty, stepped aside ;
And you who never fell, through pride ;
You who in different sects were shammed,
And come to see each other damned,
(So some folk told you, but they knew
No more of Jove's designs than you) :
The world's mad business now is o'er,
And I resent these pranks no more.
I to such blockheads set my wit ?
I damn such fools ?—Go, go, you're *bit.*'

JOHN HOPKINS

CCCLXXXI

(FROM ' *TO THE GOD OF LOVE* ')

Me my ambition only leads
Beneath the hill to seek out pleasing groves,
   The charming Muses haunt the shades
And there in laurel bowers I would reveal my
   loves.

Congreve and Wycherley are great
  Upon Parnassus' tops they sit,
Not raised by Fortune, but by Fate,
Their praise is to their merits late ;
  They lord it o'er the world of wit.
The mighty Dryden o'er their heads
  Like a vast cloud appears ;
Gilt with late sunbeams, wide he spreads,
And grateful dew upon them sheds,
  Fruitful yet shining too in evening years.
His fancy still swift does in lightnings fly,
And loudly rolling words run thundering from
    his sky.

Amasia, 1700.

ANONYMOUS

CCCLXXXII

A LOVE SONG

Sabina has a thousand charms
  To captivate my heart ;
Her lovely eyes are Cupid's arms,
  And every look a dart :
But when the beauteous idiot speaks,
  She cures me of my pain ;
Her tongue the servile fetters breaks
  And frees her slave again.

Had Nature to Sabina lent
  Beauty with reason crowned,
Each single shaft her eyes had sent
  Had given a mortal wound ;
Now though each hour she gains a heart,
  And makes mankind her slave,
Yet like the Grecian hero's dart,
  She heals the wounds she gave.

Amphion Anglicus, 1700.

WILLIAM CONGREVE (1670-1729)

CCCLXXXIII

ON MRS. ARABELLA HUNT, SINGING
Irregular Ode

I

Let all be hushed, each softest motion cease,
Be ev'ry loud tumultuous thought at peace.
  And ev'ry ruder gasp of breath
  Be calm, as in the arms of death.
And thou most fickle, most uneasy part,
  Thou restless wanderer, my heart,
  Be still : gently, ah gently, leave,
  Thou busy, idle thing, to heave.
  Stir not a pulse ; and let my blood,
  That turbulent, unruly flood,
    Be softly stayed :
Let me be all, but my attention, dead.
Go rest, unnecessary springs of life,
  Leave your officious toil and strife ;
For I would hear her voice, and try
If it be possible to die.

II

Come all ye love-sick maids and wounded swains,
  And listen to her healing strains.
A wondrous balm between her lips she wears,
  Of sov'reign force to soften cares ;
'Tis piercing as your thoughts, and melting as
    your tears ;
  And this through ev'ry ear she can impart
  (By tuneful breath diffused) to ev'ry heart.
  Swiftly the gentle charmer flies
And to the tender grief soft air applies,

Which, warbling mystic sounds,
Cements the bleeding panter's wounds.
But ah ! beware of clam'rous moan,
Let no unpleasing murmur or harsh groan
Your slighted loves declare ;
Your very tend'rest moving sighs forbear,
For even they will be too boist'rous here.
Hither let nought but sacred silence come,
And let all saucy praise be dumb.

III

And lo ! Silence himself is here.
Methinks I see the Midnight God appear,
In all his downy pomp arrayed,
Behold the rev'rend shade :
An ancient sigh he sits upon,
Whose memory of sound is long since gone,
And purposely annihilated for his throne.
Beneath, two soft transparent clouds do meet,
In which he seems to sink his softer feet.
A melancholy thought, condensed to air,
Stol'n from a lover in despair,
Like a thin mantle, serves to wrap
In fluid folds his visionary shape.
A wreath of darkness round his head he wears,
Where curling mists supply the want of hairs,
While the still vapours, which from poppies rise,
Bedew his hoary face, and lull his eyes.

IV

But hark ! the heav'nly sphere turns round,
And silence now is drowned
In ecstasy of sound.
How on a sudden the still air is charmed,
As if all Harmony were just alarmed !
And ev'ry soul with transport filled,
Alternately is thawed and chilled.

See how the heavenly choir
Come flocking, to admire,
And with what speed and care,
Descending angels cull the thinnest air !
  Haste then, come all th' immortal throng,
      And listen to her song ;
  Leave your loved mansions in the sky,
  And hither, quickly hither fly ;
Your loss of Heav'n nor shall you need to fear,
  While she sings, 'tis Heav'n here.

V

See how they crowd, see how the little cherubs
    skip !
While others sit around her mouth, and sip
  Sweet Hallelujahs from her lip.
Those lips, where in surprise of bliss they rove ·
  For ne'er before were angels blest
        With such a luscious feast
        Of music and of love.
  Prepare then, ye immortal choir,
  Each sacred minstrel tune his lyre,
  And with her voice in chorus join
Her voice, which next to yours is most divine.
  Bless the glad earth with heav'nly lays,
And to that pitch th' eternal accents raise,
  Which only breath inspired can reach,
To notes, which only she can learn, and you can
    teach.
  While we, charmed with the loved excess,
  Are wrapt in sweet forgetfulness
Of all, of all, but of the present happiness,
  Wishing for ever in that state to lie
  For ever to be dying so, yet never die.

(1692) *Poems*, 1710.

CCCLXXXIV

SONG

Love's but the frailty of the mind,
  When 'tis not with ambition joined ;
A sickly flame, which if not fed expires,
And feeding, wastes in self-consuming fires.

'Tis not to wound a wanton boy
  Or amor'us youth, that gives the joy ;
But 'tis the glory to have pierced a swain
For whom inferior beauties sighed in vain.

Then I alone the conquest prize,
  When I insult a rival's eyes :
If there's delight in love, 'tis when I see
That heart which others bleed for, bleed for me.

The Way of the World, 1700.

CCCLXXXV

AMORET

Fair Amoret is gone astray ;
  Pursue and seek her, every lover ;
I'll tell the signs, by which you may
  The wand'ring shepherdess discover.

Coquette and coy at once her air,
  Both studied, though both seem neglected ;
Careless she is with artful care,
  Affecting to seem unaffected.

With skill her eyes dart every glance,
  Yet change so soon you'd ne'er suspect 'em ;
For she'd persuade they wound by chance,
  Tho' certain aim and art direct 'em.

She likes herself, yet others hates
    For that which in herself she prizes ;
And while she laughs at them, forgets
    She is the thing that she despises.

Miscellany Poems, v. 1704.

CCCLXXXVI

SONG

Pious Selinda goes to prayers
    If I but ask the favour ;
And yet the tender fool's in tears
    When she believes I'll leave her.

Would I were free from this restraint,
    Or else had hopes to win her ;
Would she could make of me a saint,
    Or I of her a sinner.

Ibid.

CCCLXXXVII

SONG

See, see, she wakes, Sabina wakes !
    And now the sun begins to rise.
Less glorious is the morn that breaks
    From his bright beams, than her fair eyes.

With light united, day they give,
    But different fates ere night fulfil :
How many by his warmth will live !
    How many will her coldness kill !

Ibid.

CCCLXXXVIII

SONG

False though she be to me and love,
  I'll ne'er pursue revenge ;
For still the charmer I approve,
  Tho' I deplore her change.

In hours of bliss we oft have met ;
  They could not always last ;
And though the present I regret,
  I'm grateful for the past.

Poems, 1710.

JOSEPH ADDISON (1672-1719)

CCCLXXXIX

ODE

The spacious firmament on high
With all the blue ethereal sky
And spangled heavens, a shining frame,
Their great Original proclaim.
Th' unwearied sun, from day to day
Does his Creator's power display,
And publishes to every land
The work of an almighty hand.

Soon as the evening shades prevail,
The moon takes up the wondrous tale,
And nightly to the listening earth
Repeats the story of her birth ;
Whilst all the stars that round her burn,
And all the planets in their turn,
Confirm the tidings as they roll,
And spread the truth from pole to pole.

What though in solemn silence all
Move round the dark terrestrial ball ;
What though nor real voice nor sound
Amid their radiant orbs be found ;
In reason's ear they all rejoice,
And utter forth a glorious voice,
For ever singing as they shine :
' The Hand that made us is divine.'

The Spectator, 1712.

CCCXC

COWLEY'S EPITAPH ON HIMSELF

Translated

From life's superfluous cares enlarged,
His debt of human toil discharged,
Here Cowley lies ! beneath this shed,
To every worldly interest dead ;
With decent poverty content,
His hours of ease not idly spent ;
To fortune's goods a foe professed,
And hating wealth, by all caressed.
'Tis true he's dead ; for oh ! how small
A spot of earth is now his all.
Oh ! wish that earth may lightly lay,
And every care be far away ;
Bring flowers ; the short-lived roses bring,
To life deceased, fit offering :
And sweets around the poet strew,
Whilst yet with life his ashes glow.

ELIZABETH ROWE (1674-1737)

CCCXCI

PARTHENIA, AN ELEGY

With singing angels hence she posts away,
As lovely now and excellent as they.
For one short moment Death's grim looks she
  bore,
But ne'er shall see his ghastly visage more.
Released from her dull fetters, as the light
Active and pure, Parthenia takes her flight,
And finds at last the awful secrecy
How spirits act and what they do and be:
But now she's swallowed in a flood of light
And scarce endures the splendour of the sight.
Dear shade, whom Heaven did so soon remove
From these cold regions to the land of love,
To endless pleasures and eternal day:
How glittering now, how satisfied and gay
Art thou?   Methinks I do but half lament
The lovely saint from my embraces rent.
Nor can on those fair mansions cast my eyes
To which she's fled, and not recall my sighs.
My grief for her were as unjust as vain,
If from that bliss 'twould hurry her again.
For though the charmingst friend on earth I've
  lost
Yet she the while may the advantage boast:
And should her pure unfettered soul but deign
A careless glance on these dark coasts again,
'Twould smile, as conscious, where she left her
  chain,
And smile again at the surprising odds
Of her late dwelling, and those bright abodes,
Those bright abodes where now, securely blest,
She sings the anthems of eternal rest.

Philomela (2nd edition) 1727.

ISAAC WATTS (1674-1748)

CCCXCII

THE DAY OF JUDGMENT
An Ode

When the fierce north wind with his airy forces
Rears up the Baltic to a foaming fury ;
And the red lightning with a storm of hail comes
    Rushing amain down,

How the poor sailors stand amazed and tremble !
While the hoarse thunder like a bloody trumpet
Roars a loud onset to the gaping waters
    Quick to devour them.

Such shall the noise be, and the wild disorder
(If things eternal may be like these earthly)
Such the dire terror when the great Archangel
    Shakes the creation ;

Tears the strong pillars of the vault of Heaven ;
Breaks up old marble, the repose of princes ;
See the graves open, and the bones arising,
    Flames all around 'em.

Hark the shrill outcries of the guilty wretches !
Lively bright horror and amazing anguish
Stare thro' their eye-lids, while the living worm
 lies
    Gnawing within them.

Thoughts like old vultures prey upon their
 heartstrings,
And the smart twinges, when their eye beholds
 the
Lofty Judge frowning, and a flood of vengeance
    Rolling afore him.

Hopeless immortals ! how they scream and
  shiver
While devils push them to the pit wide yawning
Hideous and gloomy, to receive them headlong
                    Down to the centre.

Stop here my fancy (all away be horrid
Doleful ideas) come arise to Jesus,
How he sits God-like ! and the saints around
  him
                    Throned, yet adoring !

Oh may I sit there when he comes triumphant
Dooming the nations : then ascend to glory,
While our Hosannas all along the passage
                    Shout the Redeemer.

Horae Lyricae, 1706.

CCCXCIII

CRUCIFIXION TO THE WORLD BY THE CROSS OF CHRIST

When I survey the wondrous Cross
On which the Prince of Glory died,
My richest gain I count but loss,
And pour contempt on all my pride.

Forbid it, Lord, that I should boast
Save in the death of Christ my God ;
All the vain things that charm me most,
I sacrifice them to his Blood.

See from his head, his hands, his feet,
Sorrow and love flow mingled down ;
Did e'er such love and sorrow meet ?
Or thorns compose so rich a crown ?

His dying crimson like a robe
Spreads o'er his body on the Tree,
Then am I dead to all the globe,
And all the globe is dead to me.

Were the whole realm of nature mine,
That were a present far too small ;
Love so amazing, so divine,
Demands my soul, my life, my all.

Hymns, 1707.

CCCXCIV

MAN FRAIL, AND GOD ETERNAL

Our God, our help in ages past,
  Our hope for years to come,
Our shelter from the stormy blast,
  And our eternal home.

Under the shadow of thy throne
  Thy saints have dwelt secure ;
Sufficient is thine arm alone
  And our defence is sure.

Before the hills in order stood,
  Or earth received her frame,
From everlasting thou art God,
  To endless years the same.

Thy word commands our flesh to dust :
  Return, ye sons of men.
All nations rose from earth at first,
  And turn to earth again.

A thousand ages in thy sight
  Are like an evening gone ;
Short as the watch that ends the night
  Before the rising sun.

The busy tribes of flesh and blood
   With all their lives and cares
Are carried downwards by thy flood,
   And lost in following years.

Time like an ever-rolling stream
   Bears all its sons away ;
They fly forgotten as a dream
   Dies at the opening day.

Like flowery fields the nations stand
   Pleased with the morning light ;
The flowers beneath the mower's hand
   Lie withering ere 'tis night.

Our God, our help in ages past,
   Our hope for years to come,
Be thou our guard while troubles last,
   And our eternal home.

Psalms, 1719.

JOHN OLDMIXON (1673-1742)

CCCXCV

THE RESPECTFUL LOVER

My mistress is, I own, above
The humble proffer of my love ;
In justice yet she must confess
That nothing can disturb her less :
It never durst offend her ear,
With what she is averse to hear ;
But yielding to a just despair
'Tis modest still as she is fair.
It wishes much, and none that see
Such beauty are from wishes free.
It hopes for little, naught requires,
Nor yet discovered its desires.
It dares not, or it knows not how
To tell her what she ought to know,

How long have I endured the pain
To love and wish and not obtain :
To find my passion is unknown,
Or what she sees, she will not own ·
Or what she coldly may regard
She thinks unworthy a reward.

Poems, 1696.

CCCXCVI

TO CHLOE

Prithee, Chloe, not so fast,
Let's not run and wed in haste ;
We've a thousand things to do :
You must fly, and I pursue ;
You must frown, and I must sigh ;
I entreat, and you deny.
Stay ! If I am never crossed,
Half the pleasure will be lost :
Be, or seem to be, severe,
Give me reason to despair ;
Fondness will my wishes cloy,
Make me careless of the joy.
Lovers may of course complain
Of their trouble and their pain ;
But if pain and trouble cease,
Love without it will not please.

Ibid.

AMBROSE PHILIPS (1675-1749)

CCCXCVII

MORTALITY

Beneath the covert of a grove
Frequented much by men in love,

Careless, and supinely laid,
I took my lute and on it played.
Of Love's soft passion did I sing,
And Cupid, Love's almighty King.
When lo ! a string, that would have spoke
O' th' sudden cracked and sighing broke :
It broke, and said (methoughts) to me,
'Think of thine own mortality.'

Miscellany Poems (Rogers), 1697.

CCCXCVIII

Then never let me see her more !
In vain I sigh, in vain adore.
In some lonely desert place,
Far from sight of human race,
In some unfrequented cell,
Where neither joy nor sorrow dwell,
Oh ! let me endeavour to forget
At once myself and Amoret.

Miscellany Poems, vi. (1709)

JOHN HUGHES (1677-1720)

CCCXCIX

THE HUE AND CRY

Some wit, more folly, and no care,
Thoughtless her conduct, free her air ;
Gay, scornful, sober, indiscreet,
In whom all contradictions meet ;
Civil, affronting, peevish, easy,
Formed both to charm ye and displease ye ;
Much want of judgement, none of pride ;
Modish her dress, her hoop full wide ;
Brown skin, her eyes of sable hue ;
Angel, when pleased ; when vexed, a shrew.

Genteel her motion when she walks,
Sweetly she sings, and loudly talks ;
Knows all the world and its affairs,
Who goes to court, to plays, to prayers,
Who keeps, who marries, fails or thrives,
Leads honest or dishonest lives ;
What money matched each youth or maid,
And who was at each masquerade ;
Of all fine things in this fine town,
She's only to herself unknown.

By this description, if you meet her
With lowly bows and homage greet her ;
And if you bring the vagrant beauty
Back to her mother and her duty
Ask, for reward, a lover's bliss,
And (if she'll let you) take a kiss ;
Or more, if more you wish and may,
Try if at church the words she'll say.
Then make her, if you can, " obey."

CCCC

THE MARCH

Victoria comes ! she leaves the foraged groves,
Her flying camp of Graces and of Loves
Strike all their tents, and for the march prepare,
And to new scenes of triumph wait the fair.
Unlike the slaves which other warriors gain,
That loathe subjection, and would break their
chain,
Her rural slaves their absent victor mourn,
And wish not liberty, but her return.
The conquered countries droop, while she's
away,
And slowly to the Spring their contribution pay.
While cooing turtles, doubly now alone,
With their lost loves another loss bemoan.

Meantime in peopled cities crowds press on
And jealous seem who shall be first undone.
Victories, like Fame, before th' invader fly,
And lovers yet unseeing haste to die.
While she with careless, unelated mind,
Hears daily conquests which she ne'er designed :
In her a soft, yet cruel heart is found,
Averse to cure, and vainly grieved to wound.

GEORGE FARQUHAR (1678-1707)

CCCCI

Tell me, Aurelia, tell me, pray,
   How long must Damon sue ?
Prefix the time, and I'll obey,
With patience wait the happy day
   That makes me sure of you.

The sails of time my sighs shall blow,
   And make the minutes glide ;
My tears shall make the current flow,
   And swell the hasting tide.

The wings of love shall fly so fast,
   (My hopes mount so sublime)
The wings of love shall make more haste
   Than the swift wings of time.

Love and Business, 1702.

ANONYMOUS

CCCCII

SONG

As the snow in valleys lying,
Phœbus his warm beams applying,

Soon dissolves and runs away ;
So the beauties, so the graces,
Of the most bewitching faces,
    At approaching age decay.

As a tyrant, when degraded,
Is despised, and is upbraided,
    By the slaves he once controlled ;
So the nymph, if none could move her,
Is contemned by every lover,
    When her charms are growing old.

Melancholic looks, and whining,
Grieving, quarrelling, and pining,
    Are th' effects your rigours move ;
Soft caresses, amorous glances,
Melting sighs, transporting trances,
    Are the blest effects of love.

Fair ones ! while your beauty's blooming,
Use your time, lest age resuming
    What your youth profusely lends,
You are robb'd of all your glories,
And condemn'd to tell old stories
    To your unbelieving friends.

Miscellany Poems, v. 1704.

CCCCIII

Cupid ! Instruct an amorous swain,
Some way to tell the nymph his pain,
    To common youths unknown :
To talk of sighs, of flames, and darts,
Of bleeding wounds, and burning hearts,
    Are methods vulgar grown.

What need'st thou tell ? (the God replied)
That love the shepherd cannot hide

The nymph will quickly find :
When Phœbus does his beams display
To tell men gravely that 'tis day
Is to suppose 'em blind.

Ibid.

CCCCIV

STANZAS

This is the place where oft my longing eyes
Have charming Silvia seen.
How in that instant would my passion rise !
And with what transports did I meet her then !
What means my heart at that false name to
move ?
Have you forgot that you no longer love ?

Here, chaplets of the choicest flow'rs to make,
The meads I wander'd o'er ;
Which she with tender looks would blushing
take,
Or with feign'd coyness make her kindness
more.
What means my heart at that false name to
move ?
Have you forgot that you no longer love ?

If tender jealousies disturb'd my rest,
When e'er my doubts appear'd
How unconcern'dly would she calm my breast !
With what contempt describe the swains I
fear'd !
What means my heart at that false name to
move ?
Have you forgot that you no longer love ?

Now, conscious of her guilt, she shuns my sight ;
    To me she shuts her door ;
While worthless hirelings grossly taste delight,
And riot in the charms that I adore.
What means my heart at that false name to
    move ?
Have you forgot that you no longer love ?
Ibid.

CCCCV

THE FALSE MORNING

The morning rose bright as a blooming bride,
Flush'd with enjoyment from her lover's side ;
So warm for winter, and so like the spring,
I thought to hear the foolish cuckoo sing ;
But see how soon the blessing turned a curse,
The weather and the ways grow worse and
    worse ;
The clouds look sullen in the faithless skies,
And winds, like jealousy, in murmurs rise ;
It thunder'd in my ears, and lighten'd in my
    eyes.
Sometimes a flatt'ring minute seem'd to smile,
But lasted but a very little while.

    Such is the morning of a married life,
But such the dirty journey with a wife.
Ibid.

CCCCVI

EPITAPH ON A YOUNG GENTLEMAN WHO DIED FOR LOVE OF A MARRIED LADY

Here lies a youth, who fell a sacrifice
In his first bloom, to fair Aurelia's eyes.

Whom shall we blame ?   Her duty was her
    guard,
And his injustice was its own reward
(If he's unjust, whose reason cannot prove
Of force enough against imperious love).
Th' aspiring youth, who scorn'd to stoop so low
To take what pity only could bestow,
Still wish'd for more, till in the fatal strife
He sunk beneath the virtue of a wife ;
Resign'd his blood to quench his guilty flame.
But crimes of love deserve a gentle name,
And I must neither praise him, nor condemn,
For I would die to be bewail'd like him,
Since she, whose piety denied to save,
Now pours her fruitless tears upon his grave.

Ibid.

THOMAS PARNELL (1679-1718)

CCCCVII

ANACREONTIC

When spring came on with fresh delight,
To cheer the soul, and charm the sight,
While easy breezes, softer rain,
And warmer suns, salute the plain ;
'Twas then, in yonder piny grove,
That Nature went to meet with Love.

   Green was her robe, and green her wreath,
Where'er she trod, 'twas green beneath ;
Where'er she turned, the pulses beat
With new recruits of genial heat ;
And in her train the birds appear,
To match for all the coming year.

   Raised on a bank where daisies grew,
And violets intermixed a blue,

She finds the boy she went to find ;
A thousand pleasures wait behind,
Aside, a thousand arrows lie,
But all unfeathered, wait to fly.
    When they met, the dame and boy,
Dancing Graces, idle Joy,
Wanton Smiles, and airy Play
Conspired to make the scene be gay ;
Love paired the birds through all the grove,
And Nature bid them sing to Love,
Sitting, hopping, fluttering, sing,
And pay their tribute from the wing,
To fledge the shafts that idly lie,
And yet unfeathered wait to fly.
    'Tis thus, when spring renews the blood,
They meet in every trembling wood,
And thrice they make the plumes agree,
And every dart they mount with three,
And every dart can boast a kind
Which suits each proper turn of mind.
    From the towering eagle's plume
The generous hearts accept their doom ;
Shot by the peacock's painted eye,
The vain and airy lovers die ;
For careful dames and frugal men,
The shafts are speckled by the hen ;
The pies and parrots deck the darts,
When prattling wins the panting hearts ;
When from the voice the passions spring,
The warbling finch affords a wing ;
Together, by the sparrow stung,
Down fall the wanton and the young ;
And fledged by geese the weapons fly,
When others love they know not why.

ON MRS. ARABELLA FERMOR LEAVING LONDON

From town fair Arabella flies :
  The beaux unpowder'd grieve ;
The rivers play before her eyes ;
The breezes, softly breathing, rise ;
  The Spring begins to live.

Her lovers swore they must expire,
  Yet quickly find their ease ;
For, as she goes, their flames retire ;
Love thrives before a nearer fire,
  Esteem by distant rays.

Yet soon the fair one will return,
  When Summer quits the plain ;
Ye rivers, pour the weeping urn,
Ye breezes, sadly sighing, mourn,
  Ye lovers, burn again.

'Tis constancy enough in love
  That nature's fairly shown :
To search for more, will fruitless prove ;
Romances, and the turtle-dove,
  The virtue boast alone.

SONG

' When thy beauty appears
In its graces and airs,
All bright as an angel new dropped from the sky ;
  At distance I gaze, and am awed by my
    fears,
  So strangely you dazzle my eye !

' But when, without art,
   Your kind thought you impart,
When your love runs in blushes through every
         vein :
   When it darts from your eyes, when it pants
         in your heart,
   Then I know you're a woman again.'

   ' There's a passion and pride
      In our sex,' she replied,
' And thus, might I gratify both, I would do :
   Still an angel appear to each lover beside,
   But still be a woman to you.'

CCCCX

AN ELEGY, TO AN OLD BEAUTY

In vain, poor nymph, to please our youthful
      sight
You sleep in cream and frontlets all the night,
Your face with patches soil, with paint repair,
Dress with gay gowns, and shade with foreign
      hair.
If truth in spite of manners must be told,
Why really, fifty-five is something old.

Once you were young ; or one, whose life's so
      long,
She might have borne my mother, tells me wrong.
And once (since Envy's dead before you die)
The women own, you played a sparkling eye,
Taught the light foot a modish little trip,
And pouted with the prettiest purple lip.

To some new charmer are the roses fled,
Which blew to damask all thy cheek with red ;
Youth calls the Graces there to fix their reign,
And airs by thousands fill their easy train.

So parting Summer bids her flowery prime
Attend the sun to dress some foreign clime,
While withering seasons in succession here
Strip the gay gardens and deform the year.

But thou (since nature bids) the world resign,
'Tis now thy daughter's daughter's time to shine.
With more address (or such as pleases more)
She runs her female exercises o'er,
Unfurls or closes, raps or turns the fan,
And smiles or blushes at the creature man.
With quicker life, as gilded coaches pass,
In sidelong courtesy she drops the glass ;
With better strength on visit-days she bears
To mount her fifty flights of ample stairs.
Her mien, her shape, her temper, eyes and
    tongue
Are sure to conquer, for the rogue is young ;
And all that's madly wild, or oddly gay,
We call it only pretty Fanny's way.

Let time that makes you homely, make you sage,
The sphere of wisdom is the sphere of age.
'Tis true, when beauty dawns with early fire,
And hears the flattering tongues of soft desire,
If not from virtue, from its gravest ways
The soul with pleasing avocation strays.
But beauty gone, 'tis easier to be wise ;
As harpers better, by the loss of eyes.

Henceforth retire, reduce your roving airs,
Haunt less the plays, and more the public
    prayers,
Reject the Mechlin head and gold brocade,
Go pray in sober Norwich crape arrayed.
Thy pendent diamonds let thy Fanny take,
(Their trembling lustre shows how much you
    shake) ;

Or bid her wear thy necklace rowed with pearl,
You'll find your Fanny an obedient girl.
So for the rest, with less encumbrance hung,
You walk through life, unmingled with the
    young ;
And view the shade and substance, as you pass
With joint endeavour trifling at the glass,
Or Folly dressed, and rambling all her days,
To meet her counterpart, and grow by praise.
Yet still sedate yourself and gravely plain ,
You neither fret nor envy at the vain.
'Twas thus, if man with woman we compare,
The wise Athenian crossed a glittering fair :
Unmoved by tongues and sights, he walked the
    place,
Through tape, toys, tinsel, gimp, perfume, and
    lace ;
Then bends from Mars's Hill his awful eyes,
And ' What a world I never want ! ' he cries ;
But cries unheard : for folly will be free.
So parts the buzzing gaudy crowd and he :
As careless he for them, as they for him ;
He wrapt in wisdom, and they whirled by whim.

CCCCXI

A NIGHT-PIECE ON DEATH

By the blue taper's trembling light,
No more I waste the wakeful night,
Intent with endless view to pore
The schoolmen and the sages o'er :
Their books from wisdom widely stray,
Or point at best the longest way.
I'll seek a readier path, and go
Where wisdom's surely taught below.

   How deep yon azure dyes the sky !
Where orbs of gold unnumbered lie,

While thro' their ranks in silver pride
The nether crescent seems to glide.
The slumb'ring breeze forgets to breathe,
The lake is smooth and clear beneath,
Where once again the spangled show
Descends to meet our eyes below.
The grounds, which on the right aspire,
In dimness from the view retire :
The left presents a place of graves,
Whose wall the silent water laves.
That steeple guides thy doubtful sight
Among the livid gleams of night.
There pass with melancholy state,
By all the solemn heaps of Fate,
And think, as softly-sad you tread
Above the venerable dead,
Time was, like thee they life possessed,
And time shall be, that thou shalt rest.

Those graves with bending osier bound
That nameless heave the crumbled ground,
Quick to the glancing thought disclose
Where toil and poverty repose.

The flat smooth stones that bear a name,
The chisel's slender help to fame,
(Which ere our set of friends decay
Their frequent steps may wear away)
A middle race of mortals own,
Men half ambitious, all unknown.

The marble tombs that rise on high,
Whose dead in vaulted arches lie,
Whose pillars swell with sculptured stones,
Arms, angels, epitaphs and bones,
These (all the poor remains of state)
Adorn the rich, or praise the great ;
Who while on earth in fame they live,
Are senseless of the fame they give.

Ha ! while I gaze, pale Cynthia fades,
The bursting earth unveils the shades !

All slow, and wan, and wrapped with shrouds,
They rise in visionary crowds,
And all with sober accent cry
Think, mortal, what it is to die.
　Now from yon black and fun'ral yew,
That bathes the charnel house with dew,
Methinks I hear a voice begin ;
(Ye ravens, cease your croaking din,
Ye tolling clocks, no time resound
O'er the long lake and midnight ground !)
It sends a peal of hollow groans,
Thus speaking from among the bones :
　' When men my scythe and darts supply,
How great a King of Fears am I !
They view me like the last of things :
They make, and then they dread, my stings.
Fools ! if you less provoked your fears,
No more my spectre-form appears,
Death's but a path that must be trod,
If man would ever pass to God :
A port of calms, a state of ease
From the rough rage of swelling seas.'
　Why then thy flowing sable stoles,
Deep pendent cypress, mourning poles,
Loose scarves to fall athwart thy weeds,
Long palls, drawn hearses, covered steeds,
And plumes of black, that as they tread,
Nod o'er the escutcheons of the dead ?
　Nor can the parted body know,
Nor wants the soul, these forms of woe :
As men who long in prison dwell,
With lamps that glimmer round the cell,
Whene'er their suffering years are run,
Spring forth to greet the glitt'ring sun :
Such joy, tho' far transcending sense,
Have pious souls at parting hence.
On earth, and in the body placed,
A few, and evil years, they waste :

But when their chains are cast aside,
See the glad scene unfolding wide,
Clap the glad wing and tower away,
And mingle with the blaze of day.

MARY MONK (　-1715)

CCCCXII

From TASSO'S 'JERUSALEM'

See how on yonder bush
　　The virgin rose
Breaks from her verdure with a blush,
And does but half her charms disclose,
Which less disclosed, the brighter still appear;
　　See how grown bolder she displays
　　Her bosom bare, see how she then decays;
　　　No more that flow'r remains,
That flow'r no more which thousand nymphs
　　　　and swains
　　　　Longed in their wreaths to wear.

　　　Thus with the day
The bud and blossom of our mortal life
　　　　Passeth away,
　　And no glad spring returns to cheer
　　　　Our drooping year.
　　Come then with eager strife
　　Gather your roses this fair morn;
　　The evening soon your day shuts in.
Gather your roses and your heads adorn,
Whilst you can love and be beloved again.

Marinda, 1716.

SONETTO

From *MARINI*

Soft Sleep, thou son of Silence and of Night,
Parent of wild imaginary forms,
Thro' whose dark quiet paths the lover oft
Straying does haply find his wished-for bliss ;
   Now ev'ry heart but mine in sweet repose
Slumbers amidst these light and airy shades :
Forsake thy closer caverns, gentle Sleep,
Thy grots Cimmerian, gloomy as my thoughts,
   Approach me with thy lov'd forgetfulness,
Bring that bright form, whereon I joy to gaze,
Let it speak comfort to my lone desires.
   But if to see the semblance of the fair
In thee's denied me, I at least shall find
The image of that death I long to meet.

Ibid.

SONG

The budding rose
That smiles on Phœbus' dawning rays,
   Then blushing glows,
And her bosom wide displays ;
   Then on the ground
Scatters her fading honours round ;
Should teach coy Sylvia this great truth,
That she should make her best of youth,
   But the disdainful She no more
Is at this emblem moved, than at our plaints
   before.

Ibid.

ON A ROMANTIC LADY

This poring over your Grand Cyrus
Must ruin you and will quite tire us.
It makes you think that an affront 'tis,
Unless your lover's an Orontes,
And courts you with a passion frantic,
In manner and in style romantic.
Now, though I count myself no zero,
I don't pretend to be an hero,
Or a by-blow of him that thunders :
Nor are you one of the seven wonders,
But a young damsel very pretty,
And your true name is Mistress Betty.

Ibid.

ON A FAVOURITE DOG

Press gently on him, earth, and all around
Ye flowers spring up, and deck th' enamelled
    ground,
Breathe forth your choicest odours, and perfume
With all your fragrant sweets his little tomb.

Ibid.

EPITAPH ON A GALLANT LADY

O'er this marble drop a tear
    Here lies fair Rosalind :
All mankind was pleased with her,
    And she with all mankind.

Ibid.

THOMAS TICKELL (1686-1740

CCCCXVIII

THE FATAL CURIOSITY

Much had I heard of fair Francelia's name,
The lavish praises of the babbler Fame ;
I thought them such, and went prepared to pry
And trace the charmer with a critic's eye,
Resolv'd to find some fault before unspied
And disappointed, if but satisfied.

Love pierced the vassal heart, that durst
   rebel
And where a judge was meant, a victim fell.
On those dear eyes, with sweet perdition gay,
I gazed at once my pride and soul away ;
All o'er I felt the luscious poison run,
And in a look the hasty conquest won.

Thus the fond moth around the taper plays,
And sports, and flutters near the treach'rous
   blaze ;
Ravished with joy he wings his eager flight,
Nor dreams of ruin in so clear a light ;
He tempts his fate, and courts a glorious doom,
A bright destruction, and a shining tomb.

Miscellany Poems, vi. 1709.

ANONYMOUS

CCCCXIX

Belinda ! see, from yonder flowers
   The bee flies loaded to its cell.
Can you perceive what it devours ?
   Are they impaired in show, or smell ?

So, though I robbed you of a kiss
   Sweeter than their ambrosial dew,
Why are you angry at my bliss ?
   Has it at all impoverished you ?

'Tis by this cunning I contrive
   In spite of your unkind reserve
To keep my famished love alive,
   Which you inhumanly would starve.

The Spectator, 1712.

ABEL EVANS (1679-1737)

CCCCXX

1713

Thank Heaven at last our wars are o'er ;
We're very wise and very poor ;
All our campaigns at last are done,
We've ended where we just begun
In perfect peace : long may it last,
And pay for all the taxes past,
Refill the Exchequer, chase our fears
And dry up all the ladies' tears. . . .

Vertumnus, 1713.

NOTES

LIST OF AUTHORS

ANONYMOUS POEMS

AND

INDEX OF FIRST LINES

NOTES

1   1-3   ' THE reader needs be told no more in commendation of these poems than that they are Mr. Waller's : a name that carries everything in it that is either great or graceful in poetry.' So says the (anonymous) Editor of Waller's poems in 1690. Each generation speaks so of its Wallers, and subsequent generations are often surprised. The pre-eminence of Waller for the men of 1660 to 1700 is to be taken into account as a fact ; it is irrelevant to exclaim or wonder ; *we* should have chosen Herrick and Milton as masters gay and grave instead of Cowley and Waller. We think so, but we might be more cautious in saying so, if we would remember that Jeffrey preferred Rogers and Campbell to Wordsworth and Shelley ; our own verdicts on elder contemporaries may be severely revised by the twenty-second century. There were subsidiary reasons for the position accorded to Waller ; he had lived into his eighties, which always impresses younger men ; he wrote verse which the ordinary intelligent man could quite easily understand (*i.e.* great), and could not help liking (*i.e.* graceful). The real reason was the reason his admirers gave, that he did something new in English poetry which English poetry and its practitioners wanted done. What that was may be negatively discovered by reading Davenant's blank verse, or Cleveland's lyrics or Chamberlayne's couplets. Positively, he gave them form which is much more than merely tune, together with diction in its way as exquisite as Milton's own and far less open to abuse in imitation. ' Compositions merely pretty have the fate of other pretty things, and are quitted in time for something useful.' This generalisation, coupled with the verdict on *Lycidas*, might remind us that Dr. Johnson is infallible on every subject except poetry.

1   1   Waller's true quality is to be seen in miniature in these lines. Their grace is individual enough to deserve the term style : a cadence thin but perfect ; a choice of words fastidiously right in its cool middle style.

M 2   361

1   2   St. James's Park has still its Stuart charm of a baroque and urban Eden, and the ghost of Waller might saunter there yet. Before hotels and golf-links came to be, men took their pleasure arti-ficially in parks and palaces. Perhaps some severe reader will need to be reminded that Waller is not *quite* serious here, and was quite willing to let John Milton write about an earlier Paradise in his own way.

2   3   The reference to Turenne's campaign in 'Alsatia' dates this poem about 1674, but what actual tourna-ment of beauty it commemorates is forgotten, with-out much loss to posterity. Mazarine 'that famous beauty and errant lady' had been in England some time, and Portsmouth's 'childish simple and baby face' had by now eclipsed brazen Cleveland (England's *Chloris* ?) ; she, indeed, had already sought consola-tion in the subsidised affection of John Churchill. After all, the amours of Charles II had a spectacular interest for not too severe contemporaries, and even Evelyn shows himself here, as always, demurely and conventionally a connoisseur. Mr. Waller (quoted by Mr. Pope) said 'that he wished everything of his burnt that did not drive a moral ' ; perhaps the moral of this poem is that three mistresses are better than one. Waller cannot be acquitted of snobbery for omitting all mention of English Nell ; ' her very impudent discourse ' often gave pain to her social superiors (such as Portsmouth)—but perhaps she was 'not a Love at all but a mere Consoler,' and her lack of social status offended the morality of the day.

Pope derives always from Waller rather than from Dryden ; these poems set the tune of *The Rape of the Lock*—there is nothing else as elegantly mock-heroic between that and them.

4   4-5   Davenant, a rather untidy playwright, is a better poet than most critics admit, and a selection of his non-dramatic verse would make a pretty book. Now and then a cadence or a phrase makes ' that notion ' of his ' being more than a poetic child of Shakespeare ' seem just possible.

4   4   Mr. Massingham has 'almost against his will,' taken a song of Davenant's dated 1662 ; for compensation I choose this delightful thing, a variant of which Mr. Ault has traced as early as 1655. It may serve as an example of the rather boisterous cavalier verse in vogue between 1650 and 1670, of which Alexander Brome and Henry Bold are efficient but not very in-teresting writers. This touches the tavern swagger to a finer note ; it looks back to Drayton, forward

  to a more genial Byron, or perhaps even to a Browning somehow made free of Theleme.

5 5 This was the song with which Moll Davis sang her way into the King's ever-sensitive heart. Like so much of Davenant's it has a faint suggestion of folk-song, and of Shakespeare's transfiguration of folk-song.

6 6 Wild's *Iter Boreale* had a topical success at the Restoration, but even the not over-fastidious Pepys could only ' like it pretty well, but not so as it was cried up.' This ' In Memoriam ' from the same volume is an exercise on a theme which employs poets, like sculptors, throughout the seventeenth century. It has its own charm, which is definitely ' Restoration ' and not Caroline; its use of the heroic couplet is interesting in comparison with Dryden's, in his welcome to the returning King. Verse form is in the air at periods of change; the lesser men exemplify it as well as the greater, because it does correspond to some change in communal outlook.

8 7-9 Some words of Dr. Elton sum up the essential quality of that honest, embittered, good Englishman, Samuel Butler. ' The *Genuine Remains* unmask for us the melancholy simplicity which is the faith and honour of Butler, as dexterity and sharpness are his graces. They show the ultimate mood of a coarse, honest and irregularly learned mind, equally malcontent with the old enthusiasms and the new substitutes. The rabble who cannot rule, the doctrinaires who scheme on paper, the Kings who return to riot, are not better one than the other.' La Rochefoucauld, himself a great lord, and an actor in civil strife, was driven into an aristocratic and disdainful loneliness of disillusion. Butler, who had seen twenty years of war between rich men from the bare tub of a poor and dependant scholar, seems rather to hint by negatives at an unexpressed positive love of England, the impossible England all poor scholars are homesick for; to Right or Left, Tory or Whig, Fascist or Socialist, offering us their Englands, we can but say almost shamefacedly ' No, not just that.' Perhaps at last the satirical melancholy of such men as Butler and his greater spiritual son, Swift, comes from an unconscious yearning, not for England, but for the City of God ; they seek for ' something in the world that is there in no satisfying measure '; they know too much of life's subtlety to repose in the philosophic complacence of Hobbes and Locke; they cannot, like some greater and many lesser men, be content with the revelation of Art. Lacking the Catholic Faith they have found the truth of one half only of Southey's

       maxim ; unkind experience has taught them ' to abate their political hopes ' ; they have not learned ' to increase their religious hopes.'

8   7   This ' mere punctilio of chance ' is not a conceit ; it is a minor example of the disconcerting classical habit of saying just what one means. ' The irony of Fate ' may be tragic as in Shakespeare, or theatrical as in Hardy ; Butler can see it as rather poor comedy.

8   8   Butler somehow missed love on earth and perhaps hardly expected it in a heaven he was not very sure about.

8   9   The rabble of the seventeenth century had at least the occasional consolation of a pennyworth of entertainment from a statesman's rope and ladder. To-day, we must weep with Mr. Belloc.

> ' Here richly, with ridiculous display
> The Politician's corpse was laid away ;
> While all of his acquaintance sneered and slanged
> I wept ; for I had longed to see him hanged.'

9 10-12 John Austin must have suffered for the Faith what every English Catholic of the seventeenth century suffered—ostracism, calumny, exaction—although ' The King's Highway of the Holy Cross ' did not lead him to disembowelment, and the palm and the crown. This life-long discipline perhaps leaves him with what Mr. Belloc has remarked in the *Devotions* of James the Second, some lack of ' the gaiety of the Faith.' His *Devotions* were printed in Paris, and subsequently demurely adapted by Anglicans ; they follow the pattern of the Breviary without using its material ; the ' Psalms ' for the respective Hours are original prose compositions. The whole, if not actually Jansenist, has, like the painting of Le Sueur, a coldness akin to Jansenism, the colour of Philippe de Champaigne's austere portrait of Sœur Angelique ; we have travelled far enough from St. Philip Neri and St. Francis de Sales.

9   10   This indeed has its own sober gaiety ; its English singing of birds and streams contrasts with the noble, silent, Latin sunrise of St. Ambrose.

10 11   This paraphrase of *Adoro te devote* changes the entranced ecstatic movement of the original to an effort of more strenuous and desolate yearning ; in the thirteenth century the Body of God consecrated every village church ; in the seventeenth a man had to go further than Robin Hood before he might ' His Saviour see.'

11 12   This is a reminiscence of the famous Spanish sonnet associated with the name of St. Francis Xavier.

PAGE NO.
11 13 The Romanesque of the eleventh century is better
translated by the Augustan idiom than by the
baroque of such a Caroline as Crashaw, or by the
stained-glass sentimentality of the nineteenth century.
Here it is left bare and strong, although it loses
something of the dew-veiled morning light of the
original.

12 14 The versions of the Breviary hymns in the Primer of
1685 supplanted the earlier (1619) versions, which
have some undefined connection with Drummond of
Hawthornden ; they gave way in their turn, to the
versions of 1706 (*see* Nos. 80-83). They were perhaps
by some Benedictine of the English congregations in
France, such as the courtly and learned Serenus
Cressy. Their English has something hesitating
and formal, as of exiles recalling a mother-tongue.
Let this version stand here in memory of those holy
and courageous gentlemen, who served the English
Mission in disguise and concealment, with the noose
and the knife always awaiting them, such as Father
Huddleston, who succoured the King at Worcester
fight, and brought him reconciliation and his
Viaticum thirty-five years after. Nor should it be
forgotten how, a century later, in Paris, they wel-
comed Samuel Johnson, as if he were an ' absent
brother ' and ' appropriated a cell to him,' and how
to-day, as at Ampleforth, they keep unspoiled that
very English tradition, English Benedictinism.

13 15-17 As Waller was the Tennyson of the Restoration,
Cowley was the Browning. His critics and his
readers pardoned some harshness in diction and in
verse, in consideration of his ' wit,' just as Browning
was pardoned in consideration of his ' thought.'
Cowley was only forty-two in 1660, and his influence
was alive until 1700 and after : (two of the five poems
Mr. Massingham gives belong to this period). And
yet ' as my Lord Rochester said, though somewhat
profanely, " Not being of God he could not stand." '
His formal legacy to his generation, as appreciated as
Waller's musical couplet, was the Pindaric Ode.
' This lax and lawless versification so much concealed
the deficiencies of the barren and flattered the
laziness of the idle, that it immediately overspread
our books of poetry.' There are hundreds of such
Odes, some tolerable in spite of their form, most
intolerable because of it ; they stand, as it might be
Lot's wife, a terrible warning to all advocates of
free verse. Cowley's own Odes, indeed, must not
be ' dismissed with unabated censure,' but it is
comely and refreshing to turn from their attempts
at grandeur to the happy and Horatian sobriety of
the *Essays.*

PAGE NO.

13 15 This extract from the *Ode to the Royal Society* may remind us that the Restoration period took science seriously, and that it was Cowley's scientific sympathy which was peculiarly modern and progressive to his readers. It will also serve to illustrate the irrepressible romanticism of the scientifically-minded, which rose to its climax two hundred years later.

15 16 Cowley had no wife; he was too intelligent a bachelor not to realise his desolate state. He who can walk with Her in his garden in the cool of the evening need not regret Eden.

16 17 The Pindaric, in Cowley's hands at least, can give such admirable fragments as this, yet they are in reality fragments of prose.

16 18-19 Watkyns was a Herefordshire man (perhaps a friend of Traherne) and a physician. With Traherne and Vaughan and Wanley he indicates the persistence of a religious tradition neither Puritan nor officially Anglican. He may remind us too, how good men, from Norfolk to Brecknock, were happy and quiet in spite of drums and tramplings.

18 20-23 Vaughan's *Thalia Rediviva* appeared in 1678, the year of the Popish Plot. As an intelligent young man observed the other day, ' There must have been two Englands at that time, and they do not seem even to touch. It is all passing strange.' But there are for ever two Englands, ' the one visible and the one invisible; and when it is winter with us, it is summer in that country.' For thirty years after 1660, however the guns boomed or the rabble shouted, Henry Vaughan walked in the light of his white vision, as any man may, in any generation, if he will learn to be holy and humble.

Three dead poets I love as if I had walked with them : I could as soon criticise hawthorn blossom, or aspens, or the harvest moon, as Vaughan and Cotton and Edward Thomas.

18 20 It has been suggested that Vaughan wrote his love-verses for a friend, perhaps in the days of Orinda and her coterie, before 1660. But I would keep this broad moon to shine in a collection of poems otherwise lighted by candelabra.

20 23 The tall tulip is the pride of the Augustan garden : Vaughan's flowers are those Matilda went gathering in

' La divina foresta spessa e viva.'

21 24-6 Andrew Lang by two of his ' epistolary parodies ' sets the Christianity of *The Compleat Angler* against the Calvinism of *The Pilgrim's Progress*, a tacit criticism of the legend which ascribes Bunyan's

PAGE NO.

greatness to Puritanism. He was indeed a good and
genial Englishman, disfigured but not poisoned by an
alien malady. Calvin, like Marx, could find whole-
hearted disciples in Scotland, scarcely in England.
No doubt there are well-wishers who would have
me haled away for saying this, as poor, cheerful
Ignorance was, to the door in the side of the hill,
where ' they heard a rumbling noise as of fire, and
a cry of some tormented and they smelt the scent of
brimstone.' The *Book for Boys and Girls* brings us
nearer the unspoiled Bunyan. Apparently his
co-religionists thought so too, for they garbled it a
good deal after his death.

21 24 Bunyan is as much a man of his generation as, say,
Sedley, in his inevitably lucid and unemphatic
diction. This lovely poem suggests the just as
delicate sobriety of Cowper's *Epitaph on a Hare*, a
century later.

23 25 Did the cuckoo's call come through some conventicle
window, bringing forbidden thoughts of Maypoles
and the village green ?

24 27-33 Painful probity would compel me to leave this Thrice
Noble, Illustrious and Excellent Princess to the
unappreciative hands of Caroline anthologists, for the
first version of these *Poems and Fancies* appeared in
1653. But, to begin with, the *Golden Treasury* series
owes her reparation for a *Selection* edited in 1872 by
one Jenkins, who found ' in every page something
offensive to a fastidious or even an ordinary healthy
taste,' which he made his excuse for textual corrup-
tions at about the rate of two a line. Secondly, in
those qualities of diction and treatment which one
calls prosaic or plain according to one's personal
prejudice, she is a Restoration poet. And to conclude, I adore her and will bite my thumb at any
other Duchess's serving-man. A princess among
poetesses, a poetess among princesses, let her walk
behind La Grande Mademoiselle, and Christina of
Sweden, with Mme. de Sévigné and Madeleine de
Scudéry, ever so little charmingly silly without loss
of dignity, as a Précieuse should be.

25 28 She is a rather embarrassing ally of Waller and
Denham and, in theory, all for good sense and reason.

26 29-30 She conceives of Nature as just such another fantastical Duchess.

27 32 This landscape may be compared with Lady Winchilsea's (another fervent Royalist lady) a generation
later ; Anne Finch had much in common with
Margaret Cavendish, if the libel of Pope and Gay has
any foundation.

PAGE NO.

28 33 How pleasant a poet the Duke was may be seen in the five poems Mr. Ault prints (for the first time) from MS.

29 34 Matthew Stevenson, a Norwich man (he probably knew Sir Thomas Browne respectfully and at a distance) is often, as here, a not unworthy follower of Herrick.   I suppose the eclipse of Herrick was due to his long banishment in Devonshire, together with the comparative bulkiness and unfortunate date of publication of *Hesperides*; it need not be ascribed to any exceptional stupidity on the part of the men of 1660, who knew and read and appreciated (more or less) Carew and Herbert, and even Milton and Vaughan.

29 35 Here is a touch of the rowdiness of the younger generation of Cavaliers, who had to keep up their spirits by discreet swaggering under the Commonwealth tyranny. He is certainly thinking, with artless simplicity, to bully Boscobella a little.

30 36 How happily impudent is this defiance of ' his pale Pippin '; he would like to make the best of both worlds, in love and out of it.

31 37 A symbolic farewell to daffodils, for a century and more ; the rest of a longish poem does not live up to its opening.

31 38 His death-date is unknown ; let us hope he saw the century out with his Brown Girl ; I should like to join with the long-dead Earl of Westmoreland, in commending his taste.

31 39-40 Thomas Howard, first Earl of Berkshire, had nine sons, three of whom help to muddle literary history. Robert (who became in later life Sir Positive Atall and a well-known figure of fun) collaborated with his great brother-in-law Dryden, and is said not to be altogether negligible as a tragic dramatist.   James wrote comedies, which it is suggested owed what success they had to the acting of Mrs. Gwynn. Edward's *Heroic Poem* was furiously ragged by all the wits and commemorated at last in the *Dunciad*. Dryden married a sister of the three and his enemies said they lived unhappily ; Mr. Saintsbury's *Dryden* (English Men of Letters) traces the development of this particular libel from Shadwell to John Richard Green.

33 41-4 Dryden's character of Zimri, Pope's deathbed scene, in the *Moral Essays*, leave little to be said of Buckingham.   In brief, Pope made the best of an apocryphal anecdote he got from the gossip of Lockier, for Buckingham did in fact die in a tenant's house, and yet his picture has imaginative truth : Buckingham

spluttered out like an exhausted lamp ; he had had
his good things and at last there was nothing left.
But in 1660 all this was far off, and those who saw
him in any company had no eyes for the others.   He
had his father's grace and beauty, and more wit than
it is good for a man to have.   He was the Leonardo
of fine gentlemen, practising *virtù* itself rather than
any specific art.   His was the outstanding figure
among that last generation of the Renaissance, which
squandered itself almost furiously in mere living,
rejecting fanatically the bourgeois ideal of safety in
both worlds.   Perhaps he reckoned poetry a little
above wine and a little below wenching ; he was too
brilliant to fail in it, and far too much the amateur
to succeed.

33   41   This appeared as a broadsheet in 1677 ; I have
attempted a composite text, using also Gildon's
Miscellany Poems of 1692 and Buckingham's *Miscellaneous Works* of 1704 ;   all three are probably
unauthorised textually.   This poem, like all the rest,
illustrates the curiously old-fashioned character of
Buckingham's verse, which is in spirit a generation
older than that of Dorset or Sedley.   There is an
obstinate churlish nobility about the *Epitaph*, and
this, together with its Whiggism, suggests Marvell in
his less lovely political phase.   Fairfax was virtuous,
but he killed in cold blood gentlemen who were
prisoners of war at Colchester in 1648.

35   42   The text of this is, by permission, that of Mr. Ault's
transcript from MS. (*Seventeenth Century Lyrics*,
page 336).

37   44   This is interesting to compare with Dryden (No. 72).
The Villiers' had known both extremities of the lady's
favours more intimately than any mere poet could,
and this would account for the more energetic
wording of the Duke's defiance.

> Ma ella s'è beata, e ciò non ode :
> Con l' altre prime creature lieta
> Volve sua spera, e beata sì gode.

38   45   Mr. Ault's text, from *The Wish*, 1697 ; the poem
appeared first in 1685.   Walter Pope was a Fellow of
Wadham in 1651, under Wilkins, and (with Wren and
Petty) one of the Oxford philosophic coterie which
helped to found the Royal Society.   It is good to
think that he had his 'wish' for thirty years.   He
chooses a well-victualled and homely Paradise, with
' the ocean at distance ' ; one concludes him a loyal
Pantagruelist.

39 46-52 Cotton was Walton's disciple in more than angling ;

he too had learned ' to be free and pleasant and civilly merry.' How generous and friendly is the prose of the *Second Part* of the *Angler*, as complete in its manliness as the *First Part* in gentleness ; how happy is the fresh Northern air, and the wind that sings in the chamber-window. Cotton's style is the expression of a spirit sturdy and simple (in the nobler sense of the word). The clear and natural choice and order of words which Coleridge praises in his verse is so far personal, and yet it is of his age and akin to the more deliberate artistry of Dryden and Prior. His love poetry I would set on the other side of 1660 ; its kindly disenchantment is late Caroline, not Restoration ; it speaks a sober quotidian comradeship ' neither too rude nor yet too cold,' and yet it has not quite forgotten how to

' Murmur soft music to her dreams.'

39 46 What can be said of this glorious thing ? It is a chalienge to painters in its ' pure white mixed with red '; it is free with the manly unanxious freedom of humanism. The Blonde would call it unrefined, and the Freudian superficial, but if we ever win a new Renaissance, this will be a pattern for our treatment of what superstitious fribbles call Sex.

41 47 The emancipation of either sex is the passing effect of some happy conjunction of the stars. Puritanism bred prudes, court ladies were brazen, but between 1650 and 1680 there must have been in quiet provincial places gentlewomen as soberly free as any generation has known ; this might be their philosophy of love.

44 48 All through the seventeenth century we were doing in verse what the Dutchmen were doing in painting. All this *Summer Day* of his is Cuyp in breadth and golden light and sober splendour—and as English as Crome.

45 49 Lamb loves this with its ' purging sunlight of pure poetry.' ' How say you, reader—do not these verses smack of the rough magnanimity of the old English vein ? Do they not fortify like a cordial ; enlarging the heart and productive of sweet blood and generous spirits, in the concoction ? '

47 50 His winter poetry rings like the walker's feet on a clear frosty day. His debts were always with him, and he must have known how the neglected poet yearns for bays ; but he had considered the inscriptions before the temple-gate of the Bottle, and heard and understood that final and certain word of its Oracle.

PAGE NO.

48 51 Two stanzas omitted.

' Which most men by their *voice* disgrace.' The only edition (1687) of Cotton's verse is posthumous and so vilely printed that none of its doubtful readings are reliable. Perhaps he wrote ' vice ' here : but perhaps he heard prophetically the noise of char-à-banc parties which no doubt his own intercession with the Powers has averted just recently from his Dovedale.

' Contented die.' He thinks of Death sometimes as he might have felt when he came home and saw the firelight through the window, on a wild Derbyshire night.

> ' When Life's sun sets, Death is a bed
> With sable curtains spread,
> Where we lie down
> To rest the weary limbs and careful head,
> And to the good a bed of down.'

50 52 This passage, with its merry echo of Wither, was found for me by one who smiles with reason at its affectionate irreverence.

51 53 The Matchless Orinda (rather than her Grace of Newcastle, who went her own princely fantastic way, without caring what mere professionals said) marks the entry of women into English literature. One need not mind her being called prosaic, since many of her successors have been poetic with so much less satisfaction to readers.

52 54 No doubt Mr. Darcy felt like this, until he experienced ' happiness such as he had probably never felt before ' when he proceeded to express himself ' as warmly and sensibly as a man violently in love can be supposed to do ' (for which this book would have supplied him with precedents). How delicious it is to see our ' weakness ' discussed by one of the ' sweet enemy,' and to imagine a conversation on the subject between Mrs. Philips, Mrs. Behn, Miss Austen and Mrs. Browning.

52 55 Mrs. Frances Boothby, a Worcestershire gentle-woman, was certainly a spinster, and one would say, a governess. *Marcelia* is a tragi-comedy, rather undistinguished except for its general severity towards males.

53 56-80 The period 1660-1700 is well called the Age of Dryden, although this was not recognised by his contemporaries until the last decade of his life. To us, looking back, his work is as dominating as St. Paul's. But Dryden was less fortunate than his great contemporary and brother in art, Wren, for he had never opportunity or inspiration for one great

single poem. This was attributed (by a loyal admirer of George IV) to the perversity of ' a ribald King and Court ' ; that king did not repress Wren, although the City Fathers did. That Dryden was indolent in this matter of a great poem (what court encouraged Dante or Milton or Wordsworth ?) is perhaps rather to be ascribed to an inhibition of that generation. Dryden and his fellow-poets were the last of the Renaissance rather than the first of a new impulse ; they were overawed by Virgil and even by Tasso. And still more, they feared being absurdly epical ; in England and in France they had *Pharronida* and *Theophila, Alaric* and *La Pucelle,* too vividly in mind. A shrinking from failure, however splendid, goes naturally with the ' classical ' desire for balance and moderation. Dryden, the humblest of great poets, would feel this more than most men. Perhaps we need not lament the failure of such projects as he did entertain ; his poem on King Arthur might have been no better than the *Idylls of the King,* his epic of the Black Prince than *The Revolt of Islam.* Perhaps there are not six great poems of great length in English, or twenty in the world. As it happened, Blackmore and Glover and Wilkie (of the *Epigoniad)* rushed in where he had feared to tread.

Perhaps it is not paradoxical to suggest that Dryden, had he known the Faith earlier, might have written a great religious poem, an orthodox *De Rerum Natura* ; hardly any other theme would have attracted his whole power. His reluctance to be sublime is like Chaucer's, for across three centuries Chaucer is his spiritual kinsman. With both there is a ' lack of high seriousness ' and a refusal to repair the lack by mere solemnity. Dryden, like Chaucer, brings to the contemplation of life a disillusioned, adult soul ; he has a sense of proportion which forbids him to look too much into his own heart, or to expatiate in an individually romantic universe. Like Chaucer, like Dante, he is interested most in the world of men without him, in their deeds and thoughts rather than his own ; like Chaucer, and unlike Dante, he is unable to synthesise this world and relate it to Eternity, and too sincere an artist to repose in anything short of complete synthesis. But yet he does attain synthesis in a style as a poet should. That magnificent verse of his, if it marches instead of flying, is yet, in its brave directness, its tireless and disciplined movement, his true and sufficient creation. There is generally truth in stock epithets, and Glorious is a title the greatest English poet of the second rank has merited.

Such a book as this could not hope to ' represent '

PAGE NO.

Dryden : my selection aims at presenting him as a
poet of the Restoration only, at suggesting his
acquiescence in and his occasional transfiguration of
the conventions of his generation. From considera-
tions of space I omit *Alexander's Feast* and the Ode to
the Memory of *Mrs. Killigrew.*

53 56-65 Dryden's songs have until recently been strangely
ignored. Mr. Saintsbury (who would count not least
among the titles of honour he merits that of a good
Drydenian) drew attention to them as long ago as
1881 in the ' English Men of Letters ' *Dryden*, which
is still the best single book on its subject. Later, in
the *History of English Prosody*, that delightful
running (and leaping) commentary on all English
poetry, he analyses their forms with many citations.
It is difficult to overpraise them ; they are the best
examples of one side of the double tradition in
Restoration lyric. The other is the smooth elegant
lyric which Carew first perfected, which owes something to French example, although the French never
did anything so good. Dryden's is in the continuously English tradition of the whole period from 1580
to 1700, which for any foreign suggestion goes beyond
France to Italy; (Purcell draws a like contrast between
French and Italian models in music). Dryden is
always English, and not the less so, because, like
Jonson, he never forgets Latin.

53   56   ' A pleasant *Grotto* discovered : in it a *Fountain*
spouting : round about it *Vazquez, Pizarro*, and other
Spaniards lying carelessly unarmed, and by them
many *Indian* Women, one of which sings the following *Song.*'

He remembers Horace and Jonson (' Slow, slow, fresh
fount ' with its ' Drop, drop, drop, drop ') but the
viola-da-gamba curve of the verse is his own.

54   57   *Asteria.* Shall I sing the Song you made of *Philocles,*
           And called it *Secret Love* ?

The measure of this is used in three songs by Dryden,
and is closely akin to that of No. 59, where it is tilted
over into definitely triple time.

' And they fall silently like dew on roses.'

This exquisite line, which might not seem out of place
in *Peacock Pie*, is yet certainly in Dryden's manner ;
it exemplifies his use of ' caesura,' of word-division
overlapping foot-division, which is one of his main
devices for varying his iambic cadence. I suppose
the musicians can define something similar in Purcell
—to the uninstructed ear there is something tanta-
lisingly Drydenian in his music.

54 58 The necromancer Nigrinus calls up the soft spirit
        Damilcar to tempt St. Catherine ' in a golden dream.'

> ' Some Astral Forms I must invoke by prayer,
> Framed all of purest atoms of the air ;
> Not in their natures simply good or ill,
> But most subservient to bad Spirit's will
> . . . In airy chariots they together ride
> And sip the dew as through the clouds they glide ;
> These are the Spirits which in love have power.'

This song makes one remember Rubens and Purcell
and Grinling Gibbons all together, for they too are
baroque and this song is a baroque triumph. The
secret of baroque is its method of veiling, but not
concealing, a plain structure with ornament.

55 59 This Serenade (' On the last evening of the Carnival ')
        suggests that Dryden in love would have been
        Petrarchan, but that cheerfulness was always break-
        ing in.

56 60 This ' old song of a Lover, that was ever quarrelling
        with his Mistress ' hits off, better than any actual
        situation in his plays, Dryden's one original contribu-
        tion to comedy, the very modern couple who are in
        love, and a little ashamed of it.

57 61 Two stanzas only of five. Mr. Saintsbury calls it
        ' The very triumph of its own peculiar style, with the
        sleepy voluptuous grace of a portrait by Lely trans-
        posed into metrical expression.' But it is better
        than anything Lely ever did, and suggests rather
        something between Giorgione and Correggio.

59 65 Dryden here almost succeeds in being ' tender ' and
        ' sublime ' together ; he must have known happy
        love to write like this in his sixties ; he has conquered
        time without wrestling. But to enquire whether it is
        personally sincere is perhaps irrelevant ; observe
        rather its artistic sincerity, how the classical method
        of natural words in natural order keeps off ex-
        travagance, and leaves the human unit undwarfed
        by height and breadth, just as great architecture
        does.

60 66 He had come to the end of his life and his century.
        It had been one of the greatest of European centuries,
        but, throughout, its achievement had something
        feverish or melancholy. Its ' wars brought nothing
        about '—the Thirty Years' War, the Great Rebellion,
        the Fronde, the ' War of the League of Augsburg,'
        all had something futile about them and ended in
        draws. The ' Great Age ' was over in a generation
        in France. Dutch painting had died, Italy and
        Spain had burned out. In England Dryden could

see nothing to hearten him : in politics there was only wrangling and treachery under the cold eye of the Dutchman ; in literature Congreve would lay aside the laurel his master bequeaths him. And so Dryden lets Momus laugh off the play, and 'cousin Swift' may speak the epilogue in prose.

65   67   This is perhaps the topmost peak of the Heroic mood in English, and who shall say it is not heroic in the non-technical sense of the word ?   After all, it does but express the practice of all decent men, and its 'false' emphasis (as some would call it) is only an artistic device natural to a generation that feared, perhaps unduly, (like our own) to be consciously heroic off the stage.

65   68   Dryden was always conscious of the vanity of human achievement ; he was conscious too of its real great-ness.   He never was able to reconcile both, as the greatest can, but he can express one or the other magnificently.

66   69   A recent masterly exposition of *All for Love* by Mr. Dobree, indicates that criticism has come at last to understand the true and individual greatness of Dryden's greatest play.   These extracts suggest what a great classical tragic form we might have evolved if Dryden had found successors; it has 'form' in both senses, a verse at once sober and noble, a perception of moral necessity that can dispense with Ironies and Pities.

67   72   The last forty lines of *The Twenty-ninth Ode of the Third Book of Horace paraphrased in Pindaric Verse.* It is not Horatian, if this be an objection to so great an original form.   Dryden, one might say, only translated Lucretius ; his happy essays with other poets are always imitations or paraphrases ; one never forgets that he, and not Chaucer or Virgil, is the poet.

The verse of this is unsurpassable ; the best image of Dryden's verse is, I often think, the run and the action of a great bowler—the ordered and rhythmic energy of the stride, the balanced check, and the follow-through.

69   73   Dryden is hardly flattering or exaggerating in this magnificent address of friendship ; Congreve might have done anything, if some Whiggish malaria had not chilled him in his thirties.   The chronology of 'old Romano' is sadly out, but the comparison of Congreve to Raphael is right enough.   What a 'great hand' every couplet of this shows !

71   74   No English poet is more splendidly entombed than poor Oldham here.   And what great man of letters

anywhere has been so loyal to his craft, so generous to younger men, as Dryden was ?

72 75 *Eleonora*, like *An Anatomy of the World*, was an attempt ' to describe the Idea of a Woman.' Just as Castlemaine and Portsmouth were not typical, so such holy women as Lady Abingdon and Margaret Godolphin were exceptional, then as now. This poem, with No. 6 and No. 391, serves to illustrate the monumental sculpture of the period.

73 76 John Graham and John Churchill were born within a year, one for the silver bullet at Killiecrankie and the red heaven of Mars, the other for the tears of dotage and Antenora (as far as men may judge). Marlborough might well have given Blenheim and his millions, and even his laurels, to die as Dundee died, or Talmash on the beach at Brest, or Jeb Stuart singing in Virginia. The glorious ghost of Montrose led the other clearly out of that tangle of things, where politicians cheat soldiers, and knights are stoned. What should an old and careworn poet do but weep for dead chivalry, while Dutch guards gave the word at Whitehall ?

73 77 That a popular dramatist should turn to religious controversy in verse was not so surprising in the seventeenth century as it would be now. Dryden's elders, from Donne and Jonson to Corneille and Milton, prove that poets could not be silent as to matters of faith.

The solemn cadence of the opening of *Religio Laici* marks some spiritual experience not yet fully apprehended by the poet.

> ' La gloria di colui che tutto move
> Per l'universa penetra, e risplende
> In una parte più, e meno altrove.'

Dryden, amidst his cheerful, busy life, had seen some ray of that ' supernatural Light.' It led him first to the comfortable conclusion of *Religio Laici*, and then further and by steeper roads.

74 78-80 M. Cazamian, in that admirable *Histoire de la littéra-ture anglaise* which supersedes our vernacular manuals, says, concisely as usual, all that should be said about the greatness of *The Hind and the Panther*. ' La netteté de la pensée, l'energie directe de l'expression, une allure aisée, la qualité robuste des maximes que le poète frappe, en se jouant, le rhythme régulier sans monotonie ; des épisodes gracieux ou plaisants, une fraîcheur et comme une naïveté d'esprit sincère, une dialectique nerveuse et subtile, que le cadence poétique soutient, et qui n'en paraît pas gênée, font de cette œuvre inégale une des expressions maîtresses du génie de Dryden.'

PAGE NO.

74   78   Dryden is always inspired by his sense of history, and he sees the Church against the background of her centuries.

75   79   Dryden, like his royal master, became a Catholic from intellectual conviction; like him, too, he was prepared to sacrifice much. Conversion does not necessarily make a man a saint, and yet such lines as these prove that his was not only intellectual.

75 80-83 The translation of the *Veni Creator* was printed by Dryden himself, and a tradition of respectable antiquity asserts that (like Racine) he translated the Breviary hymns on the injunction of his director. The question of his authorship of the Hymns in the *Primer* of 1706 has been much discussed ; internal evidence, for what it is worth, goes to support tradition. Dryden's hand in translation is indeed so characteristic that, for once, it is fair to ask whose they can be, if not his. Mr. Sargeaunt's caution as to the textual immoralities of the editors of hymn-books must of course be borne in mind, but the refusal to recognise Dryden's authorship can often be ascribed to a sub-conscious reluctance to recognise his active Catholicism.

78   83   Nothing could be more unlike the honeyed languid cadences of the original than this is ; this unlikeness enhances the beauty and personal intensity of the translation.

80   84   The first version of the *Dies Irae*, published with Roscommon's name in *Miscellanea Sacra*, 1696, is so much feebler than the posthumous version of 1717, as to lend colour to Orby Shipley's suggestion of at least a revision by Dryden.

           Perhaps, as Dr. Elton suggests, the men of the Augustan age were not conscious of the mystery and awe of ' the four last things.' That they thought of the Last Judgment, four poems in this book testify ; though, indeed, they thought of it as general rather than particular, as almost political. But at least they thought of it as rational and inevitable ; only sentimental fallacies lead critics to regard such an attitude as imperfectly religious. It is no unworthy or insensitive outlook on life and death which turns for its expression to this greatest of all Latin hymns. The *Dies Irae* was remembered in the eighteenth century when so much else was forgotten. Johnson, that strong and tender and holy man, would repeat it with uncontrollable tears and Scott whispered it on his death-bed.

82   85   It is amusing to remember that, while Restoration

poets generally are condemned with all splendours of Pecksniffian rhetoric for their immorality, Roscommon is sneered at for being moral.

84 86-9 Wanley was worthy of the patient editing Mr. Martin has given his MS. To regard him as a survival is to miss his significance. He is a religious poet of the sixteen-sixties, as typical and as entitled to his chronological position as Etherege or Cotton.

84 86 Notice in this poem the struggle between imagination and the new scientific outlook. Wanley, like some even of our own contemporaries, finds difficulty in reconciling the spiritual mystery of the Resurrection with the material facts retailed by anatomists. And yet he is poet enough to understand that the impossible is true, and by way of his difficulties to come to something like Sir Thomas Browne's pre-scientific certainty, 'ready to be anything in the ecstasy of being ever.'

86 89 Is this the first occurrence of the ' York and Lancaster ' conceit ? Surely some Jacobean thought of it. Cf. Dryden :

> ' O daughter of the Rose, whose cheeks unite
> The differing titles of the red and white
> ... Whose face is Paradise, but fenced from sin.'

87 90-2 I have to confess that I shirked Thomas Ken. The four solid volumes of his *Poetical Works* (1721) drove me in cowardice to a little selection published anonymously in 1857. Ken was a Non-Juror (as honest men were quaintly called in his later years) and what is much more, he was a holy man. But like so many holy men, he thought poetry merely a pleasant change from prose, and surprisingly easy to write when you got the knack of it ; hence the four unreadable volumes.

88 91 Sacramental doctrine persisted in the Church of England even during the Age of Reason (of this Wickham Legg in his *English Church Life* gives much evidence). The wording of these verses, here and there, owes something to the prayers of the Missal, but the whole is the expression of personal and real spiritual experience. ' Languor and ardours ' might have been outside the experience of Tillotson or Burnet, but quiet souls like Ken and Vaughan knew passion and ecstasy.

' Green trees of life and living springs.'

88 92 The three famous hymns must be excluded from any censure, however mild, of Ken's poetry ; none since the ferial hymns of the Breviary, of Prudentius and the anonymous ' Ambrosians ' of the sixth century.

have so expressed the quotidian sobriety and patience and hope and grace of a holy life.

The morning and evening hymns are omitted from lack of room ; but let their peace and purity be remembered in any ' reconstruction ' of that age. For the tangled question of the texts see Julian's *Dictionary of Hymnology* ; I have preferred the revised (1709) text of the Midnight Hymn, but the earlier (1695) texts of the others have the greater beauty.

90 93-6   Traherne, six years younger than Dryden, is called ' a belated Caroline ' by literary historians who like everything fitted into neat frames.   He is a poet of his own generation, refusing to lose himself in a mystery, striving to make his perception of reality consonant with reason, articulate, fully conscious in the narrower sense of consciousness.   This is what makes him prosaic in verse ; his prose is poetic to the verge of prettiness ; the discipline of verse-pattern kept his thought truer to itself.

94 94   This vision or rather dream of a regenerated Europe shines with a happy health Puritanism could never have understood.   It is nearer William Morris than Bunyan.

98 95   How the bells ring out here !   It is almost ' Corinna's going to Church.'   We have perhaps forgotten (Traherne remembered) that from 1644 to 1659 the observance of Christmas, at home or in church, was forbidden by the Parliament.   Evelyn was arrested in church on Christmas Day, 1657, and bullied a good deal.

101 96   Wordsworth (who did indeed what Traherne tried to do) is closer to Traherne than to Vaughan.   To Wordsworth, as to Traherne, the true world is before our eyes if we could learn to look into it as it is mirrored in still water.   Vaughan looked through things, not into them ; he saw by a light beyond sun or star.

104 97-8   ' Lame Mephibosheth, the wizard's son,' had fallen into worse company when he blasphemed the Lord's Anointed, and more dangerously, his laureate.   The ' Wizard ' himself, John Pordage, was a harmless Theosophist, given over to geometrical diagrams of the Eternal, after the manner of his sect.   He was founder of the ' Philadelphians ' and the master of Jane Lead, whose *Fountain of Gardens*, 1696, is a too complacent record of exclusive revelations, not without its charm.   Young Samuel was following a more

excellent way in his *Poems,* but later on he gave himself over to Whiggery.

104 97   This poem might almost be one Herrick had forgotten when collecting *Hesperides.* ' The flowery Napææ ' are Virgilian.

> ' tu munera supplex
> tende petens pacem et facilis venerare Napæas.'

Dryden calls them ' the soft Napæan race.' They were the nymphs Eurydice danced with under the trees, ' Sweet sisters of the grove,' (R. D. Blackmore). How ingeniously the poet invokes another power to drive the beloved home again ; a lover may watch the wind kiss his lady without immedicable jealousy.

106 100-6   Two respectable critics (independently, no doubt, and after careful study) have pronounced Flatman a poetaster ; others have tasted the innocent joy of hinting at a pun without making it. Snobbery persists in travelling through English literature with a Baedeker, looking only at starred items. Even a minor poet has his own positive goodness ; St. James indeed distinguishes between ' every good gift ' and ' every perfect gift,' but he is quite positive that all are ' from above.' If you miss Flatman's ' good gift ' you miss something that Dryden, that Shakespeare himself, cannot give you.

106 100   He was a miniature-painter : his pen is following his brush in this first stanza.

108 102   ' Clouds ' and ' the sun ' in ll. 16-7 are readings given by Mr. Saintsbury from a MS. of 1659. The 1674 text is ' the stars ' and ' Phoebus.' Perhaps Flatman did not at heart wish to fly very high ; a suburb of the New Jerusalem will content poor minor poets.

108 103   Mr. Saintsbury points out that Ken and Flatman were at Winchester and New College together, and that Ken certainly took at least hints from this and Flatman's *Hymn for the Morning.* See also Sir Thomas Browne's (earlier) evening hymn (*Seventeenth Century Verse,* No. 21) ; Browne was at Winchester too. Flatman's hymn was set to music and no doubt sung. The happy obscure currents of Anglican tradition during the period have never been sufficiently explored.

110 105   Pope, who (like Wordsworth) looked everywhere for good things, used this in his once well-known *Dying Christian.* Flatman thought often of Death ; that habit is one of the ' faint survivals of the Renaissance ' which Mr. Saintsbury rather grudgingly allows

his period.   But Flatman here reminds one from afar of Villon.

' Puis sue, Dieu scet quelle sueur ! '

110 106   Here again it is perhaps not fanciful to suggest that there is something of a fifteenth-century North European tradition, untouched by the Renaissance, some hint of the Danse Macabre and *Everyman*. It is in minor artists that such survivals are oftenest found.

113 107   I had missed this, and owe it to Mr. Hamilton's *Soul of Wit* ; nothing else in *Emblems of Love* is good, and the book is an amusing contrast to Mr. Abercrombie's great poem.

Professor Mario Praz has rather unkindly revealed in detail the indebtedness of Ayres to Italian and Spanish authors.   Ayres admits that his *Lyric Poems* are ' made in imitation of the Italians ' and that ' many ' are translations.   Alas, they are all translations ; but he does them very prettily, and he recalls the often ignored fact that English poets read and imitated the Italians right to the end of the century.

113 108   ' Possibly an adaptation of Achillini's " Bellissima Mendicà ' " (The Fair Beggar—*Seventeenth Century Verse*, No. 1), ' to the theme of Bellissima Spiritata of the same poet ' (Praz).   But Ayres must be given credit for remembering Ophelia, and Fletcher's Alinda, and the *Mad Maid's Song*.

114 109   A translation from Preti, another disciple of the great Marino, the contemporary and Italian counterpart of Gongora and Donne.   Here, as elsewhere, Ayres reminds one faintly and elusively of Mr. W. H. Davies, the thin strings of his lute echoing that poignant clear fluting.

115 110   Mr. Belloc has urged upon us greater courtesy to the sensitive frog, possibly without realising that he is the teetotaller's totem, and can reasonably be called names.

116 111   Mr. Ault thinks this song more probably Dryden's ; the measure is Dryden's, but the cadence is harsher. In any case, it is good to recall the honoured name of Betterton, to whom Rochester's Apollo, in *The Trial of the Poets*, awards the bays, because

' His wit had most worth and modesty in't,
For he had writ plays, yet ne'er came in print.'

The Restoration song-writers, even the lesser and anonymous, had a knack, or rather a sound method,

of writing words for music. Purcell owed something
to his poets, who were perfectly in touch with his
splendidly straightforward approach, his glorifica-
tion of speech in song. The musicians may perhaps
explain the subtle change in the next century, which
led at last down to Haynes Bayly and his commercial
disciples of to-day. Purcell set this song, and Miss
Sylvia Nelis singing his tune in *The Beggar's Opera* is
a delicious memory.

117 112-19 With Etherege begin the 'Restoration lyrists' of
accepted tradition, 'the mob of gentlemen who wrote
with ease ' (this phrase of Pope's refers to ' the wits
of either Charles's days ' and brackets Sedley with
Carew and Sprat). In no other period of English
literature are the Gentlemen so nearly a match for
the Players. Already we have had a Duchess, a
Duke, and an Earl. We have two more Dukes to
come, half-a-dozen other peers, a countess, and
baronets, knights, ambassadors, members of parliament, and unnamed persons of quality in a crowd.
Many of them may have been from a middle-aged,
middle-class point of view ' deboshed courtiers,' or
as Milton, perfectly unsympathetic to his juniors,
called them

' the sons
Of Belial, flown with insolence and wine.'

but at least they wrote verse, and often good verse.
Never since has it been usual for the Mohock, the
Corinthian, the swell, the blood, to turn a song as an
obviously elegant and gentlemanlike exercise. It
would be vain to expect from any member of the
present House of Peers a poem as intense as one of
Rochester's, from any member of the present House
of Commons, a ' copy of verses ' as airy as one of
Sedley's. Somehow the more moral and morose
critics contrive to make this too a reproach to ' good
King Charles's golden days.'

Here, too, begin the troubles of an anthologist ;
their songs passed lightly from hand to hand

' Like twinkling stars the miscellanies o'er.'

and their ' Works ' were collected, if at all, after many
years and on dubious tradition. Some person of
improbable learning, industry, energy and leisure
combined, might analyse for us the four miscellanies
of 1672-3, *A Collection of Poems, New Court Songs,
Covent Garden Drollery* and *Methinks the Poor Town*.
All these were edited (with a pitchfork) by men in
touch with the Dorset-Etherege-Sedley set but, except
for an impression that the first has a strong flavour of
Etherege and Sedley, the last of Dorset, I have been
unable to come to any conclusions.

118 112   ' Gentle George ' is the lightest and cleverest of this group. Rochester, who was infallible when he was sober, hits off the right adjectives:

> ' Etherege writes airy songs and soft lampoons
> The best of any man.'

He is nearest ' natural easy Suckling ' as Sedley is nearest Carew. Why—I ask it in blameless ignorance—is the quality of these men ascribed to French influence ? They had better teachers at home. What Frenchman wrote as well as they ? Voiture is quite apart, even within the narrow sphere of his admirable perfection. I cannot pretend, for instance, to a thorough knowledge of the work of Montausier (who might have been Alceste) or of Charleval (who might have been Oronte), but Oronte's sonnet is apparently not an unfair sample of what the noble amateurs of France wrote and admired. Etherege and Dorset, Sedley and Rochester, owed nothing to these men, and still less to the little abbés and scribblers and lapdogs whom Boileau kicked.

Etherege's ' sense, fancy, judgment and wit ' (to quote Rochester once more) are best tasted in the graceful prose of his plays ; his personal charm shines through his songs. He was an efficient and honourable diplomat, and he did not sell his loyalty in 1688. Wherever he lies, the earth is light upon his happy good-nature.

118 114   His song flutters about her lips like a butterfly ; he affects too an engaging touch of Bertie Wooster (' if you know what I mean ') and how admirably he makes it musical!

119 115   He might have said of himself, with Boswell, that ' he had thought a great deal more than anyone supposed.' Compare this song with Rochester's (No. 206) : that is Lucretian, this Horatian.

119 116   A defect in Restoration eyes is that they never saw children ; even Marvell thought of little T. C. as grown up ; Etherege's little lady, like Sedley's, moves stiffly in a long gown and ' early glories ' already, although her English roses outshine the pale Infantas of Velazquez. As for little boys, except for a stray Cupid now and then, they vanish from English literature until Sterne ; how far has Europe travelled from Donatello's Cantoria, and the sturdy shouting of young Gargantua !

120 117   He remembered Virgil, Eclogue III.

> ' Triste lupus stabulis, maturis frugibus imbres,
> Arboribus venti, nobis Amaryllidis irae.'

The general sentiment recalls one of Mr. Jacob's

> skippers, who, being engaged to two ladies at once, sighs to the night-watchman ' Why was wimmen made ? Wot good are they ? Fancy 'ow bright and 'appy we should all be without 'em.'

120 118 How tender are the last lines ! ' Callous ' and ' libertine ' are favourite words with some critics, but few of these poets have missed the honey of bitter-sweet love. ' He whom the Cyprian loves not, knows not what roses her flowers are.'

121 119   ' Abstinence snows sand all over
    The ruddy limbs and flaming hair,
   But Desire gratified
    Plants fruits of life and beauty there.'

Blake, who could enjoy Aphra Behn, understood the virtue of Restoration love-poetry. His ' enough or too much ! ' was a hard saying to the nineteenth century.

122 120-7 Dorset's poems have never been properly collected or edited, which fact must furnish my excuse for playing at the perilous game of ascription. ' He cared not what became of them though everybody else did.' How highly his contemporaries rated his verse may be gathered from what Wolseley, that gallant squire of Rochester's, says about them. ' The severest critic might say, as some have done, that there is not altogether so much strength and closeness in My Lord's (Rochester's) style as in that of one of his friends : a person of great quality and worth, whom I think it not proper yet to name, because he has never yet publicly owned any of his writings, though none have been more generally or more justly admired.' And Pope said ' Rochester has neither so much delicacy or exactness as Lord Dorset.'

As to his character and personality there is uniform tradition ; even when he played the fool (and worse) with Sedley, the scandalmongers of the day pardoned him ; Rochester grudgingly said ' that he did not know how it was, but my Lord Dorset might do anything, yet was never to blame.' Prior, in a dedication to Dorset's son, drew his character ' largely and elegantly ' and whatever deduction must be made for flattery, there remains the portrait of a great and happy gentleman. Horace Walpole (as quoted by Hayward in his *Rochester*) sums up the tradition about Dorset. ' He was the finest gentleman in the voluptuous court of Charles II and in the gloomy one of King William. He had as much wit as his first Master, or his contemporaries, Buckingham and Rochester, without the Royal want of feeling, the Duke's want of principles, or the Earl's want of thought. It was not that he was free from the failings of humanity, but he had the tenderness of it too, which made everybody excuse whom everybody loved.' Add to all this his generosity—' he was the support of all the poets of his time.'

His work cannot be compared seriously with that of Rochester, who is almost great ; Dorset is a very complete and entirely charming minor poet. If this is allowed for there need be no deduction from the panegyric of his greater pupil Prior. ' His thought was always new, and the expression of it so particularly happy, that anybody knew immediately it could only be my Lord Dorset's ; and yet it was so easy that everybody was ready to imagine himself capable of writing it. There is a lustre in his verses, like that of the sun in Claude Lorraine's landscape ; it looks natural and is inimitable.'

122 120 Mr. Ault's text, from a MS. first transcribed by him. This delicious song, rocking like a ship on a blue sea, recalls the courage behind Restoration insolence. All through this period there is the distant thunder of guns at sea, ' like swallows in a chimney,' as Dryden and his friends heard it, from the Duke of York and stout old Monk in the North Sea to Benbow in the West Indies forty years later.

124 121 This poem charmed its own day ; Prior learned its tripping tune, and the eighteenth century never forgot it. Even Prior never bettered the run and music of this, so light and athletic ; it sets the heart leaping, as Bess herself did.

125 122 Mr. Saintsbury draws attention to the prosodic merit of ' miserably.' Whatever it is fashionable to say about accents and stresses, such felicities as these depend upon foot-construction and the spanning or breaking of the foot by the word.

126 123 This song ' by a Person of Honour ' is nowhere ascribed to Dorset. It seems to me to have his natural sunshine all over it ; others may think otherwise.

127 124 This (another ascription suggested only) was printed as Rochester's in 1707 ; but when was love ' gentle ' or ' quiet ' to that brother of Catullus ?

128 125 Mr. Ault's text from MS. I think it is certainly Dorset's ; ' gentle love ' is almost his signature. ' Delicacy and strength . . . the wit of Petronius in the softness of Tibullus,' as Prior says of him.

128 126 Dorinda was Lady Dorchester, Sedley's daughter, one of the ugly mistresses James II took ' for a penance.' But James did true penance in exile ; see Mr. Belloc's *James II* on this seventeenth-century paradox of the unchaste devout man, which used to perplex

N

PAGE NO.

Victorians so much more than the paradox of the rebellious devout man, or of the avaricious devout man. Dorset and James II were antipathetic, except perhaps on a quarter-deck in action. But I like Dorset so much that I cannot blame him for conniving at the Dutch Invasion ; *he* could ' do anything.'

129 127   The third of the ascriptions to Dorset I have risked. No one will miss the close resemblance to *Jinny the Just* (No. 359). It might be Prior's first sketch for this, or the poem that suggested it to him.

130 128-38   Sedley is the typical Restoration fine gentleman— ' everything that an English gentleman could be ' as an eighteenth-century admirer said ; perhaps it is not surprising that his whole generation is often credited with his virtues and debited with his vices. He was witty and elegant and handsome, and yet it is impossible to like him ; he had not Rochester's black blood or Mulgrave's brutality : he was too cautious to be anything but a wit and a fine gentleman. He turned active Whig after 1685 and was a person of some little political importance. He is so cold-blooded that one feels no compunction in handing over his reputation to amateurs of Restoration ' hollowness ' and ' insincerity.' His verse too is typical of himself in its smooth accomplishment : he achieves an ideal negatively, by avoiding faults. But he achieves in verse, as in life, a gesture, a manner, an exquisitely poised convention. He must be postponed to Etherege, to Dorset, and of course, to Rochester : and yet, if you can be content with poems instead of poetry, you can hardly better his. He is like his Dutch contemporaries in genre, Mieris or Netscher, beside and below Vermeer and de Hooch.

130 128   For Sedley the stars are merely ' obliging ' enough to make ' night look clear.'

131 130   The use of the heroic couplet here, and the general approach of the poem to its theme, recall Randolph and Cartwright ; the break in English poetry about 1660 is not so decided as some suggest ; Sedley too is a grandson of Ben.

132 131   My respected and respectable predecessor, Palgrave, thought this poem moral enough for his *Golden Treasury*. It is indeed immoral and an offence against Love such as is rare in this age of conscious love-technique. From Plato to Don Quixote no lover would care to give reasons for his love—and such reasons as these ! Love, like Religion, must be an act of Faith ; a man should not presume to bargain his way into either Heaven by buying a certainty.

132 132   This is, of course, a triumph and has been taken for the central lyric of the period. And yet, as has been observed, it falls off continuously from the first couplet, which is one of those amazing pieces of luck a merely competent poet may get once in a lifetime. The poem as a whole lacks ' fundamental brainwork '; the marine metaphor is dropped after the third stanza, two more quite unconnected metaphors drift in, and it finishes anyhow.

135 136   A lovely opening is again frittered away to commonplace.

136 137   This simpers a little ; it has an eighteenth-century note of self-consciousness, foreign to this period.

136 138   Whatever one says against Sedley, his elegance does afflict one with envy. How well, within his limits, he does what he set out to do. He is an indubitable Little Master.'

137 139-58   I saw someone the other day refer to Restoration miscellanies as ' dunghills ' ; if they are, I praise Heaven my moral nose is not so sensitive as to mind their honest farmyard smell. Amidst much rubbish, they contain much that is pleasant, and (I hope some readers at least will think) a little that is more than merely pleasant.

137 139   *Westminster Drollery* has a general air of Cavalier rowdiness, after the manner of Alexander Brome. This particular poem is on the way from the rowdy to the Heroic ; it combines hints from Marvell and Davenant in a manly and loverlike way.

138 140   The trochaic cadence (Sedley has it in No. 134) is uncommon enough to be noticed when it does occur, although here the poet is not happy with it. There is a rare muddle of metaphors in the middle, but a certain ramshackle nobility about the poem as a whole.

140 142   This has been attributed to old Rowley himself (see Mr. Ault's note) on evidence which it would be exaggeration to call slender. It might have been written on his behalf, for he must often have suffered the pains of the third stanza. Line 9 was perhaps the inspiration of a later anonymous poet.

141 143   I should like to risk the ascription of this to Dorset too ; the dancing sea-shining movement, and the frame of mind are alike his.

142 145   This is almost alone in its folk-song quality, but it is at least arguable that English folk-song generally took and kept until its extinction a colouring of its diction from the period 1660-1700. There is a difference between the fiddle-tune of this and the

bagpipe drone of ' Staines Morris ' a half-century before. The Maypoles were set up again in 1660, and the Puritans gnashed their teeth impotently, yet they won in the end.

> ' Where's Troy, and where's the Maypole in the
> Strand ? '

Bell's *Songs of the Peasantry of England* gives another stanza good enough to sing with the others :

> ' Goodnight ' says Harry, ' Goodnight ' says Mary,
> ' Goodnight ' says Dolly to John,
> ' Goodnight ' says Sue, ' Goodnight ' says Hugh,
> ' Goodnight ' says everyone.
> Some ran, some went, some stayed,
> Some dallied by the way,
> And bound themselves by kisses twelve to meet
> next holiday.

144 146 This sounds a little harsh after Caroline exercises in the same manner, but it has a compensating solidity, and the refrain is a gem and a joy.

145 147 The Restoration men had a surprising taste for rhymed Latin verse : Henry Bold, not a bad poet in English, published a book of lyrical translations in measures reminiscent of the Goliards, and there are others. So I should not be surprised if the writer of this had seen a poem (German, perhaps, of the seventeenth century) included by Trench in his *Sacred Latin Poetry,* ' although it is indeed little more than a mere worldling's lamentation at leaving a world which he knows he has abused, and would willingly if he might, have continued still longer to abuse.'

> Parendum est, cedendum est,
> Claudenda vitae scena ;
> Est jacta sors, me vocat mors,
> Haec hora est postrema ;
> Valete res, valete spes ;
> Sic finit cantilena.

(and eleven more stanzas) ; the matter is perhaps a commonplace, but the internal and double rhymes in both are suggestive.

146 148 Another more commonplace essay in triple-measure ; the twang of the guitar has supplanted the sighing of Wyatt's lute.

147 149-51 *Covent Garden Drollery* is for the light-hearted, not for ' the grave or the precise ones.' It claims Martial's and Herrick's allowance :

> ' To read my book the virgin shy
> May blush while Brutus standeth by,
> But when he's gone, read through what's writ
> And never stain a cheek for it.'

148 151 This poem is also in *Methinks the Poor Town,* with
several variants, of which the most important is in
the final line:

   ' I will try her again in a second amour.'

149 152-8 *Methinks the Poor Town,* ' a Collection of all the New
Songs that are Generally Sung either at the Court or
the Theatre,' is perhaps the prettiest of all the
strictly Restoration Miscellanies. It takes its title
and its keynote from Dorset's rippling laughter
(No. 121).

149 152 The stream, the shade, the Cupid, here make up a
charming landscape, as if Fragonard had been
Poussin's pupil.

151 155 The summary and the justification of all these songs.

152 157-8 The ladies then were not too coy to admit that they
also were in love ; for two centuries after they had
to keep up the affectation of not knowing or of not
caring ; perhaps we have come back nowadays to the
Restoration equality of the sexes. Are there still
clowns who would suggest that it was improper of
these warm-hearted girls to sing their love-secrets ?

153 159 A certain N.C. was apparently the sole writer of
Bristol Drollery ; he apologises for his ' fresh country
Muse ' but the whole book is as sweet as Gloucester-
shire air.

154 160 How happily and naturally does this express what
every lover knows ; he accepts and rejoices in love
like forenoon sunshine.

154 161 He was too humble a lover, and he was going to lose
Phyllis. The date and ' the length of the street '
colour the picture—the chill clear Bristol day, the
maiden as light and cold as the wind.

155 162 This is a triumph of combined unselfishness and
optimism.

156 163 A perfect example of the Restoration middle style.
Its gay disillusion would have been spoiled earlier by
extravagance and later by sentimentality.

157 164-9 Aphra Behn is the first professional woman of letters
in England ; her male colleagues regarded her, not as
a phœnix or a portent, but as a rival or a friend.
Literary cliques abused each in their obscure and
shifting rivalries, and Aphra too was maligned,
as sex-equality would demand ; one result of these
contemporary blackguardings is much edifying
shaking of heads by innocent literary historians.
Mrs. Behn was no chaster than her critics ; her
earlier adventures and her establishment with the
ambiguous and transitory Mr. Behn have some air of

Roxana; but she can never be accused of meanness or treachery. An idle sneer of Pope's was a convenient basis for later judgments, and some bright young ladies of to-day may be treated similarly some other day. As a matter of fact, her work (like theirs) is shot with an impulsive and sentimental virtuousness which is feminine in the derogatory sense of the word.

Her reputation has perhaps done a service to her poetry, which, though charming, hardly deserves the position it is sometimes given. In lyric she is below Dorset and Sedley, to say nothing of Dryden and Rochester. She has an engaging warmth and enthusiasm, easily mistaken for true lyric rapture and cry; her facility makes her easier to read, but harder to remember, than less attractive contemporaries. It is only comparatively that she must be depreciated thus; the Restoration discipline often controls her flights and gives them poise and direction.

157 164-5 These are from her translation of the two parts of *La Montre* (1666-71) of Balthasar de Bonnecorse, a minor Frenchman and one of Boileau's butts. She probably improved upon her original, for *The Lover's Watch* and *The Lady's Looking Glass* are delicious; they would make a pretty reprint, and, if this is a merit to-day, they are very and consistently proper. She writes the easy lucid prose of her day, with dainty differences proper to her theme; the poems, these and others, are as pretty as any poetess could write; they deserve the recurrent epithets of *The Looking Glass*—' natural ' and ' charming.'

158 166 One would be loath to call this poem overpraised, and yet its magnificence is rather that of the prima-donna. The ' did ' of line 3 is ' not a mere expletive ' as Mr. Saintsbury points out; and how admirable are the open vowels of line 8.

158 167 The glow-worm light of this from afar suggests Blake; he knew Mrs. Behn, at least from the extracts in Bysslie's *Art of Poetry.*

160 168 There is evidence for the ascription of this to a Mr. Ouseley, but a lady should have the benefit of any doubt.

160 169 This lights up the rambling prose of *Lycidus* wonderfully : Byron might have been proud to have written it. How well quatrain and couplet are welded together! Her characteristic open vowels make music in lines 5 and 13.

161 170-5 Nothing seems to be known about ' Ephelia '; Sir Edmund Gosse's suggestion that she was a daughter

of Katherine Philips is unsupported, and she certainly
was not the Lady Worsley who corresponded with
Lady Winchilsea under that name. Robert Gould
in a foul-mouthed lampoon calls her

> ' Ephelia !   Poor Ephelia !   ragged jilt '

and from other allusions it seems that her contemporaries knew all about her. Her ' J. G.' behaved
badly to her, and went to Africa (Tangiers, I suppose).
Apart from the novel-interest of her book, it proves
that the Restoration verse-manner (called ' prosaic ')
lends itself to a plain love-story without conven-
tionality or sentimentality, and yet keeps it at the
level of poetry. The women of this generation have
said in verse what women since have only said as well
in prose. Ephelia's emblem might have been the
declaration of Anne Elliot, ' All the privilege I claim
for my own sex (it is not a very enviable one : you
need not covet it) is that of loving longest, when
existence or when hope is gone."

163 172   She had probably heard of Sappho, and knew

> ' Lingua sed torpet, tenuis sub artus
> Flamma demanat, sonitu suopte
> Tintinant aures, gemina teguntur
> Lumina nocte '

yet here this is no mere literary reminiscence ; she
slips for a little into conventional metaphor, but
returns to plain speech at the end.

165 174   This is very subtly feminine ; Mopsa's inferiority
was probably noticed only when Strephon began to
notice her. But Ephelia cannot get the best out of
any measure except the couplet.

165 175   This has in it half the mystery of women's love ; they
can love us without liking us.

166 176-9 Wycherley is a little dull and heavy in verse ; he was
a crypto-Puritan, as Alceste was a crypto-Jansenist.
His poems obviously belong to the 1670's ; young
Pope claimed to have touched them up, but we have
only his word for it ; yet as there are longer versions
of most in the collection of 1702, it is possible that he
advised in the abridgements of the later posthumous
edition. The text here is, by permission, from the
Nonesuch edition.

168 178   This song, perhaps unconsciously, has the portentous
solemnity and self-explanation of one stage of a
cheerful evening.

169 179   Love's Golden Age has always been the day before
yesterday.

169 180   Rymer is surprising ; who would have expected the
critic of *The Tragedies of the Last Age* (a ' pert and

arbitrary fool' says Butler quite rightly), or the
learned editor of the *Foedera*, to write anything so
sincere and charming. His reverence for Nature
and Sense, which had led him all astray with Shakespeare, kept him straight here. Love which

'gives to every power a double power
Above their functions and their offices'

made him a poet.

171 182   This is adorable; it is a perfect 'minor' poem, its
narrow range justified by its individuality.

172 184-6   Shadwell deserved what he got from Dryden;
the 'satire' which called forth *MacFlecknoe* is
monumental in imbecility. But when he is not being
professionally true blue and Protestant he can
be very friendly and entertaining; even Dryden
must have laughed over *The Virtuoso*, where Shadwell's own absurdity reinforces that of his fools
with overwhelming effect. And sometimes he is
a not bad poet when his dullness is merely
lambent.

172 184   It is strange to see him kissing the hand of the
Duchess; by another irony, he was buried in Westminster Abbey, as most of us will not be.

172 185   This must be kept for Purcell's sake; and should
not Shadwell too have credit for a poetical Bank
Holiday?

173 187   John Rawlet speaks for many obscure good men,
conveniently overlooked by the Macaulays and the
Gosses. He was lecturer at St. Nicholas, Newcastle-
on-Tyne, and a devoted preacher all over North
England. Perhaps he had a touch of the Puritan,
but he never snuffles; his portrait has a strange
far-off look of the young Donne. This poem is
attractive by a slight likeness to a sonnet by Gerard
Hopkins.

175 188   How soberly Horatian is this poem, yet another
success in the Restoration middle style. Like all
southern exiles in the North he has to keep his spirits
up by deliberately making the best of things, but
he does it with a Christian and gentlemanly courtesy
and goodness of heart.

177 189   Wright's lines come best after Rochester's terrible
beauties. It is good to be humble, and easily content, for all but poets.

'It's wiser being good than bad,
It's safer being meek than fierce,
It's fitter being sane than mad.'

177 190   Wright was a Papist, but he probably thought of
St. Paul's as English rather than Anglican.

178 191-3 Mason often deviates toward doggerel, but his hymns,
very popular for a generation, are much better than
the run of Puritan verse—witness those amazing
Psalms Milton did in 1648, between *Lycidas* and
Paradise Lost.

179 193   Sometimes, as in the third, the eighth and the
last stanzas here, Mason is on the verge of great
poetry.

181 194-6 Mary Southworth (perhaps a kinswoman of Blessed
John Southworth, martyred in 1654), was one of the
early members of the Society of Friends in Lanca-
shire; that she was a humane scholar is less than the
character her husband gave her (they were married
in prison).   ' She was very loving, diligent, tender-
hearted and kindly affectionate towards me and
our children; and generally loving and tender
towards all people, especially such as were in
any distress, sickness or affliction, though never
so poor.'

It is worth noting that she was an exact contemporary of St. Margaret Mary Alacoque and
of Madame Guyon in France, as her master George
Fox was of Miguel de Molinos.

181 194   This very beautiful poem has the idiom of John
Woolman, and the sweet austere quietism of the
primitive Friends, set as never since, to its own tune
in verse.   It is difficult to reconcile that with the
fretful Pharasaism about hats and the days of the
week and the rest of the superstitions of that revolt
against superstition.

183 197   Dean Aldrich may stand as a symbol of the genial
Oxford of that age ; perhaps these verse-jests of his
are the main evidence for its indolence.   He edited
Clarendon's *History*, he wrote much music, he built
All Saints Church and Peckwater Quad ; although he
was not always quite quite serious, yet another side
of his life is revealed by Hearne's note.   ' He
constantly received the Sacrament every Sunday,
rose to five o'clock Prayers in the morning, Summer
and Winter.'

184 199   Thomas Heyrick, A.B. of Peterhouse in 1670, A.M.
in 1675, was a Leicestershire man, a Heyrick of
Beaumanoir ; he was therefore a kinsman of Swift
and of the Vicar of Dean Prior (who somehow never
achieves this particular variant of the name in his
numerous signatures).   Thomas Heyrick shows no
sign of having studied *Hesperides*, but his *Miscellany
Poems* are very attractive and individual.   He is

N 2

crazy about natural and unnatural history; he
allows the crocodile to compare himself at length to
the Tyrant, and the Phœnix to lament somewhat
angrily an inevitable chastity, while he himself will
willingly moralise about any other animal.   As befits
a Leicestershire man, he has a *Chase of the Fox*, which
agreeably links Chaucer to Surtees and Mr. Masefield.
He is an angler too, at great Pindaric length, and indeed all water, fresh or salt, excites his buxom Muse.
Of all the fantastic amusing things I found in ranging
Restoration verse, I give the palm to Heyrick's
Submarine Voyage, a poem in four fairly long Books
of Pindaric verse.   A dolphin bears him away into
a fantasy that mixes Keats and Jules Verne with
clots of geography, a complete treatise on fish,
and the Court memoirs of Neptune and the
mermaids.   Heyrick ought to be reprinted; he is
decidedly what our great-grandfathers called ' an
original.'

The *Tomineios*, as is proper, is all Heyrick's verse in
miniature.   He is of his generation in being ' scientific ' and in welcoming evidence for the Ruck
(Aladdin's benefactor): like Sir Thomas Browne, he
hoped for scientific confirmation of the fantasies he
cherished.

185 200-12 The legend of Rochester began in his lifetime; it
owed something to the malignity of the enemies he
chose to make, and something to the other legend of
Don Juan.   After his death, any ribald song or
outrageous anecdote could be fathered on Rochester;
the eighteenth century was edified, the nineteenth
shocked, until at last, in the moral paroxysms of
Sir Edmund Gosse, Rochester becomes ' a veritable
devil' (as distinguished from the Devil one need not
believe in) and ' a plague-spot in English literature.'
Herr Prinz's monograph in *Palaestra* (1923), and Mr.
Hayward's introduction to his Nonesuch edition of
the poems, give material for the reconsideration of
his life and his tragedy, the tragedy of the

' genti dolorose
Ch'hanno perduto il ben dello intelletto.'

He wasted himself in restless and joyless debauchery,
driven on by the intensity of his temperament.
Lesser men could drink and riot, and forget it
with next day's headache; he could not forget and
dared not think; he could but return to ' the expense
of spirit in a waste of shame ' for which the psychologists have many names, which the theologians call Sin.
Sick in mind and soul, he could but tell Burnet at last
that ' he was sorry he had lived so as to waste his

strength so soon, so that he had brought such an ill name upon himself ; and had an agony of mind about it, which he knew not well how to express.' And so he repented as well as he could, and died at thirty-two.

In the last mad years of his life he could be insolent and treacherous and brutal to real or fancied enemies, but he could keep his friends.   One of them was Robert Wolseley, who chivalrously defended him after his death, whose words show what those who loved him felt.   ' His poetry has everywhere a tincture of that unaccountable charm in his fashion and conversation, that peculiar becomingness in all he said and did, that drew the eyes and won the hearts of all who came near him.'   This ' unaccountable charm ' is his lesser merit.   The subtlety and intensity of his experience, the clear and swift verse that is its inevitable expression, these set him at moments beside Catullus.   His individuality makes the idiom of the Restoration classical and gives it the dignity of a form indispensable to the completeness of English poetic tradition.

185 200   Rochester has much in common with that other great and passionate lover Donne.   His work expresses not a series of experiences, but one experience—love—in successive ' states of the soul.'   Now in modish persiflage, playing with easy conquests, now in the bitterness of love given and unreturned, now in the sharp memory of love returned and then lost, he seeks to resolve the unreason of circumstance into something significant and final.

186 201   This, otherwise only a malicious jest, is transfigured in one faultless couplet by the antithesis of ' morning ' and ' night '   He looks northward ;   he sees only black and white, darkness and light :   his imagination of this has something of the passion with which the damned in the Inferno recall the ' dolce lome,' down there where the sun is silent.

186 202   Kindness in love he could hardly give and so could hardly get.

187 204-5 ' Death ' and ' life ' are more here than the counters of traditional conceit ;   he is more in earnest than he cares to say, for he might cry with Mr. Abercrombie's Holofernes

> ' under passions of fleshly pleasure
> I hide myself from my desiring soul.'

It is this hidden intensity and reality that gives these songs their perfect poise and hovering breadth of wing.

PAGE NO.

188 206   This in its bareness is more intense than Marvell's fancy of ' Time's winged chariot.' There is no imagery to colour its terrible arithmetic—the ' flying hours ' that perish and are reckoned, the ' livelong minute ' that outweighs them.

> ' Every time less than a pulsation of the artery
> Is equal in its period and value to six thousand years,
> For in this period the poet's work is done.'

(Mr. Saintsbury draws attention to the peculiar quality of the quintet in stanza-form, from Sidney's serenade at the window to Browning's at the villa.)

189 207   This compares with Cowper's *Castaway* in the expression of despair ; but despair here is clear-eyed and conscious, the ' maggiore dolore ' of Francesca. It is not fashionable to quote Mr. Kipling (the intelligent refer to him sometimes as Webster did to Shakespeare) but *Love-o'-Women*, for all the melodrama of its slang, speaks of the same damnation. ' Walkin' round and round, to considher (him that was beyond all touch av bein' happy this side hell !) how happy he wud ha' been wid *her*.'

190 208   This very great poem suffers from slight incoherence ; its three movements are not given unity. But for all this it is the greatest short poem between Donne and Blake.

A winter's day. The imagery of the stanza is cosmic. The vast sweep of the retreating sun is the symbol of something vaster in the soul.

But pain can ne'er deceive. The whole philosophy of a classical view of life is implicit in this. Common conceptions of love, of art, even of religion, count pain the only evil, pleasure the only good. This vast delusion is behind all minor delusions, from Socialism to Christian Science.

The stanza has a reminiscence of Donne's great forerunner, Fulke Greville.

> ' For thought is not the weapon
> Wherewith thought's ease men cheapen
> Absence is pain.'

191 209   One unnecessarily objectionable stanza omitted. This is Rochester's one essay in landscape, and in Pindaric. It is not Horatian at all, but it has Rochester's strength of line and harsh true diction.

192 210   Rochester, like most of the great lords, was a Whig at heart, and if he had lived would have scrambled

for power at the Glorious Revolution, but he was too
clear-sighted not to see what constitutional monarchy
meant.

193 211   This is not mere paradox, but the philosophy of
Hobbes taken to the logical absurdity of its end ;
Rochester was not innocent enough for the mater-
ialist's child-like faith in matter.

I have seen no direct evidence of his acquaintance
with the work of Donne ; *Nothing* seems to owe a
hint in substance to Donne's *Will* and in manner to the
Epistle to Lady Bedford, just as *The Mistress* has a
faint echo of the *Ecstasy.* It is fairly clear that
Rochester had studied Carew's verse.

195 212.   The *Satire* runs off at last into mere abuse of knaves ;
something fundamental is the theme of these opening
lines ; much as they owe to Hobbes and Lucretius
they express a personal disillusion.   It is instructive
to read them after Dryden's lines (No. 77).   It needs
an effort to remind oneself that Dryden is in the right
after all ;   cannot Lucretius sometimes make Virgil
sound sentimental and Horace frivolous ?

196 213-9 ' The valiant, brutal, honourable, covetous, long-
lived, many-titled John Sheffield, Earl of Mulgrave,
Marquis of Normandy, Duke of Buckinghamshire '
was Rochester's unforgiving enemy, as such an
' homme moyen sensuel ' could hardly fail to be,
given contact and provocation. Sheffield was a friend
and a patron of Dryden, who took a cudgelling
for the *Essay on Satire* and complimented his patron
with what one would like to take for Chaucerian
irony.

' How will sweet Ovid's ghost be pleased to hear
His Fame augmented by a British Peer.'

Sheffield made love, not unacceptably, to the young
Princess Anne, and might have been an incon-
veniently vigorous Prince Consort.   He was a Tory,
and behaved not badly in 1688, although he was not
Quixotic enough to run any serious risk ;   he was
honest enough at least to earn from Macaulay the
compliments of ' poetaster ' and ' libertine.'   He had
no delusions about the ability or the morals of
William III, on whom he looked, according to
Johnson, with a reasonable compromise between
' malevolence ' and ' contempt ' ;   characteristically
he got a Marquisate and a pension from William, a
Dukedom, a job, and the site of Buckingham Palace
from his royal mistress later on.   His prose is cheerful
and natural ;   his verse, edited after his death by an
admiring third wife, is just as normal and straightforward and efficient.

PAGE NO.

196 213   His enemies might call him knave, but never fool.

197 214   Sheffield can be honest and impudent by turns or together, and leave a lady or a reader in doubt as to which. The opening couplet, as Mr. Saintsbury notes, is (appropriately) one of the last successful attempts at the great Caroline cadence in ' Common Measure.' If Gloriana was the Princess, stanza two is hardly courteous.

198 215   The last four stanzas of nine—a long way from Donne's *Apparition*.

198 216   A sober and happy statement of true love ; Sheffield was a wise enough lover to understand the friendship of love.

199 217   As often he starts well, the relapse is at the end. The first quatrain is shining, but significantly he leaves wonder and delight at the stars to children.

200 219   ' His character is not to be proposed as worthy of imitation ; his religion he may be supposed to have learnt from Hobbes '; and yet a Latin epitaph he wrote for himself suggests something better. Hobbes ' irritated all speculation' for this generation. The popular estimate of his ascendancy is illustrated by the fact that, in dramatic convention, he succeeds Machiavelli as the intellectual sustenance of the villain. Vizard, in Farquhar's *Trip to the Jubilee* reads in a pocket Hobbes, to indicate his hypocrisy.

The noble disciple here shows a suggestive unwillingness or inability to expound his master's philosophy, and slips away into remarks on style.

202 220   Wolseley, Rochester's friend, editor and defender, did some diplomacy for William III ; his father had been one of Cromwell's ' House of Lords,' his uncle a ' staunch Protestant,' and the victor of Newtown Butler. For all these grave family connections of his he must have credit for several pretty songs, and this is perhaps the prettiest.

203 221-2   Duffett was ' a milliner in the New Exchange '; he travestied plays by Dryden, Shadwell, and even Elkanah Settle, which pain the editor of *Biographia Dramatica* by ' indulging a vein of scurrility ' and so are relegated ' to a perpetual obscurity and contempt.' His *New Poems, Songs, Prologues and Epilogues*, ' set by the most eminent Musicians about the Town ' made a hit in 1676.

203 221   Duffett often hits on a tune but cannot keep it up ; this is rather break-neck but just scrambles home. Waller's elegance or Dryden's majesty never chilled his vein.

205 223-4 Webbe is only a name, but two such songs as these give him an enviable modicum of immortality.

206 225 Richard Leigh, after taking his B.A. at Queen's College, Oxford in 1669, became an actor, but he must not be confused with ' the great Leigh ' (who was Anthony). He is perhaps a poet only of the class of Hooke, but the passage of twenty years since Hooke has brought about interesting changes in method.

207 226 Leigh has difficulties with grammar—as Thackeray says of a much duller person, ' I don't mean merely his grammar of language, but his moral grammar, so to speak, his grammar of the mind.' This is my excuse for extracting seven stanzas out of sixteen here. There is delicious colour ; tulips were still a passion in Holland, but Dutch flower-painters never excelled this.

209 228 This is perfect in its clear daintiness ; ' sixes ' are rare in English verse, but Leigh handles them as delicately as Herrick does. (Gerard Hopkins has a poem in sixes, ' Our Lady compared to the air we breathe,' which brings something like the same character out of the measure in a very different manner).

210 229 The dynasty of Playford—John I, 1623-86, John II, 1656-86, Henry, 1657-1706—almost monopolised the publication of music in London from *The Dancing Master* of 1650 until Henry's death. Their song-books begin to be interesting about 1676, when Purcell takes the town by storm. They are pleasant and mellow and dignified books, with their suggestion of a society in which men and women are frank and happy together. Anyone turning them over will wonder where are the ribaldry and the offensive rubbish literary historians have told him to expect.

There is something particularly attractive about tender feminine poems like this song ; it may have been by a man who wanted to think women felt like that, but one would prefer to imagine some true-hearted forgiving gentlewoman as the writer.

212 232 These collections have several Mad-songs ; (the greatest of all, *Tom of Bedlam*, is now proved to be Jacobean) ; most of them, like Durfey's famous *Rosy Bowers*, are too obviously concocted for the sake of the composer. This (also set by Purcell) was certainly written by a poet ; it might be before 1660, but the opening couplets sound post-Waller.

214 234 Robert Gould, whose *Works* were collected in 1709 by his Relict, was ' nine years a servant of the Duke of Dorset,' and afterwards a country schoolmaster.

PAGE NO.

His noble master did not teach him to be light and airy, but his own downright and sometimes heavy-handed manner has its own successes.

This, like many other Restoration poems, cannot keep up to its charming opening ; these poets start with a theme, in music and meaning ; they work it out carelessly, and bungle the one in developing the other.

216 237 Gould had seen the stars (see No. 236) and this is noticeable in an age that preferred candlelight. He knew Horace's Neæra too, but the humour of the last stanza is both original and poetical.

A change in conditions is suggested by the fates of the group of poets born in the sixteen-fifties ; Otway, Lee, Allestree, Oldham, Coppinger—even Tate and Durfey—they are all poor lousy rogues, starving in garrets or dodging bumbailiffs, shabbier descendants of Greene and Peele. The Renaissance tradition of patronage was beginning to fade, and the public as distinct from the town had not begun to buy books.

217 239 This is a poem that may be fairly called conventional; it is a rather competent professional piece of work wearily done to a pattern.

218 240 Dr. Elton calls this ' very pathetic and skilful in its movement ' ; it has the interest of landscape, a Dutch etching of bare, sandy country. It is actually the first stanza of a weary Pindaric Ode.

219 241 This keeps up its original measure well ; Lee is really a belated Jacobean, who would have found himself at home in the company of Marston and Dekker, if not of Shakespeare and Jonson.

220 243 Three out of forty-two stanzas. Dr. Elton praises :

' So chaste, the dead are only more,
    Who lie divorced from objects and from power,'

' a couplet which, with its doubtful rhyme and syntax, its anachronistic praise of chastity, and its large splendid thought and phrasing, is altogether in the extinct manner.' This judgment is in the terms of the conventional Restoration thesis, some day it is hoped to be extinct in its turn. What is old-fashioned here is the clumsiness alone, which, as Dryden thought, was a fault of the poet's immaturity ; had Oldham lived he would have kept largeness and splendour, and found a better organised form.

222 244 Allestry, who was at Westminster and Christ Church, died in poverty, ' of a poet's vices ' as Anthony à Wood severely says. This strong and splendid poem is " metaphysical " ; Allestry had read Lucretius and felt for himself.

223 245-6 Matthew Coppinger's book is dedicated to the
Duchess of Portsmouth, in lines amusing either as
irony or sober compliment. According to a MS. note
in the British Museum copy, he lived to be hanged,
'and now, poor man, he is among the Otamys at
Surgeon's Hall.'

223 245 One stanza omitted ; this very pretty poem owes
something to Spenser's *Epithalamion*, for Spenser
was never entirely neglected. The tune of it (which
eluded me for months) is from an 'Emblem' of
Quarles.

225 247-9 Tom Durfey, as accommodating as the Vicar of Bray,
supplied entertainment for five monarchs. In nearly
fifty years he wrote thirty-one plays and 'more odes
than Horace.' He had to send the hat around often
in his genial and unreverend old age, but is chirping
as cheerfully as ever in the last edition of *Pills to
Purge Melancholy* (1719). He died in 1727, and an
epitaph for him says

> ' His tale was pleasant and his song was sweet :
> His heart was cheerful but his thirst was great.'

Only the very severe can dislike him, in spite of his
tendency to confuse the emetic and the erotic. As
Steele says, ' He had a peculiar talent in the lyric way
of writing, and that with a manner wholly new and
unknown to the Greeks and Romans.''

225 247 The omission of one stanza leaves this a very pretty
poem indeed. ' Poetry was in the air ' then as
always, a fact convenient for anthologists, but in-
convenient to literary historians.

226 249 Charles Lamb, who had not the advantage of modern
text-books, never knew that English poetry suffered
an eclipse in 1660, and so he included this song, with
praise, in his Garrick Extracts. Tom turned it off
to liven up a play of his just as cheerfully as he
turned off the poems which offended Shadwell's
decency ; this was the Elizabethan way of doing
it—Shakespeare's way.

227 250-6 Nahum Tate confirms a Shandean hypothesis ; with
a more picturesque Christian or given name—Maurice
for instance—he might have earned more respectful
treatment from the critics : as it is, he is a very
pleasant, sober minor poet. His *Poems* were published in 1677 ; a second edition in 1682 makes many
changes in the direction of smoothness, from the
rather down-at-heels Caroline to the decent Augustan.
The texts here (except No. 253) are from the later
edition.

227 250 Suggestions from Herrick and Cotton here just fail
to blend into something original.

PAGE NO.

228 251   This is indispensable to the anthology of Love ; and lucky is the lover who has done such penance and received such absolution. Fanaret is very amiable and credible, midway between the Goddess and the Pretty Creature.

229 253   The earlier text is given because Tate spoiled it in revision ; the lesser men began increasingly from now onwards to think sobriety dull and to swell into the pompous; thus in a generation or so the classical heritage of natural clear idiom is dissipated.

230 254   The ' dull round ' of the verse fits his theme, which is boredom, and not the fierce Epicureanism of No. 163.

    ' Ah ! que la vie est quotidienne ! '

230 255   Tate's hymn-writing is parallel to the Latin work of Santeuil in France, which began those Gallican hymns so often translated and imitated by the Anglicans of the Oxford Movement.

  The *New Version* is complete and harmonious and comfortable, like Wren's contemporary city churches. Like them it expresses a transition from the soaring baroque of the seventeenth century to the well-built homeliness of the eighteenth. The piety of that day began to reconcile *Christian Morals* with *The Whole Duty of Man,* or rather a humbler humdrum spirit of religion displaced the nobler extravagance of the seventeenth-century spiritual aristocrats, with the inheritance of some of their dignity. And yet there is an ardour under the coolness of the verse. as in this extract, that speaks of unchanging human needs ; plump merchants in pews yearned for the living God as surely as hermits in the Thebaid.

  If Tate were no poet, how did he come to vary Common Measure, as he does in this poem and the next ? How different is the cadence and movement, and yet how subtle the differences of balance and foot-division that distinguish them.

231 256   Familiarity can never dull the shining beauty of this : it is as direct and simple as the singing of children. The Joyful Mystery of the Nativity found poets in the eighteenth as well as in the other centuries. In Manchester (that Jacobite town) under George II ' Christians awake ! ' rang out its happiness to the midnight stars ; in the France of Louis XV perhaps awoke the silver sweetness of ' Adeste Fideles '— for as Verlaine sings it, the age of Louis Racine was an age of faith.

    ' Quand poète et docteur, simplement, bonnement,
      Communiaient avec des ferveurs de novices,
      Humbles servaient la Messe, et chantaient aux
        offices.'

PAGE NO.

The same spirit stirred in the England of the Non-jurors, when Johnson was learning his catechism at Lichfield. For another expression of the religion of the first decade of the eighteenth century beside its churches and its hymns, consider two tunes, the majesty of Croft's ' St. Anne,' the joy of ' Jesus Christ is risen to-day.'

232 257-8 *Philander and Eirene* is a long and perhaps over-sweet poem, in spirit not unlike *Britannia's Pastorals*, for all the regularity of its couplets.

233 260-4 Norris has been called a survival, a belated mystic in an unmystical age; on the contrary he is up-to-date and all too contemporary. He gets his philosophy from the Cambridge Platonists, still a powerful influence, and from Malebranche. He had his public too, for the general philosophic standpoint he expressed was that of a large section of serious Anglicans. Like many others he attacked Locke; no less would have been expected of him by that public. Literary history is simplified by the assumption of an immediate revolution in poetry after Dryden, and an immediate revolution in philosophy after Locke, but such a simplification falsifies; the older transcendentalism lost ascendancy, yet Law and Swedenborg and Blake testify to its survival even in the days of the ' philosophers.'

Norris is of his own day as a poet, too ; indeed, he dates too accurately. He was trying to express his philosophical outlook in a style as contemporary and popular as he could make it. He even uses those colloquial abbreviations which the better judgment of his generation always condemned. He can paraphrase the Song of Songs thus

' Come, thou divinest object of my love,
This noisy region don't with us agree;

and in this and other things he is not a poet spoiled by a bad convention, but a poet choosing to use a bad convention although a better was to hand.

233 260 He hits on a new thought here, the strangeness of dying rather than its terrors.

234 261 This takes something from Cowley, and something from Milton (who was read, though not yet cited as a classic). His darkness has nothing of the mystery of Donne's or Vaughan's ; it is conceived and explained by negatives.

Thomas Yalden has a *Hymn to Darkness* only six years later than this, one stanza of which Dr. Johnson thought ' exquisitely beautiful'; I, too, would like to say as much for a Tory poet, but my Toryism is not as stout as that.

PAGE NO.

236 262   Norris's beloved ghost was a thirteen-year-old niece ; he is very kindly here in his escape from the superstition of anti-superstition.

237 263   Here alone his Platonism becomes Platonic. His poverty in stanzaic invention is noticeable : he cannot fly far from couplet.

238 264   No doubt he knew Donne (although he has little to do with his predecessor at Bemerton, George Herbert, a son of Donne's spiritual mistress, Magdalen Herbert) ; perhaps he remembered the *Anatomy of the World.*

> ... Think thy shell broke, think thy soul hatched but now,
> And think this slow-paced soul which late did cleave
> To a body, and went but by the body's leave
> Twenty perchance or thirty miles a day,
> Dispatches in a minute all the way
> 'Twixt heaven and earth. . . .
> But ere she can consider how she went
> At once is at and through the firmament.

240 265   It would be ungallant to suggest any twentieth-century application of this.

241 266   Some one may be able to guess who Lady E——M—— was ; she perhaps wrote No. 265.

241 267   From *To the Nightingale on the Return of Spring,* written by a Person of Quality in 1680. This may recall Mr. Shanks' *Fête Galante.*

243 270-1   This Sackville was a Colonel in 1684, a Major-General in 1695 ; I looked no further ; it was sufficient for my immediate purpose that he could write a good song, with more of Sedley in it than of his great kinsman.

244 272   This was Jack Howe, the politician, who is reproved by Macaulay, not so much for having been ' the most rancorous and unprincipled of Whigs ' as for becoming ' the most rancorous and unprincipled of Tories.' He made love unsuccessfully to Queen Mary herself (perhaps he is the Endymion of No. 268).

245 273   Henry Cromwell was one of Pope's mentors, of whom Johnson could learn ' nothing particular but that he used to ride a-hunting in a tye-wig.' He was fond of amusing himself with poetry and criticism. There were humble and harmless Cromwells ; Richard, like Romulus Augustulus, was living in obscurity and did not die until 1712.

245 274-6   Richard Duke, an Oxford man, was a friend of Otway's, and one of the young men about Dryden, a business-like sub-contractor for verse transla-

tion. He took orders and became a prebendary of Gloucester. Like Dr. Grant, he found ' institutionary dinners ' too much for him, and Swift notes his death with dry contempt for poets and fat beneficiaries. ' He was one of the wits when we were children, but turned parson and left it, and never writ further than a prologue or recommendatory copy of verses. He had a fine living given him by the bishop of Winchester about three months ago ; he got his living suddenly and he got his dying so too.' No doubt a man would rather die of overeating than of starvation, but if Duke had lived as poorly as Otway he might have written something worth while. Dr. Johnson thinks ' some of his compositions such as he must have reviewed with detestation in his later days ' ; indeed, his best poem is too good a following of Carew's *Rapture* for inclusion here.

245 274 This looks back to Spenser and forward to Browning.

247 276 Is this conventional, or is it a half-satirical version of what emancipated ladies were likely to say, then as now.

248 277 This is like ' The lady prayeth the return of her lover abiding on the seas ' in *Tottel's Miscellany*, and unlike the conventional idea of a Restoration love-poem.

248 278 Too early to be Prior's, but not unworthy of him in its arch and artful simplicity.

249 279 Is this the first mention of champagne ? Poets (when in funds) should rather drink Burgundy, with Herrick and Cotton.

250 280 This is a little silly, but charmingly so ; fancy must set Purcell's tune to its echoes and trills.

251 281 This gossamer thing was printed for the first time from MS. by Mr. Ault, who dates it ' before 1687.'

253 285 I had doubts about this ; but the period is hardly ever jolly in verse, for all its tavern-reputation.

253 286 There are other stanzas ; the point of view is rare in verse since La Belle Héaulmière ; this lady leaves others to moralise about her.

253 287 This is perhaps a reject from Purcell's *Fairy Queen* ; it is ' school of Davenant ' ; Bishop Corbet's *Popish Lament* was premature ; some domestic fairies survived until 1700.

254 288 Lady Mary Chudleigh reminds me of Lady Catherine de Burgh, for no sound reason except something in the tone of voice. Her ' Paraphrase of the song of the Three Children ' is the longest and dullest of all Pindaric Odes, and what that means only a few will understand.

255 289   Perhaps addressed, under a misapprehension, to Mr. Darcy.

256 290-3 Jane Barker is not in the *Dictionary of National Biography*, but her book of verse tells something of her earlier life ; later on she wrote novels which have attracted a German monograph. She had friends at Cambridge, and may be guessed at for the daughter of a country clergyman, like a greater Jane a century later. She walked and talked with E. D. (who died young) like Helena with Hermia.

> ' Nor riches hoped, nor poverty we feared,
> 'Twas innocence in both, which both revered.
> Witness this truth ye Wilsthorp-Fields, where we
> So oft enjoyed a harmless luxury,
> Where we indulged our easy appetites
> With pocket-apples, plums and such delights.'

She had ' a little money of her own ' ; Dr. R. S. came courting her, but she found him out and he was rude ; if it is fair to judge from the lady's verses, he had about him something of Mr. Elton and something of Mr. Collins as well. Then she had settled down to be an Old Maid, but her peace was disturbed by a young lover, who would heed not her protest against the adoration of ' a superannuated deity.' There her love-story ends ; we are left to hope the best for her, whether with her young worshipper or more safely with some middle-aged and disinterested admirer. She was merry and wise ; it will be worth while calling on her in Elysium, where certainly she sits by Miss Austen and John Oliver Hobbes.

256 290   This fixes her birth-date about the late fifties.

256 291   This is ' out of *Scipina*,' ' a most delightful and excellent Romance now in the Press,' which makes J. N., Fellow of St. John's College, cry out:

> ' Hail ! Fair commandress of a gentle Pen
> At once the Dread and dear Delight of Men
> Who'll read with transport those soft joys you've writ.
> ... Yet all this while, such are thy harmless Flames
> As neither Age itself, nor Envy blames,
> The Precise-Grave-Ones cannot disapprove
> Thy Gallant Hero's honourable Love.
> Thy lines may pass severest Virtue's test,
> More than Astræa's soft, more than Orinda's chaste
> —Young Country Squires may read without offence. . . . '

Once a lady has given herself for better or for worse, she makes the best of her bargain, and it is to spinsters we must go for an impartial feminine estimate of the clumsy sex, which would hardly vary through the centuries.

257 293 This is to be compared with Astræa's *Caution* (No. 164). The last stanza is an admirable defiance of those rationalists who confound the actual with the real; " really ' is the significant word.

258 294 The text is that of *Examen Poeticum*, 1693; the poem had already appeared in 1685, together with No. 295. ' Mrs.' was of course, used for unmarried women as well as married.

259 295 How well these Restoration ladies write! A contemporary damsel would dilute this situation into a novel.

260 297 Mrs. Lovelace (who perhaps wrote No. 297 also) is kinder and softer than Mrs. Taylor. Was she blonde and the other brunette ?

261 298 Anne Lee, an heiress, was only fourteen when they married her to Thomas Wharton, a ' libertine ' and ' the most universal villain ' Swift ever knew, though he knew so many Whig politicians. (The *D.N.B.* has apparently confused her with her mother-in-law.) Her married life was unhappy; Burnet helped her to religious consolation and Waller praised her verse.

261 299 Very seldom since this century have women been so frank with their own hearts as these all were.

263 301 Dryden's memorial ode for Anne Killigrew is, of course, one of his greatest things. Perhaps readers of it have assumed that he flattered her poems; he did, but not unduly. She wrote ' all like a man '; her strong, sober, plain, sixth-form face explains her verse, which is scanty but has ' noble vigour '; I wish, too late, I had made room for more.

264 302 Probably this is not hers; it is one of these poems of which her 1685 editor says, ' These three following Odes being found among Mrs. Killigrew's papers, I am willing to print them, though none of hers.' Another of them is a surprising thing called *Cloris's Charms dissolved by Eudora*, which very reluctantly I had to omit as too long; it will be found in Arber's *Dryden Anthology*. It is full of fantastic power and suggests now Crabbe and now Shelley. It might be Anne Killigrew's, and if so, she was indeed a considerable poet.

265 303-7 Lady Winchilsea was praised by Wordsworth and has never since been neglected. She was Maid of Honour to Mary of Modena when she married Heneage Finch, the fourth of that name. After the betrayal of 1688, her husband and she withdrew to Eastwell Park in

Kent, where they lived as guests of their cousin, the Earl, until in 1712 he died and Heneage Finch succeeded him. Her long retirement and its leisure taught her to write, but not to prune ; she is never exquisite and often dull, but everywhere in her verse is the expression of a loyal and kind nature. This and not 'external nature' is the charm of her rambling water-colour landscape, as well as of her pleasant plain moralising.

Her *Poems* were edited in 1903 by Miss Myra Reynolds for the Chicago University Press ; the volume includes much printed for the first time from MS. and it is by the courtesy of the Press that I am enabled to reprint here No. 305 and No. 306.

265 303   This first appeared in *The Gentleman's Magazine* of 1693. It is interesting to compare it with Orinda's poem thirty years earlier (No. 112). In the 1650's rapture needed repression, in the 1690's encouragement.

265 304   This is Mr. Squire's admirable excerpt from an endless Pindaric Ode entitled *All is Vanity*. I do not think she was pacifist in the modern way ; like her contemporary, Lady Castlewood, she had no enthusiasm for Whig wars. Those were hard years for loyal English men and women who could not be true at once to their legitimate King and to their country.

266 305   From *An Epilogue to Jane Shore*. Anne Finch was not always merely amiable ; Pope knew this one, as well as other poems of hers.

266 306   ' An Invitation to Daphnis to leave his study and usual employments—mathematics, painting, etc.— and to take the pleasures of the fields with Ardelia.' The lady loved to explore the park ; she once had quite an adventure, and walked so far that she had to come home in a woodcutter's cart. Poor Finch is drawn gently away from some fascinating, useless task he had settled down to that morning, but he comes without complaining. They were quietly happy together, dear friends rather than passionate lovers.

268 307   This charming poem has often been praised by those who, like the great Wordsworth himself, are stating a case against Augustan poetry generally. Theirs is the undying heresy of the subject ; those who praise a portrait because the sitter is good-looking, or a poem because it reminds them of a pleasant place, should be content with essays and photographs and leave alone the transubstantiations of art. ' The images of external nature ' in this poem are never symbols of a revelation ; they are but notes of pleasant impressions. The ' sedate content ' of this

PAGE NO.

after-dinner walk in a park is as far from Wordsworth's 'fleeting moods and shadowy exultations'
as from Vaughan's rapture in 'deep but dazzling
darkness.'

There is a double tradition of landscape in the
seventeenth century, expressed in poetry as well as
in painting. One side of it is the golden classical
landscape of Claude and Milton (the last lines of
Lycidas are pure Claude). The other is the quieter
naturalistic landscape of the Dutchman, of Cuyp and
Ruysdael and Rembrandt himself ; the expression of
this tradition in poetry is often overlooked. It
begins in France about the sixteen-twenties with
Théophile de Viau and Tristan l'Hermite, and (a little
differently) with Saint-Amant. The influence of
these poets in England from about 1640 has never
been traced. Marvell, especially in *Appleton House*,
shows signs of it, and Cotton is sometimes actually
a translator. The double tradition persists in
England, to culminate at the beginning of the nineteenth century with Wordsworth and Crome on one
side, Shelley and Turner on the other.

Lady Winchilsea's landscape is in the quieter manner
and possibly she was directly influenced by painting
rather than poetry. Dutch painters like Jan
Siberechts were working in England. The *Nocturnal
Reverie* may be set beside the delightful minor Dutch
landscape of the century, the work of Adrian Van de
Velde, or that magical shadowed Camphuysen which
is a glory of the Wallace Collection. Her clear, dainty
water-colours of the foxglove and the glow-worm are
in that vein ; the 'ancient Fabric' and the 'falling
waters' lead on to the romantic classicism of Collins.

270 308   John Cutts, the renowned Whig soldier, Anne Finch,
the recluse Tory lady, furnish one of those engagingly
complete contrasts the accident of contemporary
birth often brings about. When his poems were
published in 1687 he had already earned in Hungary
against the Turks his reputation for headlong valour ;
he was the Bayard, or perhaps to avoid anachronistic
suggestions of chivalry, one should say the Ney, of
English soldiers. His nickname of 'Salamander'
was justified on every battlefield for twenty years ;
at the Boyne, at Steenkirk, on the bloodstained beach
at Brest, in the ditch at Namur, under the stockade
at Blenheim. He was consistently a Whig and ran
some risks to bring over William III, and he knew
how to keep his feet in the slippery ways of Revolution politics. He had some excuse for conceit, even
if he became 'the vainest old fool alive,' as Swift
called him years after his death.

His poems are a cavalryman's ; he makes a spirited protest in *La Muse de Cavalier* on behalf of ' such gentlemen as make their poetry their diversion, not their business.'

' My Muse is but my Mistress, not my Wife.'

But for all his ostentatious amateurism he knew what poetry was.

' Is it the noblest truths, the best expressed,
Or Nature in harmonious numbers dressed ?
Is it the strongest thought, the most refined,
Like cordial drops to fortify the mind ?
. . . 'Tis (like the strange effects of heat and cold)
Something in Nature better felt than told.'

271 310 This is Cutts' bravest gallop in verse. His admirer Steele makes ' honest Cynthio ' quote this, since he unfashionably has " a devotion rather than love for his Mistress.'

271 311 Cleland fought on the side of the Covenanters at Bothwell Bridge ; he was the first Colonel of the Camerons and died in battle at Dunkeld. He has been credited with the earlier version of *Hallo ! My fancy* which Mr. Ault has now traced back to 1639. The original poem owes a good deal to Burton's *Anatomy*. Cleland has another point of view ; he changes the individual humanism of his model into something alternately political and scientific.

275 312 *The Dispensary* gave something to the *Dunciad*, but is well worth reading for its own sake. This fragment on death is interesting, for Garth, behind his cheerful good-nature, was weary of life and ' willing to let it go.' ' It was usual for him to say that if there was any such thing as religion, 'twas among the Roman Catholics,' and he seems to have died a Catholic.

275 313 John Smith published his poems in 1713, with a preface defending himself from the suspicion of plagiarising Prior : ' I had finished mine long before his excellent compositions were published in the world.' He has very virtuous Pindarics on the Shortness of Life and for contrast a lively version of Chaucer's *Miller's Tale*, which is perhaps subsequent to Dryden's *Fables* but prior to Pope's *January and May* (Chaucer too had his vogue about 1700). I found nothing to my purpose in Smith's book, except this, which Mr. Iolo Williams had found before.

276 314 Hawkshaw is rather puzzling ; he was at Cambridge and Trinity College, Dublin ; he got a living in Dublin and lived till 1738, a neighbour of Swift. He was in verse a disciple of Cowley ; the subsequent generation of English poets hardly existed for him. Cowley was respected and popular up to 1700, but

there is nothing elsewhere like Hawkshaw's adoration and imitation.

This poem was written ' the night Limerick surrendered ' (so perhaps he was there with Captain Shandy) ; it is strangely rhapsodic for 1691.

276 315   One stanza omitted. A commonplace, perhaps, but written with a restraint and absence of irrelevant ornament his master Cowley seldom managed.

277 317   Elsum's book, which is perhaps mostly translation, is generally dull, and of more interest to the historian of art than of literature. This one epigram is incredibly good. The " cymbal " is the *cembalo* or *clavicembalo*, an elder cousin of the clavichord. In Paolo Veronese's ' Marriage Feast ' in the Louvre, tradition gives, as among the musicians, Titian the double-bass, Paolo himself the violoncello, and Tintoretto the viola.

280 322   Purcell set this song twice ; all through this decade—perhaps because of Purcell's fame—there is praise of music. Cp. No. 368 and No. 383.

280 323   This poem may be cited as evidence of the mercenary outlook of ladies then ; a contemporary of Griselda Grantly's noticed something like it in Victorian England.

> ' And the angels in pink and the angels in blue,
> In muslins and moirés so lovely and new :
> What is it they want and so wish you to guess ?
> But if you have money, the answer is Yes.'

282 326   The engaging contrast between this and No. 325 illustrates the way these songs run up and down the gamut of love.

283 327   De la Sale, from his name, would appear to be one of those surprisingly bi-lingual Huguenots, like D'Urfey and Motteux ; he keeps up his pretty tripping measure without a slip.

284 330   This dates from the sixteen-nineties ; the Prince and Princess are ' Est-il possible ? ' and Anne.

' Whalebone airs.' The corset returned with the Revolution ; Kneller's beauties have not the languishing and opulent charm of Lely's. They come like Millamant, ' full sail with her fan spread and her streamers out.' The revolutions and eclipses of the corset might attract a Historian of Civilisation, and a dozen inconsistent hypotheses could be developed in the high Hegelian manner. Just after 1715 it moved one of Pope's dunces, John Breval, to a piquant trifle of real poetry.

> ' When you put on, to grace a solemn day,
> Your best attire, and every charm display,

> Each due convenience for your ease prepare,
> But most, ye nymphs, of lacing close beware ;
> Lest by a fit surprised, you swooning fall
> Disturb the feast, or interrupt the ball.
> Then the breast heaves, the blush the cheek
>   forsakes,
> Till some kind hand the whalebone prison breaks,
> Meanwhile an amorous youth may steal a kiss,
> Or snatch, unfelt, perhaps, a greater bliss.
>   I much approve, when snowy breasts are seen
> Of fragrant sprigs a nosegay stuck between ;
> The scent and object make us half despair
> And ardent lovers wish their lips were there.'

The last couplet recalls one of Panurge's law-suits against the ladies of Paris.

Costume, no doubt, has its historical importance. The periwig is rather a surprising phenomenon ; for a century Europeans wore it as consistently as ancient Egyptians ; this perhaps moved the Victorians, who preferred Assyrian ideals, to condemn their artificiality.

285 331 Motteux translated Rabelais ; he gave up literature for business and came to a bad end. He was editor of the *Gentleman's Journal* of the sixteen-nineties, and some of his songs appeared in it. This one is tender and faultless,

285 332 No period of English literature could show a poem kinder and more gracious than this.

286 333 This is probably by Horatio Townshend (1630-87), (Viscount Townshend from 1682) and if so it is chronologically out of place here; although not published until 1694, it has a touch of the archaic and a plain debt to Drayton.

287 334 This is as subtle in its way as a ' metaphysical ' poem of a generation earlier, with its own timid clavichord-like evenness of touch.

288 335 Samuel Wesley, the son of one of Cromwell's intruded ministers, the father of John and Charles and seventeen other children, would seem to have enjoyed a brief springtime of frivolity while at Oxford. *Maggots* is a whimsical and light-hearted little book. It owes something to Butler, but the *Pindaric on Three Skips of a Louse* and the *Dialogue between Frying Pan and Chamber Pot* are good fooling without too pedantic a satirical intention.

How athletic and light are the couplets of this scrap from the *Tobacco Pipe*. Dryden was only the best exponent of the couplet of the day, neither its inventor nor its teacher.

PAGE NO.

289 336 If he had managed his double rhymes better this would have been an altogether admirable light poem. Its measure and treatment are based on popular song and not on literary precedent. The scholar's ' sums ' in stanza 4 would be ' summas ' like St. Thomas's : his ' sentences ' would be Peter Lombard's.

290 337 I did not explore the *Works* of the fatally facetious Tom Brown ; I found this in a Percy Society anthology ; it is an exposition of the best practical Toryism. The Lime Street chapel (the Palatine Ambassador's) was gutted by the London rabble in 1685. Macaulay is quite pleased to record the desecration of a crucifix, for ' the city had not within living memory been polluted by any idolatrous exhibition.'

292 338-40 King was a Tory wit. ' His purpose is to be merry; but perhaps to enjoy his mirth it may be sometimes necessary to think well of his opinions.'

292 339 King got some jobs in Ireland, but apparently they were not sinecures ; the Civil Service has never had the easy times its outside critics speak of. Johnson is always austere to poor King. He ' soon found a friend as idle and thoughtless as himself in Upton, one of the judges, who had a pleasant house called Mountown, near Dublin, to which King frequently retired ; delighting to neglect his interest, forget his cares, and desert his duty.' Mully was ' the red cow that gave him milk.' There must be something in the Irish air which encourages hearty eating. Compare ' The Vision of MacConglinne ' in Kuno Meyer, with the Gargantuan meals which oppressed the Irish R.M.

293 340 Top-Knots ' had just come in, and as new fashions do, had somewhat troubled the moral. He is imitating Ovid in the *Art of Love*, but Ovid never thought of this pretty consonance with the seasons. The ladies of Theleme indeed ' varied their head-dress with the season of the year, according to which they decked themselves.'

294 341 Swift thought Stepney as a poet ' scarce of the third rate,' but even a fourth-rate poet might take precedence of the second-rate diplomatist he was otherwise. Sir John Fortescue, generally so accurate, calls him ' Arthur Stepney ' and ' a bawdy poet '; the first charge is perhaps more easily refuted than the second; his best poem, on dreams, is too Freudian for admission here. This has its own very late Hellenistic prettiness.

294 342 Dryden called Walsh ' the best critic in the nation ' and he was Pope's preceptor, urging ' correctness.'

' Granville the polite
And knowing Walsh, would tell me I could write.'

Johnson says, ' he had more elegance than vigour, and seldom rises higher than to be pretty,' With all proper deference, I think this an unfortunate judgment. Walsh has a ' natural acidity ' (as a good old wine-merchant used to say when selling the cheaper Burgundies) which does keep him at least from being pretty. But it is his sole virtue ; he is timid and never allows himself to write a poem as he really wanted to write it. He has too much ' cool judgment ' in poetry as in love.

296 345 *The Despairing Lover* has some sort of vogue in anthologies ; it illustrates the metrical originality he might have made more of. Mr. Saintsbury says, ' He need not be taken seriously as a poet ; as a versifier he must always hold a respectable position.

297 346 This is perhaps the only sonnet between 1670 and 1750. The octave is almost considerable poetry, but the sextet, with its protest against any risk of being damned, does not convince.

298 347 *Delia* was Mrs. Tempest ; she died in 1703, on the night of ' that terrible tempest we call by way of distinction the Great Storm.' Walsh persuaded Pope to dedicate his *Winter* pastoral to her memory. ' I should take it very kindly of you to give it a little turn as if it were to the memory of the same lady.' She seems to have been good and handsome and clever, which need surprise only conventional critics of the Englishwomen of the period.

299 348-59 It is hard to say anything profitable about Prior's verse, which is with Herrick's the most perfect in English, made to be enjoyed, not to be explained or explained away. It is easy to praise him amiss, to emphasise an art which so wisely avoids emphasis. At his best he has a detachment from the merely contemporary which is seldom found even in the great ; whenever he had lived he would have created the same secure, candid, limited art. And yet his period did much for him ; it encouraged him to write verse, when earlier or later he might have been led aside into drama or novel ; it gave him that brief perfection of English speech ' at once vigorous and delicate, coloured and lucid,' which with him is just enough consciously artful to run no risk of colloquialism or of stiffness ; it gave him metrical form just as golden in its middle way. His is the last refinement of the whole period ; the clear diction of his master Waller made crystalline, the natural, easy measure of his master Dorset disciplined to the final grace of the ballet. He has been called Horatian : ' his song and his philosophy, his happy easy turns and melody, his love and his Epicureanism, bear a

great resemblance to that most delightful and
accomplished master.' But this is only half the
truth about him or Horace ; the Roman has a
foundation of nobility and gravity Prior lacks.
The parallel with La Fontaine is closer, but La
Fontaine too has more of the universal and the
seriousness of great art. Prior's art is that of a lesser
poet ; its perfection is its limitation.

' In small proportions we just beauties see.'

299 348   The lightness of the touch makes this tragic

> ' As when, both arms beside her held,
> Feet straightened out, some gay French lady
> Is caught up from life's light and motion,
> And dropped into death's silent ocean.'

' Et rose elle a vécu; far off, Donne's bell is tolling
for ' all the beautiful Queens of this world.'

301 350   Prior (Mr. G. R. Hamilton notes) shows imperfect
taste in some of his epigrams, jesting at beauty's
pathetic subterfuges, some lingering taint of
Puritanism even in him. Phyllis ought to be
praised for conquering Time, and someone owed her
more than praise. ' Be constant in something and
love her who shows her great *love* to thee, in taking
this pains to seem *lovely* to thee.'

301 351   This tiny sea-piece owes something to Sedley and to
Dorset in its first suggestion ; but see how the final
triplet of the stanza averts gravity with its happy
iteration of exaggeration.

302 352   ' The ugly hard rosebud,' with the flowers Sappho
carried in her apron, and that ripe rose

> ' just washed in a shower
> Which Mary to Anna conveyed,'

these bloom for ever in a more earthly Paradise than
that where Matilda went ' adding flower to flower.'

304 356   Thackeray could understand and praise Prior, another
' virtuoso of the muffled drum.' The *Invalides* here
is an essential touch : you must see the veteran
against Mansard's stately dome, the individual
against the stately pageant of history.

305 358   These stanzas from *Down Hall* for once bring magic
into the clear world of Prior's verse ; they go by like
the wind, as the ghosts walk at noonday in the
sunshine of the inn courtyard.

306 359   Delightful as the verse is, one could wish Jinny
celebrated at length in the leisure of a novel ; Prior
could have written novels a century later, and he
would have given Jinny her rights ; in most novels
good, easy women are pushed aside for the tantrums

of young madams in love. How she would have wandered through *Tristram Shandy* if Sterne had had Prior's serenity!

311 360 Vanbrugh is of the decadence in verse ; he is slipshod while he tries to be downright. Seldom does one find in him such a light, happy touch of comic poetry as the ' charming weather ' of the end of this, with the Columbine kick of the double rhyme.

312 361 La Fontaine's *Fables* found no English imitator, though Prior had followed the *Contes* ; this is hard and merely witty, but perhaps barely worth including as a reminder of one thing the French did better.

313 363 ' Nature ' and ' the gods ' are mere algebraic symbols ; the abstractions of the eighteenth century are drawing near.

314 364-7 Glanvill, a Devonshire man, and at last a wealthy Whig lawyer, has been unjustly forgotten as a poet ; perhaps this is because his poems, which date from the eighties and nineties, were not collected until 1725.

314 364 This poem has its own sober splendour and deep music ; it is the last re-statement of the Renaissance commonplace of fading youth. The swift octosyllables of Carew's *Pervasions to A L* and Marvell's *To his Coy Mistress* in their raptures contrast with these grave, slow couplet-quatrains, which now and then suggest the cadence of the *Rubaiyat*.

315 365 That he died a bachelor is perhaps to his credit as a lover.

316 366 The substitution of ' mind ' for ' soul ' marks how far these post-Revolution lovers have travelled from *The Ecstasy*.

317 367 Even such losses have their compensating gains ; what a ' sober certainty of waking bliss ' is here ; it is unforgettable and perfect.

317 368 Thomas Fletcher, Fellow of New College, a friend of Ken's, but not a Non-Juror (he became a Prebendary of Wells) is a very interesting minor poet, giving all sorts of hints of new winds soon to blow. Music is a pre-occupation of his ; he wrote one of the numerous Odes for St. Cecilia's Day which followed Dryden's. (The Musical Society, which commissioned them, celebrated its annual festivals at Villiers Street and at St. Bride's Church from 1683 to 1703.) There are suggestions of Shelley's *To Constantia Singing* in this.

318 369 This is interesting to compare with Congreve's *Arabella Hunt* of about the same date (No. 383).

318 370   In his preface he discusses at some length an experi-
           ment of his in translating Virgil into blank verse.
           ' Methinks blank verse carries in it somewhat of the
           majesty of Virgil; when rhymes, even the most
           happy of them (after tedious pumping for them and
           having good expression balked for the lack of them)
           do but emasculate heroic verse and give it an un-
           natural softness.' It is significant that in his blank
           verse he cannot keep clear of rhyme.

           He goes on to justify his experiment (quoted here) of
           an unrhymed Pindaric ode. ' Whether I have
           carried this humour of mine too far in writing a
           blank Pindaric Ode, let others judge ; only this I
           have to say, that the licentiousness of rhyming,
           which is usual in that sort of poetry among us, will
           make the want of it less discerned.' As a matter of
           fact, it is difficult to hear the rhyme in the average
           loose and clumsy Pindaric. Fletcher gets a real
           nobility in the passage quoted ; it is best to cut it
           short here, for it goes on

              ' Not so thee, William, best of British Kings.'

320 372   This has Miltonic reminiscences, which, taken
           together with his experiment in blank verse, has its
           significance. In 1694 appeared Gildon's *Vindica-
           tion of Paradise Lost* (reprinted in Mr. Spingarn's
           Critical Essays of the Seventeenth Century). The
           eclipse of Milton's fame between Dryden and Addison
           was hardly more than the inevitable reaction against
           any great poet just after his death. The published
           judgments of official critics in any generation are
           always a little out of date ; true critical opinion is
           being formed silently outside their hearing or
           understanding.

321 373-7 ' Granville the polite ' was the grandson of Bevil
           Granville, the Lion of the West, and the title the Tories
           gave him in 1711 recalls the battle in which that good
           Cavalier fell.   Granville himself would willingly have
           fought for his King in 1688, and had the honour of im-
           prisonment as a suspected man in 1715.   For all this,
           and discounting the praises of Pope and Gay, Johnson
           speaks severely of his poems, as he had of Waller's,
           Granville's master. Addison, who had less cause to
           be fair to a Tory poet, makes good fun of ' Ned
           Softly ' in a *Tatler*. There is no need to apologise for
           his verse, in spite of these august censures. It is
           polite in a good sense of the word ; Mr. Saintsbury
           ascribes to it ' a faint shadow or flavour, a sort of
           distant rose-scent, of the cadence and the melody of
           older days '; I see rather the rococo charm of coloured
           porcelain, bright and dainty. Like Waller's verse,
           it has been blamed for its merits. Johnson, a good

lover himself, was unduly contemptuous of 'the common cant of lovers'; he forgot that his own etymology derived cant from *cantus*.

321 373 These epigrams, as early as Prior's, are among the first of their kind in English, and for once it is safe to assume French models.

322 375 This is present-day in its psychology, if indeed women novelists are psychologists.

322 376 According to one account Myra was Mary of Modena, 'whose charms appear to have gained a strong prevalence over his imagination, and upon whom nothing ever has been charged but imprudent piety, an intemperate and misguided zeal for the propagation of popery.' If this is true, it puts Granville with Howe and Sheffield as the last in a troubadour tradition.

323 378-80 It would be irreverent to represent Swift by his Pindaric odes, which earned him Dryden's kindly condemnation, 'Cousin Swift, you will never be a poet'; his mature verse is eighteenth-century in manner. These fragments will serve to recall that he was older than Congreve, and chronologically a man of the seventeenth century.

323 378 'Mrs. Floyd looked out with both her eyes, and we had one day's thaw: but she drew in her head, and it now freezes as hard as ever.'

324 379 I fear I can hardly agree with the view of the critic who saw in this a prophecy of *The Waste Land*; it is an essay in the style of Ostade, which gave Crabbe a hint. *The Tatler* is not to be taken too seriously—'Such janty scribblers are so justly laughed at for their sonnets on Phillis and Chloris, and fantastical descriptions in them, that an ingenious kinsman of mine . . . has to avoid their strain, run into a way perfectly new, and described things exactly as they happen.' Steele's caution may have its value, even to-day. 'I foretell any man who shall go about to imitate him, that he will be very insipid.'

325 380 This no doubt dates from Swift's last years, but it so admirably supplements the other poems on the theme of *Dies Irae* that I had to include it. Its sudden splendid bitterness, and especially the terror and strangeness of its opening lines, recall the Scherzo of Beethoven's Fifth Symphony, when the trumpets of archangels wail over human vanities.

325 381 The *Amasia* of John Hopkins (whose brother Charles was an intelligent dramatist) is the dullest book of verse I have ever seen; even *To Amasia tickling a gentleman* is lugubrious. This Pindaric fragment, with all the clumsiness of its lumbering kind, has

its critical interest, and the cloud-simile for Dryden is
right as well as fine.

326 382   I wonder whether Congreve wrote this ? ' Beauteous
idiot ' is in his verse-vein, and the poem suggests a
sister to Lady Froth in some unwritten comedy.

327 383-8 Congreve dominates the last decade of the century,
and all Dryden said in his praise is but sober truth.
He is to the rest of his generation as Vermeer was to
Rembrandt and the lesser Dutch painters, aloof in
a subtle, cold, exquisite perfection, with something of
what is called unreality in his art, as if, like Vermeer,
he painted not life, but its reflection in a mirror.
And sometimes it seems that his silence dominates
the first twenty years of the eighteenth century ; he
sits apart, Olympian, smiling, silent, while Addison is
reigning ' with a certain crafty propriety—policy let us
call it,' uneasily as earthly monarchs must, while Pope
is flaunting in restless, flattering brilliance.   His
silence, like Racine's a generation earlier, is sometimes
ascribed to pique, and simple indolence is not an
impossible explanation.   Pique and indolence might
be the expression of a great artist's contempt for the
Philistine ;   Vermeer himself would perhaps have
stopped painting but for the eight young Vermeers
and the baker's bill ; to be regarded as an under-
study to Gerard Dou or Ravenscroft would arouse
the disdain of either.   It is permissible to see in
Congreve's silence something deeper, something
inevitable, given the man and his time.   Congreve
is the last Englishman of the seventeenth century ;
he found himself, still young, in a world which had
nothing for him.   The politics of faction, the
ethics of commerce, were all around his detachment.
His ideal, whatever it was, some modish Theleme,
some unenthusiastic Urbino, was out of tune with
such a world.   He had passed into a mysticism of
elegance, a Trappist renunciation of the vanity of
achievement : he would be no author, like those whom
fools applauded ;   he chose to be but a Gentleman ;
this pride of his is the last exercise, strangely inverted
in an inverted world, of Renaissance *virtù*.

327 383   He wrote verse as it were with his left hand ; it was
the drawing of a sculptor.   But in 1692 he was young
enough to play at enthusiasm, to be almost as if he
was in earnest about Arabella Hunt's singing.   He
writes in the manner of Crashaw, with a fantastic
irony ;   he too can be baroque as well as classical.
This mood towards music, this conscious excitement,
is a prophecy as well as a retrospect ;   it is the
beginning of Romanticism as well as the end of
Baroque.   Shelley really felt like this, and most of

the criticism of the nineteenth century in all the arts is an exposition of the critic's admirable emotions. Boswell's was being romantic about music, when the Doctor corrected him classically and rationally. ' I should never hear it, if it made one such a fool.' But perhaps all this is considering too curiously a delicious mock-serious poem.

330 384   *Millamant* ' not that there's any great matter in it—but 'tis agreeable to my humour.'

330 385   This is perfect rococo ; the second stanza expresses one ideal the eighteenth century pursued and some-times achieved.

331 386   Selinda might have been Anne Bracegirdle, and that Austenian woman was perhaps not as dazzled by Mr. Congreve as she let him think; he paid her the supreme compliment of Millamant, an admission that he could not be Mirabel, except on paper. This was set by Purcell in 1695, almost his last song.

331 387   Thackeray—he does it to perfection in that wonderful prose of his—is yet merely sentimental about Con-greve's artificial world, and the Coming of Death and Fate to destroy it. That world has gone with the snows of so many years. And where is the sunshine of Victoria's days ? The crinolines have followed the hoops into darkness.

           ' Nox est perpetua una dormienda.'

           The Park survives, and these Victorian streets Thackeray knew, ' built by an architect and under-taker,' to remind us of the two ages and their differences.

332 388   ' And flesh is flesh was flame before,
               And infinite hungers leap no more
               In the chance swaying of your dress :
               And love has changed to kindliness.'

           Regret and gratitude are the ashes of a lover's fire.

332 389   Addison commenced to write verse as early as 1692, and was a collaborator of Dryden in ' the subordinate parts ' of the *Virgil*. But he is of the eighteenth century, and his substantial poems, the *Letter from Italy* and *The Campaign*, are as certainly in a new manner as is the luminous prose of *The Spectator*. He was the first considerable man of letters to write verse as if it were prose, and for his poetry one must go to his shorter things.

           Addison is as deceptively lucid to us as he was to his contemporaries ; there must have been achievement and defeat behind the serenity of those features, some ' house ' behind the successful ' shop ' of his public career. This *Ode* reveals something of his

inner life ; ' these verses shine like the stars : they
shine out of a great deep calm.'

334 391   Elizabeth Singer married Thomas Rowe, thirteen
years younger than herself, in 1711, and was left a
widow in 1712. Her vogue as a religious poet was
considerable, and survived her for half-a-century;
even Johnson took her seriously. He speaks of her
' copiousness and luxuriance ' and indeed preferred
her to Watts. Of Heaven she says—or sings—or
cries—

'Gay banquets in thy splendid courts '

(which in *sense* is not so far from ' Sunt Sion atria,
conjubilantia,' if sense were all); of stars (in com-
petition with Addison)

'The active lights that shine above
  In their eternal dance,
Reveal their skilful Maker's praise
  With silent elegance.'

She excels herself in political verse.

On the picture of KING GEORGE I.

Such native goodness, such a regal grace,
Was never stamped in any vulgar face :
The sacred characters so clearly shine
'Twere impious not to own the *right divine.*'

Parthenia is interesting in comparison with Wild's
elegy (No. 9) ; it has its own polished and unsatis-
factory efficiency, and suggests how easy it is for
artistic conventions to pass from the significant to the
absurd ; it reminds one of the awkward reclining
sepulchral statues of the same date in York Minster.

335 392   Watts was perhaps not a great poet, yet he certainly
wrote great poetry. This particular poem is conventionally sublime, but our own ideas of the sublime
are as conditioned and conventional as those of other
generations.   This is baroque sublimity, like Padre
Pozzo's painted ceilings, or the Abbey of Melk ; we
begin to understand that kind of painting and
architecture once more, and by analogy, this kind of
poetry.   Probably he got the idea of Sapphics from
some Jesuit Latin poem ; the whole is strangely in
contrast with the *Dies Irae.*   It is public, impersonal;
there is nothing in it like

' Quaerens me sedisti lassus.'

336 393   This surely takes rank with the great sacred poetry of
all the centuries ; the only parallel to it in another
art would be a Spanish crucifix of the seventeenth
century of Montañés or Pedro de Mena.

337 394   Watts would have been surprised to find this a kind
of supplementary National Anthem, inseparably

connected with the idea of areas coloured red on a
map, and of a Chosen People divinely exalted above
foreigners. The good folk who sing it with conviction hardly realise that it is pure poetry, diction
and verse, that moves them so: if they stop to
consider its meaning, it makes them uneasy, so that a
military gentleman has suggested a rewriting of the
seventh stanza, to read:

> ' But not forgotten, as may seem,
> ' They live in endless day.'

The poem is a paraphrase of Psalm xv, verses 1-10;
it has the majesty of its original, with its terrible
rebuke of human vanity, but stopping where it does,
it omits the humble and consecrated hope of the
Psalm's last verse, which the Benedictines say every
day at Prime, ' Prosper thou the work of our hands
upon us, O prosper thou our handywork.'

It must be remembered that the sublime Common
Measure of this poem is also the stanza of ' Love still
has something of the sea ' and of ' While shepherds
watched their flocks by night.'

338 395-6 Oldmixon is in the Dunciad; but could anything be
pleasanter in their modest way than these? The
spirit of Wither is not yet exorcised from English
poetry, though it dwells now only in a pleasant
suburb.

339 397 I am not quite sure that this is by Philips; a
version in *Miscellany Poems* (1709) is inferior to this.
The pseudo-Anacreon was popular all through the
seventeenth century, and this ' Anacreontic ' has a
little of Herrick's own grace.

340 399 John Hughes ' was a good humble-spirited man, a
great admirer of Mr. Addison.' He practised all the
unheroic virtues, which in Queen Anne's day, included
the composition of heroic tragedy. This poem and
the next (text from *Chalmers' Poets*) set the prose
of the *Spectator* to a pleasant enough tune.

341 400 This has the very flaunt of a triumphant petticoat
about it.

342 401 This song is better than any of those in Farquhar's
plays; his place at the end of the canon of Restoration dramatists involves this also, that he is the
last who felt songs to be demanded from him as part
of the action of the play. The eighteenth century
inclined to treat the song as mere inserted entertainment, because it had temporarily lost its sense of the
necessity for lyrical poetry. We have not revived it
yet in the theatre; if we had, perhaps Mr. Shaw's
songs would be as good as Congreve's.

343 403   This is a confession before suicide on the part of Erato ; the need to 'tell the nymph' is always present, and if old methods are grown vulgar, we must find new ones.

344 404   This is translation from Boileau's only love-song.

345 405   This is quite a fresh and realised landscape, and agreeably suggests a contrast to Coventry Patmore. Had the cuckoo already given over his traditional message to the married ?

345 406   The outrageous Jeremy Collier called the *Miscellany* poems 'horribly licentious.' I suppose he would have disliked this delicious thing. Observe how poet, lady and lover alike ignore the insignificant husband.

346 407-11   Parnell is often spoken of as eighteenth-century, and treated as a bewildered March swallow of Romanticism. Goldsmith's view is truer. 'He appears to me to be the last of that great school that had modelled itself upon the ancients.' He is the last English poet of the Renaissance. Latin was then the birthright of every educated man ; Parnell knew and understood as well the *Pervigilium Veneris* and the sixteenth-century Neo-Latins, Joannes Secundus and the rest. He was a good Grecian, too, in an age when it was particularly true that a man had only as much Greek as he could get. All this went into his verse, as a vital influence. His 'simplicity' which Hume praised, is not merely the 'easy sweetness' to which Dr. Johnson reduces it ; it comes of real restraint and selection. True, he is the last and heirless scion of an old and decayed line ; he had no power ; he is minor, if you will, but still an unreplaceable and unique poet. He is an Augustan in a truer sense than Pope was ; he was more truly correct, for he observed traditional principles, whereas Pope innovated, like the genius he was. 'His poetical language is not less correct than his subjects are pleasing. He found it at that period in which it was brought to its highest pitch of refinement ; and ever since his time it has been gradually debasing.' So Goldsmith says, whose own verse-diction shows a conscious effort which he knew well enough was far from Parnell's instinctive felicity.

346 407   This, Goldsmith says, is translated 'from a French poet whose name I forget.' It is far more in the spirit of the *Pervigilium Veneris* than Parnell's avowed translation. The only thing in English to be compared with it is Tennyson's strangely overlooked 'Guinevere' fragment. And how strangely, behind its contemporary wit, does it go

back to *The Parlement of Fowles* and all the *Romaunt of the Rose.* Nature is here almost for the last time a Goddess, as Alain de Lisle and Chaucer and Spenser saw her ; she is soon to become an abstraction, or as she is to-day, almost a Government Department.

348 408 Arabella is Pope's Belinda. Parnell quite properly observes all phenomena impartially; an unpowdered beau and a leafless tree are equally natural symbols of the retirement of one sunshine or another.

348 409 The last lyric of the school of Dryden ; the triple movement in English verse-form was to be frivolous for a century, and then magnificent from Shelley to Swinburne, but it has never recovered this beauty ' in its graces and airs.'

349 410 This might be French, if the French poets of the seventeenth century had ever been able to master a movement so light, so airy, so strong. Satire, even Pope's, is shrill beside it, and yet it has more gravity than Prior cared to essay.

351 411 Goldsmith by implication, prefers this to Gray's *Elegy* ; he saw the romanticism of Gray, whose churchyard landscape is to Parnell's as a Cozens is to a Poussin.

Parnell has been undervalued or overlooked. It is possible to imagine him writing great poetry, but as it is, what he has left is satisfactory rather than satisfying. His sensibility hampered him : ' He wanted that evenness of disposition which bears disappointment with phlegm and joy with indifference. He was ever very much elated or depressed, and his whole life spent in agony or rapture.'

354 412-17 Mary Monk was the daughter of Robert Molesworth (detested by Swift and ennobled by George I). She married young and lived quietly in the country with her children and her books ; her father published her poems after her death, with a preface full of tender grief and pride. Her verse is interesting as showing the range of a cultured woman's reading then, and the importance Italian yet retained. She translates from Petrarch, Tasso, Guerini, Marino, Filicaia, and many others ; these translations, apart from their not negligible beauty, illustrate the diction of 1700 as compared with that of 1600.

354 412 The original of this is the original of the ' Lay of the Rose ' in the *Faerie Queene*, Book II, canto 12.

355 413 This sonnet is paraphrased by Drummond of Hawthornden. The absence of rhyme in Mary Monk's version is perhaps due to indolence, not art ; yet

hers is better-balanced, clearer, swifter than the
elaborations of the Jacobean.

356 415   The *Grand Cyrus* was out of date in town by 1700,
but they still read it in the country; a rural
heroine of Farquhar's read *Cassandra* with an unfortunate result.

356 416   The last four lines of a longer poem ; her parallel
Latin version may be of interest.

> Flore novo circum tellus se vestiat omnis,
>   Gramine gemmato tota nitescat humus.
> Vos herbae, suaves miscete et spargite odores.
>   Ad tumulum vigeat verque perenne tuum.

357 418   The great elegy for Addison reveals in Tickell something of an elder gravity, and this poem of his
twenties moves back in its three stanzas from 1710
through 1660 to 1600 ; the last line flames up
magically.

357 419   I cannot be sure if Addison meant this to be taken
seriously ; one never can be sure with these demure
Augustans.   By this time it was hardly well-bred to.
do more than pay a pretty compliment to a lady in
verse ; Mr. Timothy Stanza's letter with the song
reveals a double ambition unworthy of a lover.   ' You
professed authors are a little severe upon us who write
like gentlemen ; but if you are a friend to love, you
will insert my poem.   You cannot imagine how much
service it will do me with my fair one, *as well as
reputation with my friends,* to have something of
mine in the *Spectator.*'

358 420   Seventy years had passed since Falkland ingeminated
Peace, Peace ' with a shrill and sad accent.'   Men
had grown so weary of war that they would purchase
peace at the price of the old loyalty and the old
religion.   All Europe was weary and the guns were
silent for nearly a generation ;   the other parallels
between 1713, 1815 and 1918 must be left to historians.

In letters too, the ardencies of an epoch are quenched,
its graces faded.   Millamant and Mirabel are middle-
aged ;   Mr. Congreve has the gout and sits smiling
and silent.

Plaudite Amici : the Restoration Comedy is over.

LIST OF AUTHORS

	NO.	PAGE
ADDISON (Joseph)	CCCLXXXIX–XC	332
ALDRICH (Henry)	CXCVII–VIII	183
ALLESTRY (Jacob)	CCXLIV	222
AUSTIN (John)	X–XII	9
AYRES (Philip)	CVII–CX	113
BARKER (Jane)	CCXC–XCIII	256
BEHN (Aphra)	CLXIV–IX	157
BETTERTON (Thomas)	CXI	116
BLOUNT (Sir Walter Kirkham)	XIII	11
BOOTHBY (Frances)	LV	52
BROWN (Tom)	CCCXXXVII	290
BUCKINGHAM (George Villiers, Duke of)	XLI–IV	33
BUCKINGHAMSHIRE (John Sheffield, Duke of)	CCXIII–XIX	196
BUNYAN (John)	XXIV–VI	2
BUTLER (Samuel)	VII–IX	8
CAVENDISH (Margaret), *see* NEWCASTLE		
CHEEK (Thomas)	CCCXIX	278
CHUDLEIGH (Mary, Lady)	CCLXXXVIII–IX	254
CLELAND (William)	CCCXI	271
CONGREVE (William)	CCCLXXXIII–VIII	327
COPPINGER (Matthew)	CCXLV–VI	223
COTTON (Charles)	XLVI–LII	39
COWLEY (Abraham)	XV–XVII	13
CROMWELL (Henry)	CCLXXIII	245
CUTTS (John, Lord)	CCCVIII–X	270
DAVENANT (Sir William)	IV–V	4
DE LA SALE	CCCXXVII	283
DILLON (Wentworth), *see* ROSCOMMON		
DORSET (Charles Sackville, Earl of)	CXX–VII	122
DRYDEN (John)	LVI–LXXX	53
DUFFETT (Thomas)	CCXXI–II	203
DUKE (Richard)	CCLXXIV–VI	245
DURFEY (Tom)	CCXLVII–IX	225
ELSUM (John)	CCCXVII–XVIII	277
EPHELIA	CLXX–V	161

	NO.	PAGE
ETHEREGE (Sir George)	CXII–IX	117
EVANS (Abel)	CCCCXX	358
FARQUHAR (George)	CCCCI	342
FINCH (Anne), see WINCHILSEA.		
FLATMAN (Thomas)	C–CVI	106
FLETCHER (Thomas)	CCCLXVIII–LXXII	317
GARTH (Sir Samuel)	CCCXII	275
GLANVILL (John)	CCCLXIV–VII	314
GOULD (Robert)	CCXXXIV–VIII	214
GRANVILLE, see LANSDOWNE.		
HAWKSHAW (Benjamin)	CCCXIV–XVI	277
HEVENINGHAM (Colonel)	CCCXXII	280
HEYRICK (Thomas)	CXCIX	184
HOPKINS (John)	CCCLXXXI	325
HOWARD (James)	XL	32
HOWARD (Sir Robert)	XXXIX	31
HOWE (John)	CCLXXII	244
HUGHES (John)	CCCXCIX–CCCC	340
KEN (Thomas)	XC–XCII	87
KILLIGREW (Anne)	CCCI–II	263
KING (William)	CCCXXXVIII–XL	292
LANSDOWNE (George Granville, Lord)	CCCLXXIII–VII	321
LEE (Nathaniel)	CCXLI–II	219
LEIGH (Richard)	CCXXV–VIII	206
LOVELACE (Mrs)	CCXCVI–VII	259
MASON (John)	CXCI–III	178
MOLLINEUX (Mary)	CXCIV–VI	181
MONK (Mary) (Molesworth)	CCCCXII–XVII	354
MOTTEUX (Peter Anthony)	CCCXXXI	285
NEWCASTLE (Margaret Cavendish, Duchess of)	XXVII-XXXIII	24
NORRIS (John)	CCLX–IV	233
OLDHAM (John)	CCXLIII	220
OLDMIXON (John)	CCCXCV–VI	338
OTWAY (Thomas)	CCXXXIX–XL	217
PARNELL (Thomas)	CCCCVII–XI	346
PHILIPS (Ambrose)	CCCXCVII–VIII	339
PHILIPS (Katherine)	LIII–IV	51
POPE (Walter)	XLV	38
PORDAGE (Samuel)	XCVII–VIII	104
PRIOR (Matthew)	CCCXI·VIII–LIX	299
RAWLET (John)	CLXXXVII–VIII	173
ROCHESTER (John Wilmot, Earl of)	CC–CCXII	185

	NO.	PAGE
ROSCOMMON (Wentworth Dillon, Earl of)	LXXXIV–V . .	80
ROWE (Elizabeth) (Singer) . .	CCCXCI . .	334
RYMER (Thomas)	CLXXX–III . .	169
SACKVILLE, see DORSET.		
SACKVILLE (Major-General) .	CCLXX–I . .	243
SEDLEY (Sir Charles) . . .	CXXVIII–XXXVIII .	130
SHADWELL (Thomas) . . .	CLXXXIV–VI . .	172
SHEFFIELD, see BUCKINGHAMSHIRE		
SINGER, see ROWE		
SMITH (John)	CCCXIII . .	275
STEPNEY (George) . . .	CCCXLI . .	294
STEVENSON (Matthew) . .	XXXIV–VIII . .	29
SWIFT (Jonathan) . . .	CCLXXVIII–LXXX .	323
TATE (Nahum)	CCL–LVI . .	227
TAYLOR (Mrs.)	CCXCIV–V . .	258
TICKELL (Thomas) . . .	CCCCXVIII .	357
TOWNSHEND (Sir Horatio) .	CCCXXXIII . .	286
TRAHERNE (Thomas) . .	XCIII–VI . .	90
VANBRUGH (Sir John) . .	CCCLX–III . .	311
VAUGHAN (Henry) . . .	XX–XXIII . .	18
VILLIERS, see BUCKINGHAM.		
WALLER (Edmund) . . .	I–III . .	1
WALSH (William) . . .	CCCXLII–VII .	294
WANLEY (Nathaniel) . .	LXXXVI–IX .	84
WATKYNS (Rowland) . .	XVIII–XIX .	16
WATTS (Isaac) . . .	CCCXCII–IV .	335
WEBBE (Charles) . . .	CCXXIII–IV .	205
WESLEY (Samuel) . . .	CCCXXXV–VI	288
WHARTON (Anne) . . .	CCXCVIII–CCC	261
WILD (Robert) . . .	VI . .	6
WILMOT, see ROCHESTER.		
WINCHILSEA (Anne Finch, Countess of)	CCCIII–VII .	265
WOLSELEY (Robert) . .	CCXX . .	202
WRIGHT (James) . . .	CLXXXIX–XC	177
WYCHERLEY (William) . .	CLXXVI–IX .	166

ANONYMOUS POEMS

	NO.	PAGE
Merry Drollery, 1661	XCIX	106
Westminster Drollery, 1671	CXXXIX–XLVIII	137
Covent Garden Drollery, 1672	CXLIX–LI	147
Methinks the Poor Town, 1673	CLII–VIII	149
Bristol Drollery (N.C.), 1674	CLIX–LXIII	153
Choice Airs (J. Playford), 1679-83	CCXXIX–XXXIII	210
Poems by Several Hands (Tate), 1685	CCLVII-IX	232
Miscellany (A. Behn), 1685	CCLXV	240
Primer, 1685	XIV	12
Theatre of Music (H. Playford), 1685-7	CLXXVII–LXXX	248
Miscellany of New Poems (A. Behn) 1687	CCLXVI–IX	241
Banquet of Music (H. Playford), 1689-91	CCLXXXII–VI	251
Miscellany Poems (Gildon), 1692	CCXX–XXI	279
Gentleman's Journal, 1692-4	CCCXXIII–VI	280
Examen Poeticum (Dryden), 1693	CCCXXXII	285
Miscellany Poems IV. (Dryden), 1694	CCCXXXIV	287
Pills to Purge Melancholy (Durfey), 1699	CCXXIX–XXX	284
Orpheus Britannicus, 1700	CCLXXXVII, CCCXXVIII 253, 283
Amphion Anglicus (Blow), 1700	CCCLXXXII	326
Miscellany Poems V, 1704	CCCCII–VI	342
Primer, 1706	LXXXI–III	77
The Spectator, 1712	CCCCXIX	357
B.M. Addit. MS. 32339 (Mr. Ault's transcription)	CCLXXXI	251

INDEX OF FIRST LINES

PAGE

A Band, a Bob-wig, and a Feather 311
A beauteous face, fine shape, engaging air . . . 245
Absent from thee I languish still 189
Adieu, my Cordelia, my dearest, adieu 150
After the pangs of a desperate lover 55
Ah Cloris ! that I now could sit 136
Ah cruel Strephon, now give o'er 260
Ah fading joy, how quickly art thou past ! . . 53
Ah ! happy grove ! Dark and secure retreat . . 82
Ah ! who can the joys discover 282
Alice is tall and upright as a pine 39
All my past life is mine no more 188
All the flatteries of fate 139
All thoughts of freedom are too late . . . 279
All over I'm in love with thee 166
All own the young Silvia is fatally fair . . . 283
A lover I am, and a lover I'll be 141
Although thou now putt'st me in doubt . . . 257
A merry cup ('faith) let us drink 168
A milk-white Hind, immortal and unchanged . . 74
Amintas, to my grief I see 210
An age in her embraces passed 190
And now, my Lord, my God, my all . . . 11
A poet I am neither born nor bred 28
As Cloe came into the room t' other day . . . 302
As he lay in the plain, his arm under his head . . 126
As pants the hart for cooling streams . . . 230
As poor Aurelia sat alone 107
As precious gums are not for lasting fire . . . 72
As the snow in valleys lying 342
A thousand martyrs I have made 160
A thousand several ways I tried 213
At the sight of my Phillis, from every part . . 127
Aurora spreads her cheerful rays 77
Authority, which did a body boast 13

Behold how eager this our little boy . . . 23
Believe, Posterity, believe it true 319
Belinda ! see, from yonder flowers 357
Beneath a myrtle shade 57
Beneath the covert of a grove 339
Best of thy sex ! if sacred friendship can . . . 161

431

	PAGE
Bewitching sin, hadst thou not been	86
Blest Poetry ! immortal soul refined	87
Blush not redder than the morning	220
Boast not your fresh unmingled sweets	171
Break, break, sad heart, unload thy grief	242
Bright as the day, and like the morning fair	321
Bright star ! by Venus fixed above	294
Bring, all ye dear-bought nations, bring	11
But, gracious God, how well dost thou provide	75
But how much better they	318
But I have lost my reason, have disgraced	66
By the blue taper's trembling light	351
Caelia is chaste, yet her bright eyes	216
Can death be faithful or the grave be just	84
Can life be a blessing	57
Can nothing, nothing move her	315
Celimena, of my heart	56
Celinda, think not by disdain	252
Chloe, be kind, I say	277
Chloe's a Nymph in flowery groves	225
Chronos, Chronos, mend thy pace	60
Cloris, I cannot say your eyes	130
Cloris, let my passion ever	138
Come here my sweet landlady, pray how d'ye do ?	305
Come into us, Holy Ghost	12
Come, lasses and lads	142
Come, let us now resolve at last	198
Conquered with soft and pleasing charms	191
Corinna, in the bloom of youth	321
Creator Spirit, by whose aid	75
Cupid ! Instruct an amorous swain	343
Cupid, the slyest rogue alive	248
Dear Love, let me this evening die !	4
Democritus, dear droll, revisit earth	304
Dim, as the borrowed beams of moon and stars	73
Dispatch, and to the myrtle grove convey	229
Distracted with care	296
Divine Thalia, strike th' harmonious lute	264
Dorinda's sparkling wit and eyes	128
Eirene's eyes had purified the air	232
Enough, enough of this world's fruitless care	320
Ere I thy charming visage saw	215
Eugenia young, and fair and sweet	41
Fade, flowers, fade, nature will have it so	1
Fair Amaranta, wert thou not to blame	131
Fair Aminta, art thou mad	134
Fair Amoret is gone astray	330
Fair, and soft, and gay, and young	214
Fairest, if you roses seek	153

PAGE

Fairfax the valiant ; and the only he 33
Fair Iris ! all our time is spent 121
Fair Iris I love and hourly I die 59
Fair shining mountains of my pilgrimage . . . 19
Fair though you are 65
False though she be to me and love 332
Farewell, all joys, when he is gone . . . 248
Farewell thou busy World, and may . . . 48
Farewell, too little and too lately known . . . 71
Farewell ungrateful traitor 58
Fear not, my dear, a flame can never die . . . 130
Fie, Chloris ! 'Tis silly to sigh thus in vain . . . 151
Fly, fly, you happy shepherds fly ! 313
Fly swift, ye hours, ye sluggish minutes fly . . . 245
Forbear, bold youth, all's Heaven here . . . 51
For naked truth let others write 289
Fortune, made up of toys and impudence . . . 37
For what to-morrow shall disclose 303
From Life's superfluous cares enlarged . . . 333
From silent shades, and the Elysian groves . . . 212
From three dark places Christ came forth this day . 16
From town fair Arabella flies 348

Give me leave to rail at you 186
Give o'er, foolish heart, and make haste to despair . 146
Give o'er, my dear Phillis, to whisper and smile . 154
Go, little book, and to the world impart . . . 294
Go, lovely pair of roses, go 275
Grave fops my envy now beget 196

Hail, April, true Medea of the year . . . 29
Hail, thou most sacred, venerable thing ! . . . 234
Hail to the myrtle shade 219
Happy art thou whom God does bless . . . 15
Happy the man, and happy he alone . . . 67
Hark my soul, how every thing 9
Hark, the cock crows, and yon bright star . . 45
Hears not my Phillis, how the birds . . . 134
Hence Cupid, with your cheating toys . . . 52
Here lies a youth, who fell a sacrifice . . . 345
Here lies little . . . a yard deep and more . . 129
Her face young, airy, fleering, licked and patched . 278
Her name is at my tongue, whene'er I speak . . 113
How charming are those pleasant pains . . . 147
How desolate 90
How dull a thing this world would prove . . . 154
How happy's that lover, who, after long years . . 252
How happy was that age of old 169
How hardly I conceal'd my tears ! . . . 261
How long, great God, how long must I . . . 237
How many coronets of daffodillies 31
How old may Phillis be, you ask 301
How quick the minstrel's fingers play ! . . . 277

PAGE

How shall I sing that Majesty 179
How sweet is harmless solitude ! 182
How sweet is the air and refreshing 250
How vain a thing is Man whom toys delight . . 230
How various and innumerable 8
How wretched is the slave to love 173

I cannot change, as others do 188
I care not, though it be 236
I did but look and love awhile 217
I dwell in groves that gilt are with the sun . . 27
If all be true that I do think 183
I feed a flame within which so torments me . . 54
If I live to be old, for I find I go down . . . 38
If music be the food of Love 280
If vows could keep a heart secure 217
If we could open and intend our eye 16
If wine and music have the power 300
If you complain your flames are hot 257
I gave her cakes and I gave her ale 253
I'll tell her the next time, said I 323
I love, but she alone shall know 285
I loved fair Celia many years 283
I love variety, 'tis true 167
I'm made in sport by nature, when 184
Impatient with desire, at last 322
I must confess I am untrue 197
In all humanity, we crave 192
In Cloris, all soft charms agree 244
In conceit like Phaeton 271
I never saw a face till now 243
In such a night, when every louder wind . . . 268
Insulting Beauty, you misspend 187
In that deep gulf, where all past times are thrown . 208
In unexperienced infancy 101
In vain, Clarinda, night and day 321
In vain, Clemene, you bestow 243
In vain, poor nymph, to please our youthful sight . 349
In vain she frowns, in vain she tries 284
In vain would Man his mighty patent show . . 256
In vain you tell your parting lover 301
I once had virtue, wealth and fame 253
I pass all my hours in a shady old grove . . . 140
Is Celadon unkind ? It cannot be 152
I strove in vain ! Here, take my heart . . . 259
It is not, Celia, in our power 119
It must be done, my soul, but 'tis a strange . . 233
It was the spring, and flowers were in contest . . 6
I will not tell her that she's fair 224

Jesus, the only thought of thee 78
Judgement ! two syllables can make 110

Know, Celadon, in vain you use 164

PAGE

Ladies, farewell ! I must retire 32
Ladies ! though to your conquering eyes . . . 117
Last Sunday at St. James's prayers . . . 284
Late when Love I seemed to slight 170
Let all be hushed. each softest motion cease . . . 327
Let Fortune and Phillis frown if they please . . . 141
Let other beauties boast in vain 279
Let other cities strive, which most 77
Let those with cost deck their ill-fashioned clay . 171
Liberty, Liberty ! 204
Life of my Soul ! return, return 152
Like children in a starry night 199
Lilies and roses, let who will go suit ye . . . 31
Look here, my soul, how sparkling and how bright . 173
Love in fantastic triumph sat 158
Love is too great a happiness 8
Lovely Lucinda, blame not me 270
Love's a dream of mighty treasure . . . 278
Love's but the frailty of the mind . . . 330
Love still has something of the sea . . . 132
Love, thou art best of human joys . . . 265
Love, thou chief good of human kind . . . 316

Madam, I love and truly, should I not . . . 29
Man is supreme lord and master 8
Many thousand follies are 151
May the ambitious ever find 128
Me my ambition only leads 325
Men with much toil and time and pain . . . 240
Methinks the poor town has been troubled too long . 124
Methought I heard the charming Echo say . . 276
Mistress of all my senses can invite . . . 247
More love or more disdain I crave . . . 205
Most of our modern writers nowadays . . . 25
Mountown ! thou sweet retreat from Dublin cares . 292
Much had I heard of fair Francelia's name . . 357
My Damon, if your heart be kind . . . 157
My God, now I from sleep awake 88
My life, my love, my joy 181
My little bird, how canst thou sit 21
My lodging it is on the cold ground . . . 5
My mistress is, I own, above 338
My mistress so bewitches me in love . . . 317

Naked I came, when I began to be . . . 109
No, I'll to tavern, where being come . . . 30
No more this dallying and suspense . . . 314
No, no, poor suff'ring heart, no change endeavour . 59
Nor didst thou those mean spirits more approve . 220
Not an angel dwells above 312
Not Celia, that I juster am 132
Nothing ! thou elder brother even to Shade . . 193
Not to the hills where cedars move . . . 108

PAGE

Not your eyes, Melania, move me 282
No warning of th' approaching flame . . . 322
Now from the altar of my heart 178
Now hardly here and there an hackney coach . . 324
Now, I confess, I am in love 106
Now to the secret groves is Lydia gone . . 104
Nyctimine now freed from day . . . 44
Nymph Fanaret, the gentlest maid . . . 228
Nymphs and shepherds, come away . . . 172

O'er this marble drop a tear 356
Of all the torments, all the cares . . . 295
Of the first paradise there s nothing found . . 1
Oh, ecstasy divine ! I cannot hold ! . . 317
Oh ! how the hand the lover ought to prize . . 157
Oh the bonny Christ Church bells . . . 183
Oh then let my Cloe know 241
O last and best of Scots ! who didst maintain . . 73
O Love ! that stronger art than wine . . . 160
O my Philander, ope your breast . . . 232
On all my flock both great and small . . 179
Once beauteous, and still reverend pile . . 177
Once on a time a nightingale . . . 312
Only tell her that I love 271
O Thou who didst deny to me . . . 20
Our God, our help in ages past . . . 337
Out of the wine-pot cried the Fly . . . 115
O you powerful Gods ! If I must be . . . 52

Pale Shadow once in love fell with bright Light . . 27
Pastora's beauties when unblown . . . 211
Peace, Cupid ! Take thy bow in hand . . . 149
Phillis, be gentler, I advise 186
Phillis is my only joy 135
Phillis, men say that all my vows . . . 136
Phillis, since you can ne'er be mine . . . 155
Phillis, the time is come that we must sever . . 148
Phillis, though your all-powerful charms . . 35
Phillis, you have enough enjoy'd . . . 133
Phyllis appearing 169
Phyllis, for shame, let us improve . . . 125
Pious Selinda goes to prayers . . . 331
Poor Celia once was very fair . . . 106
Poor hapless emblem of Amyntor s heart . . 203
Poor little, pretty, fluttering thing . . 305
Press gently on him, earth, and all around . . 356
Prithee, Chloe, not so fast 339

Reason at last has got the day . . . 242
Released from the noise of the butcher and baker . 306
Roses in their first crimson dress appear . . 207

Sabina has a thousand charms . . . 326
Say, nymph divine, for whom I burn . . . 202

PAGE

See how Damon's age appears 285
See how on yonder bush 354
See how the wanton Spring 17
See my fortune, see my fortune 105
See, see, she wakes, Sabina wakes ! 331
See there the taper's dim and doleful light . . . 262
See where enamoured Thirsis lies 229
See where 'tis fallen among a ring of boys . . . 288
See you that beauteous queen, which no age tames ? . 18
Shall dumpish melancholy spoil my joys . . . 98
Shall we die, both thou and I 145
She that would gain a constant lover 241
Since, O ye Powers, ye have bestowed on me . . 256
Since you, dear friend, wonder how here I live . . 175
Sleep ! downy sleep ! come close my eyes . . . 108
Sleep, sleep, poor youth ! Sleep, sleep in peace . . 226
Smiling Phillis has an air 210
Soft Sleep, thou son of Silence and of Night . . . 355
Sometimes (dear friend) this riseth in my heart . . 181
Some vex their souls with jealous pain 200
Some wit, more folly, and no care 340
So the long absent winter sun 287
Spite of thy godhead, powerful Love 261
Strephon hath fashion, wit, and youth 259
Strephon I saw, and started at the sight . . . 163
Such is the mode of these censorious days . . . 200
Surely that is a stately frame 85
Sweet, be no longer sad 205
Sweetest bud of beauty ! may 119
Sweet Marmalade of Kisses newly gathered . . . 26
Sweet Vesper, bring the night 223

Tell me, Aurelia, tell me, pray 342
Tell me no more, I am deceived 120
Tell me no more of Venus and her Boy 270
Tell me once, dear, how it does prove 31
Tell me then the reason, why 185
Tell me, thou safest end of all our woe 263
Thank Heaven at last our wars are o'er 358
The budding rose 355
The day of wrath, that dreadful day 80
The grove was gloomy all around 158
The lilies have more springs than one 276
The Moon, in her pride, once glancèd aside . . . 144
The morning rose bright as a blooming bride . . . 345
Then let the chill Scirocco blow 47
Then never let me see her more ! 340
The nymph that undoes me, is fair and unkind . . 118
The pride of every grove I chose 299
There is a season, which too fast approaches . . . 266
The spacious firmament on high 332
The Sun crowns Nature's head with beams so fair . . 26
The sun far sunk in his descent 227

PAGE

Think we have had a clear and glorious day . . . 66
This is the place where oft my longing eyes . . . 344
This poring over your Grand Cyrus . . . 356
Those verses still to me do seem the best . . . 24
Thou art so fair and cruel too . . . 150
Thou booby, say'st thou nothing but Cuckoo ? . . 23
Though she's so much for beauty famed . . . 215
Thou shepherd, whose intentive eye . . . 286
Through mournful shades, and solitary groves . . 246
Thus lovely Sleep did first appear . . . 206
'Tis an ambition above mortal state . . . 172
'Tis done, Urania, I am free . . . 281
'Tis no small art to give direction . . . 293
'Tis sweet to die, when they would force life on me . 67
To a high hill where never yet stood tree . . 218
To all you ladies now at land . . . 122
To die, is landing on some silent shore . . . 275
To little or no purpose I spent many days . . 118
Trail all your pikes, dispirit every drum . . . 265

Victoria comes ! she leaves the foraged groves . . 341

Waters above ! eternal springs ! . . . 20
We all to conquering beauty bow . . . 226
We are born, then cry . . . 156
Well then, the promised hour is come at last . . 69
Were I, who to my cost already am . . . 195
What a dull fool was I . . . 36
What a plague d'ye tell me of the Papist's design ? . 290
What art thou, Love ? whence are those charms ? . 222
What a strange moment will that be . . . 238
What care I though the world reprove . . . 137
What do I wish ? No more than what I have . . 177
Whate'er thy countrymen have done . . . 304
What has this bugbear, Death, that's worth our care ? . 297
What lover in his mistress hopes to find . . 298
What miracles this childish God has wrought ! . . 162
What shall I do to show how much I love her . . 116
What spendthrifts are we of the day . . . 86
When all alone in some belov'd retreat . . . 254
When at Thy altar, Lord, I prostrate fall . . . 88
When Cupid did his grandsire Jove entreat . . 323
When first I saw Lucinda's face . . . 233
When first mine infant ear . . . 94
When first my free heart was surprised by desire . . 148
When I consider life, 'tis all a cheat . . . 65
When in thy lonely bed . . . 198
When I survey the wondrous Cross . . . 336
When, lovely Phillis, thou art kind . . . 249
When on my sick bed I languish . . . 110
When slaves their liberty require . . . 296
When spring came on with fresh delight . . . 346
When such a day blessed the Arcadian plain . . 266

PAGE

When the cock begins to crow 253
When the fierce north wind with his airy forces . . 335
When thou dost dance the spheres do play . . . 251
When through the world fair Mazarine had run . . 2
When thy beauty appears 348
Where do these voices stray 209
While on these lovely looks I gaze . . . 187
While shepherds watched their flocks by night . . 231
While with labour assiduous due pleasures I mix . . 302
While you with music and with beauty charm . . 318
Whilst I gaze on Chloe trembling 251
Whoe'er thou art, thy lord and master see . . . 321
Why, Damon, why, why, why, so pressing ? . . . 255
Why do I love ? go ask the glorious sun . . . 165
With all the powers my poor soul hath . . . 10
With a whirl of thought oppressed . . . 325
With hairs, which for the wind to play with, hung . 113
With singing angels hence she posts away . . . 334

Ye happy swains, whose hearts are free . . 120
Yet with me 'tis out of season 50
Ye virgin powers, defend my heart . . . 258
Ye Winds that in your hasty flight . . . 114
You pleasing dreams of love and sweet delight . . 54
You say you love ! Repeat again 292
You understand no tender vows 280
You wrong me, Strephon, when you say . . . 165

PRINTED IN GREAT BRITAIN
BY ROBERT MACLEHOSE AND CO. LTD.
THE UNIVERSITY PRESS, GLASGOW.

Samuel H. Monk
1946